Minute Six

Also by Kevin Fong

Extremes: Life, Death and the Limits of the Human Body

Minute Six

How High-Performance Teams Navigate the Unknown

KEVIN FONG

BH

THE BODLEY HEAD
LONDON

1 3 5 7 9 10 8 6 4 2

The Bodley Head, an imprint of Vintage,
is part of the Penguin Random House group of companies

Vintage, Penguin Random House UK, One Embassy Gardens,
8 Viaduct Gardens, London SW11 7BW

penguin.co.uk/vintage
global.penguinrandomhouse.com

Penguin
Random House
UK

First published by The Bodley Head in 2026

This book is a work of non-fiction based on the life, recollections and experiences of the author as a doctor. Where necessary, the names and case details of patients, the names of staff and other individuals, and certain places, dates, sequences and details of events have been changed to protect patient confidentiality and the privacy of others.

Set in 12/14.75pt Dante MT Std
Typeset by Six Red Marbles UK, Thetford, Norfolk

Printed and bound in Great Britain by Clays Ltd, Elcograf S.p.A.

The authorised representative in the EEA is Penguin Random House Ireland,
Morrison Chambers, 32 Nassau Street, Dublin D02 YH68

A CIP catalogue record for this book is available from the British Library

HB ISBN 9781847923684
TPB ISBN 9781847923691

Penguin Random House is committed to a sustainable future for our business, our readers and our planet. This book is made from Forest Stewardship Council® certified paper.

MIX
Paper
FSC® C018179
FSC
www.fsc.org

Contents

Strategy, to be quite frank, you will have no hand in.
It is done by those up above, and it merely refers to
The larger movements over which we have no control.
But tactics are also important, together or single.
You must never forget that, suddenly, in an engagement,
You may find yourself alone.

Henry Reed, *Lessons of the War*, Part III, 'Movement of Bodies'

Introduction: What we call Monday

I have been a lot of different things in my time and have worn many different hats, but I am first and foremost a doctor of medicine. On most Monday mornings at 7.45 a.m. you can find me standing outside our emergency operating theatres at University College London Hospital with a team of fellow clinicians, trying to triage the cases and come up with a plan.

This early-morning meeting draws in a couple of dozen health-care professionals: anaesthetists, surgeons, theatre nurses and more besides, all huddled in our surgical scrubs, paper hats and clogs, waiting for kick-off. We stand around the giant computer screen that hangs on the wall, displaying a list of all the patients in the emergency queue. Everyone on the board – because of illness or injury – needs urgent surgery; the question is how soon and in what order of priority.

The meeting is a negotiation between all present. We discuss who gets to go first, why, when, how long it will take. The list is long: abdominal surgeries to snip out diseased loops of bowel; complicated fractures in frail, elderly patients with failing hearts; ectopic pregnancies that threaten to bleed torrentially; children who have swallowed batteries; appendixes on the verge of rupture; gangrenous limbs in need of amputation, and so on. It never ends.

There's a messy logic to it all. Children before adults, unless the adults are sicker than the children. And the sickest adults go before the less urgent cases, unless the right equipment hasn't yet arrived or the right surgical expertise isn't present, or we have failed to set aside enough blood to transfuse a major case, or some other snarl-up. And all of that before you factor in how many of our staff are off sick, whether we actually have any unoccupied beds available in the hospital and whether or not wards upstairs are closed because of a norovirus outbreak or flu epidemic.

And while we're trying to box around all of that, we will occasionally be interrupted by the shriek of emergency pagers, whining before their tiny loudspeakers crackle to life and speak to us, ordering the on-call anaesthetic team to drop everything and run to a ward somewhere far away to deal with a cardiac arrest, or a drug overdose, or a patient whose physiology is about to crash.

There is always a plan, a pre-formed idea of how the day will run. But that never survives for very long. Nothing is for sure. We take risks here, because we have to; we trade certainty for time; we make guesses, knowing that if we are wrong, people may come to harm or die.

This is a narrow glimpse of the uncertainty and complexity of the world that everyone working in healthcare lives in, and the dilemmas that we face all day, every day, while trying to do the right things for the people in our care.

Like anyone in other high-risk, high-reliability, high-performance organisations, we have evolved strategies and behaviours to help us deal with that reality. This book is about those strategies: how we deal with uncertainty, how we cope with surprise, how we form teams to help us do that, how we lead and follow, how we succeed and why we sometimes fail. It is about the truth of the world that we all work in today, in teams operating in partnership with technology, embedded within complex systems.

The world is uncertain and, by some measures, only getting more so. The World Uncertainty Index (WUI), created by economists to track factors that contribute to economic uncertainty, is on the rise and has been since the start of the twenty-first century. In the recent past it spiked after key historic events, such as the 2001 attacks on the World Trade Center in New York City, the outbreak of Severe Acute Respiratory Syndrome (SARS) in 2003, the global financial meltdown in 2008, Brexit in 2016 and, most recently, the Covid-19 pandemic. Right now the WUI is running at an all-time high. Many things contribute to this: geopolitics, conflict, global health and disease. In recent years technology has been added to the mix, with the advent of Artificial Intelligence (AI) and its impact on the economy making it still harder to know how best to place your bets.

This is not a book about economics, but the ripples of that uncertainty spill over into all our lives. We are fast getting used to the impermanence of everything. Institutions and global relationships and alignments that have stood solid for decades are shifting. The ways we work, and the organisations we work within, are changing, too. And while it is difficult to know precisely where it will all land, this forces us to develop new and better strategies for dealing with the rapidly changing world in which we now live.

In the wake of the fall of the Berlin Wall in 1989 and the collapse of the Soviet Union that followed shortly thereafter, American war colleges coined the concept of VUCA, a world that was now more Volatile, Uncertain, Complex and Ambiguous than it had been before – a multi-polar geopolitical environment in which you could no longer be sure who your friends and enemies were; one in which life was decidedly unsure, and the landscape could transform suddenly and without warning. Today that concept looks roundly prescient. We all live in the VUCA world and, to stay on top, we and the organisations we work within are having continuously to recalibrate.

I have spent much of my career working with or alongside high-risk, high-performance organisations: from the United States' National Aeronautics and Space Administration (NASA) and its human space-exploration programme to helicopter emergency services, from aviation to healthcare and the military.

It has been a strange safari. I have stood at NASA's Kennedy Space Center with the emergency medical teams, crossing my fingers while they blasted crews into orbit; sat next to flight directors in mission control in Houston as they fought their way through punishing mission simulations. I have spent many hours interviewing astronauts who once walked on the Moon, and the NASA flight-control teams who rescued Captain James Lovell and the crew of *Apollo 13* from the jaws of certain death.

I have found myself on the scene at major incidents: on motorway pile-ups and at terrorist bombings. During the war in Afghanistan I spent a little time with the British military at Brize Norton and in the desert at Camp Bastion, studying their medical teams. And somehow these roads together led me to my role as National Clinical Adviser for the Covid-19 pandemic, helping to guide the NHS's response from the frontlines. Wherever I have been – however I have fared – I have always looked for lessons that we all might learn, in search of ways to improve everything that we do in the practice of medicine and elsewhere in the world.

But when it comes to volatility, uncertainty and complexity, the medical profession knows more than a thing or two. The human body is among the most complex systems in the known universe. The processes that keep us alive are fragile and legion; in illness and injury, they can fail quickly and irretrievably in ways that are often hard to fathom. There is no black and white in the work that medics do, just shades of grey, and decisions that have to be made in the moment. Medicine has evolved strategies and behaviours to cope across the whole of the profession, from community care and general practice all the way to our hospital operation suites and emergency departments. They have learned to deal with the unknown and the unknowable, and how to manage in the midst of that uncertainty the cocktail of science, technology and risk to human life that they, and the people in their care, depend upon. And so this book is about trying to extract and share some of those strategies, behaviours and lessons.

This book isn't an autobiography, but most of it stems from experiences I've lived through or have learned from directly. I have learned a great deal from scholars in the field of organisational theory, who have done the hard yards in formally studying and analysing modern industries and teams and codifying that knowledge. I have engaged with that literature and those people wherever possible, poring over their papers, grappling with the theory and trying to ascertain what it means to me. But to make sure that I am seeing the right things and learning the right lessons from an organisation,

I have tried wherever possible to be more than a casual observer, embedding myself with the people and teams doing the work, wherever the work is done. This book is written primarily from that perspective: from my seat at the sharp end of practice, looking back at the organisations I have worked with, trying to make sense of the gap that inevitably opens up between the plans laid down by system designers and architects and the messy reality of the front-line endeavour.

In the nineteenth century the Prussian field marshal and famed strategist Helmuth von Moltke the Elder taught his armies about the uncertainty of war and the folly of expectation. His 1871 monograph, written while reflecting on a string of wartime victories, included the following words, '*Kein Operationsplan reicht mit einiger Sicherheit über das erste Zusammentreffen mit der feindlichen Hauptmacht hinaus*', which translates to: 'No plan of operations extends with any certainty beyond the first encounter with the main enemy forces.'

Von Moltke's maxim survives today in abbreviated form, and continues to be taught to British military officers. In the process it has become a more familiar aphorism: 'No plan survives the first five minutes of battle.' Which begs the question: what happens after that?

Where does the carefully laid strategy end, and when must improvisation begin? How do we equip ourselves to be agile and adaptable in the face of an ever-changing, ever-challenging world? How do you prepare your team, your organisation and yourself for uncertainty? What happens when you arrive at *minute six*?

PART ONE

I.

After the first five minutes

We arrive overhead, aboard our helicopter, turning hard in the air, staring down at the wreckage from a few hundred feet. It's a mess. I can't quite make sense of it. There's a car, maybe two, possibly a van as well. There's a lorry on top of it all, but I'm not sure where it ends and the smaller vehicles start.

Our pilot begins his descent, threading us past pylons, wires and tall motorway lights. Seated in the back, I pull together the beginnings of a plan of action. In less than a minute we are on the carriageway, landing in a deafening roar of turbines and rotor blades, unsure – as usual – of precisely where we are or what we've been sent to.

Within the rear cabin of the aircraft, strapped in with all our gear locked down, there is a sense of order and procedure. Everything in its place, and a place for everything. But once on the ground, with the engines quiet and the rotors at a standstill, we slide the door open and fall through the looking glass into chaos.

The fire crews are already at work. Pneumatic jaws bite down on crushed bodywork. The sound of chuntering compressors dominates a motorway now filled with silent, stationary traffic, making it hard to hear the handover from the paramedic crew already on the scene. The first thing we need to establish is how many vehicles there are, how many casualties are trapped inside them and who is in most urgent need of care. This is harder than you might imagine.

'Two PLE in the back of that car, and one trapped,' says the paramedic as he walks, leading us through the carnage. PLE: 'Pronounced Life Extinct'. It's one of our more hideous contractions. I look again at the vehicle he's gesturing at. It's just about recognisable as the remains of a red car.

'How do you . . .' My boss, Alex, pauses, trying to find the right assembly of words. He sighs and resigns the effort. 'Who pronounced them dead?'

The paramedic stops for a moment and turns to look him in the eye. He knows where we're going with this. We're the attending pre-hospital medical team – what they call an 'enhanced resource': two doctors and a critical-care paramedic trained to deliver advanced, immediate care at the roadside. It's our responsibility to be sure, which means that we should check all of them ourselves.

'They're *dead*,' says the paramedic firmly. That might be a note of indignation; more likely, though, he's trying to spare us from seeing what he has seen.

Sometimes, in the heat of the moment, it's surprisingly hard to know the difference between dead and alive. Right now, we have to trust the judgement of our colleague. This is a simmering mess, threatening to boil over, and the paramedic's view is the closest thing to a piece of information that we can rely on. We move on. Everything here is impression and uncertainty. And yet soon we need to start making some of the most important decisions we will ever make.

My boss sighs and turns to me. 'Write it on the bonnet.'

I take out an indelible marker and write in giant block capitals on the bonnet of the wrecked red car:

2 DEAD
1 TRAPPED P2

We move on, repeating the process for each vehicle, counting the dead and injured, deciding on the priority with which they should be treated. There are three triage categories, which broadly break down like this: P3, the walking wounded; P2, those seriously injured, but whose treatment can be delayed for now; and finally P1, those whose lives are urgently at risk and who will die without immediate medical intervention. There is a fourth category: P4. Those still alive, but whose injuries are so grave that nothing can be done; we rehearse it often in training. But in practice that judgement about the impossibility of life and the inevitability of death is next to impossible to make. There are, we decide, no P4 casualties today.

After our walk around the crash site, we regroup and take stock. I use the side of the crashed lorry as an improvised whiteboard and scribble down all of the casualties and their triage scores in a list for everyone to see. This temporarily reduces tragedy to a cluster of numbers. We stare at the figures, making sure everyone is accounted for. There is a sense of order in sterile numbers, the illusion of something to which logic might be applied. We need to decide where to focus our attention first. I wish for all the world there was a device that could make that decision for us, an automatic process that would help us through moments like this – but there is none.

I stare at the numbers until Alex turns me around, points me at one of the cars and tells me to lead the team there and start treating casualties, according to priority. The illusion of stability vanishes.

In the sixty minutes that follow we remove people from the crumpled remains of cars, attempting to strike the right balance between urgency and care. There is no narrative in my memory for that time, just the wordless experience of events. I'm not sure what it is that I remember when I try to recall them: short flashes of moving images, sounds, smells, impressions onto which I have since superimposed something with more structure. The resulting memories are largely false, or at the very least plastic. This is what the neuroscientists and psychologists tell us: that I can't really trust what I remember about that day. I feel as though I was carried through it on automatic – consciously unconscious.

This is what real decisions feel like in the moment. This is the edge of chaos. Ungoverned, it will descend into anarchy. That we can put something in its way – that we can maintain any semblance of order, caught up in the terror – is remarkable in itself. But to do that, we have to go beyond our traditional ideas of leadership, teamwork and human performance. All of those things are necessary, but in the face of a threat like this, they are not sufficient.

And to understand how our Helicopter Emergency Medical Service (HEMS) team is able to arrive at a scene like this with a set of procedures and protocols, and training sufficient to do some good, you have to look past the individuals and take in the wider system – specifically, how it draws information and feedback from frontline experience, and how it uses that feedback to evolve over time; how it makes sense of its successes and failures, and how it turns that sense into something useful in the future. This, ultimately, is the way that you prevail in a world where every elegant game of chess eventually degenerates into a bar-room brawl.

Matters come into sharper focus as we lift from the motorway, watching the ground and all its wreckage disappear below us. I'm strapped into my seat, facing backwards in the cramped rear cabin of our helicopter with the rest of the medical crew and our patient, who is dying. The air ambulance is still in its early phase of flight, transitioning between the slow, lumbering take-off and the relative stability of fast, forward flight. On the monitor I watch my patient's blood pressure drop away to nothing. I strain forward in my harness and press my fingers into the skin of her neck. I cannot find a pulse.

'She's arrested,' I blurt into my microphone, momentarily forgetting myself. Martin, the paramedic, raises his finger to his lips and frowns. We are below 500 feet, still pulling power, still accelerating, still climbing, and the pilots are working hard, guarding against the possibility of mechanical catastrophe. I am a rookie making a rookie's mistake: talking before we're safely airborne. Nothing, not even this turn of events, warrants breaking that taboo.

There are protocols for a reason: the safety of the entire crew is at risk, and that clarity of process is what ensures the success of the system, the extraordinary and unlikely survival of four passengers in a metal box in the sky. I keep quiet.

Another ten seconds pass, and then we're finally aloft and moving at well over 100 miles an hour, heading for London. 'Your call,' says the pilot, letting the paramedic know that he's done with the take-off procedures, finally giving us permission to speak across the cabin intercom. Paramedic Martin radios the dispatchers in the control room, letting them know that we've lifted from the scene, and then asks the pilots for permission to remove his harness. It's far from ideal, moving around unrestrained in the back of a small aircraft, but our patient is in trouble.

She is a woman in her forties and wasn't wearing a seatbelt at the time of the crash. As far as we can tell, her chest hit the steering wheel and now some part of her anatomy is broken and bleeding enough that we can no longer find any signs of life. But in this cramped cabin, with the equipment at hand and the crush of time, diagnosis boils down to educated guesswork. We are dealing in estimates and assumptions. We have already rendered her unconscious with anaesthesia and cut holes on both sides of her chest, in an attempt to relieve pressure that might have built up from the air trapped around her damaged lungs. We have started a blood transfusion as well. Two units have already run in, and another two are up. Paramedic Martin holds one in each hand, squeezing the bags desperately, trying to get the blood in faster. I check her breathing circuit, making sure it is still intact and that we can still deliver oxygen. Alex, meanwhile, reopens the finger-sized holes in her chest. It is all that we can think to do. The monitor searches in vain for a measurable blood pressure. Underneath my gloved fingers, once again resting across the carotid artery in her neck, I catch the impression of a weak pulse. There is the rising hope that what we're doing is working.

We cross a low ridge that divides the gentle countryside from the edge of the city. Rolling fields give way to patches of asphalt grey and high-rises. We push across the boundaries of suburbia, now finally in sight of our destination. Silence falls again, this time for landing.

The pilot begins his approach to the helipad on the hospital roof, dodging clear of the forest of cranes surrounding the site, watching for the fluttering of the orange windsock, turning us into wind, trading the stability of our straight-line cruise for something more precarious to get us out of the sky and onto the helideck. The pitch of the engine changes, the nose lifts and the gusts of wind against the machine start to make themselves felt, licking around us as we continue our descent.

I glance over my shoulder. The grey landing pad and its illuminated H now fill our view. Our aircraft touches down, the frame sagging gently as it is forced once again to bear its own weight. The blades spin down and the aircraft is suddenly silent. We tear off our helmets, now able to communicate without headsets. A narrow, regular rhythm beats out across the screen of the ECG monitor, with a rate high enough to be mistaken for signs of life. But our patient is once again without a pulse.

We search again for a cause. It may be due to blood loss – cardiac arrest triggered because she is losing blood faster than we can replace it. But there is no obvious source for the haemorrhage and there are other possibilities. With such a significant blunt injury to her chest, we begin to wonder if she has bled into her pericardium – the fibrous sac of tissue that surrounds the heart and ordinarily fits like a glove against its surfaces.

There is a chance that a small volume of blood has entered the space between the two, and that this is compressing the heart, causing it to arrest. This is cardiac tamponade, something very different from bleeding to death from the loss of litres of blood. As little as half a Coke can's worth of blood trapped in the pericardium could prove lethal.

And there are some signs that this might be the case: the veins in our patient's neck look a little engorged, telling us that there might be some sort of obstruction to the flow. But it's so difficult to tell. Here, in the moment, we can't be sure if we're simply seeing what we want to see, confirming our own biases to shut out the uncertainty. People talk of volatility, complexity and ambiguity, but this is where those rivers converge.

Alex steps away to call our boss. Even though we're on top of the hospital, we're still perhaps ten minutes or more from the security of the emergency room and its fully equipped and staffed resuscitation bays, separated from safety by the ramps, corridors and lift shafts that lead there. It has taken dozens upon dozens of decisions just to get us to this point. And there will be more to come.

Alex ends his phone call as we finish getting our patient out of the helicopter and onto the hospital trolley. We haven't got time to get her to the operating theatre. We have to act now. Alex has discussed it with our boss, and the decision is made.

He runs a scalpel across the full width of her torso, from right to left, making a superficial incision. He then starts work on the left side, paring the tissues back to the plane of muscle that lies between the ribs. I unwrap a scalpel of my own and deepen his incision on the right side, finding the same plane. From there I make a hole big enough to admit the lower blade of a large pair of scissors. I have never done this before. I'm trained for it. I've read the books and I've sat in the classrooms. But none of that matches up to the tremulous performance of this moment.

I press the scissors home and begin to cut through the muscle between the ribs, taking care not to lacerate the gossamer-thin lungs and heart immediately beneath. Alex and I hit the breastbone at the same time, but neither of us can get through it with the scissors. We unpack a saw, the sort of item you might find in an outdoors survival kit, a couple of rings joined by a serrated wire. Together we cut through the sternum.

With gloved hands and a sterile towel, Martin pulls the top of the chest open, as though it were the bonnet of a car. Alex hunts with his eyes around the revealed contents of the thorax, before seizing upon the heart and opening the sack of tissue that surrounds it. A large clot of blood spills out. The blood had collected in the sac, encircled the heart and was stopping it from filling and contracting. Unimpeded, it now has a chance to beat.

Now we run. I squeeze the woman's heart with my hands, trying to coax it to beat harder. Alex reaches in and holds her aorta low in her chest, clamping it shut temporarily, to make sure that what little circulating blood there is supplies the vessels of her heart and brain. We arrive finally in the emergency room and hand over to the assembled team. This is the mother of all baton-passes, to a much bigger and more capable team, with the hope that we have formed enough of a bridge to make the difference.

It is only afterwards that I notice the trail of bloody footprints we have left around us, and the gloves on my shaking hands, dripping crimson onto the floor. There is more than the clot around her heart at work here, I realise. There must be another injury. She is haemorrhaging torrentially, somewhere deep inside her chest. The team in the resuscitation bay do all they can. But our patient doesn't survive.

A hot debrief follows immediately, over tea in polystyrene cups, with the hospital team and our crew crowded into an office without enough chairs. We go around the room, retelling the events as best we can, beginning the search for answers.

In this world there is no such thing as a flawless performance; there are always actions that could, and should, have gone better. The trick here is not to go too easy on yourself, or too hard. But it's difficult to pull off. As medics, in a crisis like that, you make dozens of decisions in quick succession, each one a Schrödinger's box with lethal potential, steeped in uncertainty. That's why you debrief in the receding heat of the moment; still trembling as you sip your tea. It would be all too easy to say, 'Now is not the time.' But you have to ask the difficult questions – even though you may not like the answers – because you were there, because the lessons that you learned are written in someone else's blood, and because a patient's last gift to you is the chance to do better for someone else.

High-performance, high-reliability organisations operate at the edge of chaos. It is hard to learn to be comfortable on that edge, and harder still to make it work for you. It is the goal shared by the teams who operate in real time at the sharp end – the doctor, the astronaut, the teacher, the trader, the salesperson – and by those who work to improve systems at the blunt end – the managers, the strategists, the executive teams – to strive to make the whole greater than the sum of its parts, to deal with the uncertainty and to overcome the challenges that threaten to overwhelm us.

So the first thing to note is that success and failure in the face of a complex and deadly threat like the one we faced on the motorway that day, unfolding in real time, are not about elite individual performance. Even teamwork can only get you so far. To properly unpick these events you need to be able to step back and see the system as a whole.

When we say 'system' we mean a collection of components, linked together for a specific purpose, forming a whole that is capable of being greater than the sum of its parts. A laptop computer is a good example: a motherboard with some memory slotted into it, a processor, a hard drive, a fan, a power supply, a liquid-crystal display screen, a battery, a keyboard and a case. Individually these components aren't particularly useful. But connected together in the right way, they form one of the most powerful technologies the world has ever seen. Systems can be physical – like the laptop – social or biological. So a creature such as a dog, a cat or a human being is a system, too.

Even though we don't pay them much heed, we are surrounded by systems upon which we depend: the cars that we drive, the network of roads that we use to move around, the power grid that brings electricity to our homes, our mobile devices and their connections to the internet – they are all systems – right down to the natural world we live in: the weather and woodland on the hill, and the heart that beats in your chest.

The writer Douglas Adams once said that 'if you try and take a cat apart to see how it works, the first thing you have on your hands is a non-working cat', highlighting, in Adams's inimitable fashion, two more critical properties of systems. First, the removal of component parts – or destruction of the linkages between them – affects the function of the system as a whole, sometimes irreversibly and fatally. Second, unpicking a system to try and understand how it works is often easier said than done.

Nevertheless, if we're to properly understand how to deal with uncertainty – and why we succeed and why we fail in the face of it – it is essential that we recast ourselves in this context, as component parts of the complex systems that we live and work within. Almost all such systems today are composed of teams of people working in conjunction with technology. These systems create new possibilities, providing a kind of mechanical advantage for the human in the loop; acting like a lever multiplying our efforts manyfold. But they also create new jeopardy. This has a complicating effect. When things go wrong, there is no Colonel Mustard standing in the Billiard Room with a bloodied candlestick in his hand that we can blame. None of this absolves us of responsibility as individuals, nor does it rob us of our agency, but it should change the way we see ourselves and the way others see us, as well as our ideas about how we might improve.

The point is that unpicking systems and understanding how they work takes time and effort. The time I spent with NASA, early in my career as a doctor, exposed me to a much-mythologised organisation. It was like pulling back the curtain on the Wizard of Oz to find him less fantastic and no less wonderful – though a very different and more complex creature than I had ever imagined. The same was true of HEMS. So while there is plenty to be learned from organisations that manage to maintain high levels of reliability and performance, despite the inherent risks of their endeavours, it is important, too, to ensure that you are learning the right lessons. Divining the source of another tribe's power is an ancient pursuit; and in this there are cautionary lessons, too.

2.

Learning the right stuff

Every year on 15 February an army parades ceremonially on the island of Tanna in the South Pacific. Although their troops are natives of the Melanesian island, they march with the letters 'USA' emblazoned on their chests in red paint. They carry bamboo batons, holding them as they would rifles, and conclude by hoisting a tattered flag, which, despite its poor state, is unmistakably America's own star-spangled banner.

The Tanna Army isn't an army at all. It doesn't possess any real weapons, neither does it fight; their business is not the defence of the archipelago. The display is instead an apparent act of worship, by way of mimicry, of the spirit and once-glimpsed culture of plenty, which they believe will one day return.

During the Second World War, in the wake of the Japanese attack on Pearl Harbor, nearly 300,000 US troops deployed to the South Pacific. The spectacle, for rural-dwelling islanders, was overwhelming. Overnight outsiders had arrived in their thousands, borne by technology of a scale and sophistication they had never seen before, bringing with them plentiful supplies of food, shelter and technological marvels. This bounty arrived rapidly, raining from the sky. It brought new infrastructure and opportunities to people who had been largely isolated from the march of the technological revolution that had transformed so much of the world beyond their shores.

For a while the islanders were able to bask in the seemingly limitless supplies and new-found convenience. But the war moved on and, with it, the temporary garrisons. The Americans vanished as quickly as they had arrived, taking with them their source of wealth and power.

The departure of the US military from their hastily established, and then hurriedly dismantled, military bases on island chains in the Pacific during the Second World War left elements of the indigenous population struggling to adjust to what had happened to them. When times became hard in the years that followed, there were, among the Melanesians, those who sought to re-create the conditions that had seen bounty rain upon the islands from the sky during the Americans' presence.

They mowed mock-runways into grassy plains, erected wooden facsimiles of air-traffic control towers and spoke into sticks whittled to resemble the radio-set microphones they had seen the Americans use. All of this in the apparent hope that they might again understand how to summon cargo planes from the sky, the way the Americans once had.

There have been many attempts at explaining why some Melanesians appear to have been so readily seduced by the offerings of community figures who promised wealth through these strange acts of imitation. At first it was assumed that these social structures were simply that: technology cults, organised by civilisations who couldn't comprehend the phenomena they were trying to conjure. Indeed, the Melanesians, and their counterparts elsewhere in the Pacific, came to be referred to generically as 'the Cargo Cults', and their behaviour was the subject of fascination and ridicule in news articles and television documentaries. But in time social scientists came to realise that what underpinned these rituals wasn't stupidity or cultism.

Today sociologists believe that the Melanesian ceremonies we observe stem from an attempt to rationalise the seismic and rapid transformation of the islanders' way of life brought about by the arrival of modern warfare and the intrusion into their world of the planet's highest-income nations, with all their technology and excess.

We should pause, then, before laughing too readily at the islanders, and ask ourselves how different we are from them when we attempt to draw lessons from other spheres and apply them to our own. We may not be out there trying to summon air traffic with fake radio sets, but we are suckers for trying to learn from – and imitate – the grandiose success stories of others, even when the true roots of that success are difficult, if not impossible, to divine. Too often we look for tricks and shortcuts, copying behaviours and procedures the same way the Melanesians mowed their runways.

This has never been more true than now and in the recent decades of the information age, as new technologies arrive apace, creating new possibilities and problems. The risks in these state-of-the-art systems are difficult to understand, and even harder to mitigate. Today medicine stands, as we all do, in that transformed landscape, desperately searching for answers wherever it can. We are deluged by stories about elite teams and elite people, about pilots and astronauts, doctors and Olympians, soldiers and Silicon Valley CEOs. Too often we have been guilty of behaving in much the same way as the Melanesians did, as the medical profession has come to learn.

In 1999 the United States' Institute of Medicine published a seminal report, 'To Err is Human: Building a Safer Healthcare System'. It shone a much-needed spotlight on the spectre of medical error and the harms that followed. It urged us to recalibrate our understanding of medical practice as that of *good people working in bad systems that needed to be improved*. But for the most part that is not what the world of medicine adopted as its take-home message.

In passages elsewhere in the report, 'To Err is Human' compared medicine to other high-risk industries, which – on the surface – appeared to be faring much better than us: nuclear power, the military and aviation. Instead, that comparison became the unintended principal focus of our efforts at improvement. Unfortunately it was hard to peer inside nuclear reactors and our secret militaries, but the world of commercial aviation seemed familiar and more readily accessible. And so we set about trying to understand what it was that our flying brethren did and to import those behaviours without actually appreciating the depths and complexities that underpinned them.

We were quick to introduce safety checklists of the type that captains and their first officers run through before take-off; we flattened hierarchies in the way their flight crews had learned to; and we tried to report and investigate incidents more like they did. But despite our many years spent trying to translate lessons from the aviation industry, I was never convinced that we were seeing the right things, or learning the right lessons. Indeed, I wasn't sure how much we could ever truly learn about flight operations without actually getting inside the fence, the way I'd been able to at NASA. There was more to human space exploration than one could glean from Hollywood lore, and I was convinced there was more to airline safety than simple standardisation and checklists.

I knew that I needed to immerse myself in the culture of aviation and, if not work within it, at least find a role that sat adjacent to it. And so I decided to try and spend some time embedded with one of the UK's regional HEMS teams. I had always wondered how air-ambulance teams managed the formidable threats and challenges they faced daily; enough that they could safely launch and travel low and fast over undulating terrain in changeable weather, and then deploy medical teams who created chances at survival for their patients that otherwise wouldn't exist.

This seemed like a good place to start my amateur ethnography: here was an organisation where the worlds of medicine and aviation, with all of their attendant risk, were woven together. If aviation had anything at all to teach us, then the helicopter emergency medical crews should have learned it.

Around a decade ago, to sate this curiosity, I managed to talk my way into getting a seat as an observer within a HEMS team in the south-east of England. I would learn a lot from my observer's seat, I thought, like an ecologist sequestered in a hide in a safari park, scribbling notes and watching as they wrestled with the unknown and the unknowable.

But what I would find was some of the best teamwork I had seen in any organisation, in an outfit that had truly discovered how to learn from its successes and, more importantly, from its failures. It was too compelling; I would not remain an observer for long.

3.
Connections

The Kent, Surrey and Sussex Air Ambulance is one of the UK's oldest helicopter medical systems. The service covers a population of more than five million people, spread across 8,000 square kilometres, in a region spanning from the seaside towns of Margate to the eastern mouth of the Solent.

Each morning you could stand in their hangar and watch the pilots crawling over their vehicle, peering under engine cowlings, shining torches into the depths of the clockwork, inspecting rotor heads, tugging on aerofoil blades. This meticulous daily review – their so-called 'Check A' – was how they set up the aircraft and prepared it for action; how they made sure that it would perform optimally when launched and driven into crowded skies and a fickle British weather system. And the question that I found myself asking was, 'How do you go about setting up a human crew to be ready in the same way?'

For a system to function correctly, its component parts must be connected. In a mechanical system those linkages are easy to see and inspect: the teeth of the gear wheels, the rotor shaft, the control column with the blades, the pedals with the rudders. But the HEMS system is more than the machines. How do you ensure a helicopter medical team is properly connected?

These linkages are harder to establish and inspect, but essential nevertheless. Without the free flow of information, there is no connection. Without connection, there is disintegration. With disintegration comes failure, and the stakes were too high to be casual about failure. Setting up for uncertainty and volatility starts with being able to build teams and teamwork quickly, and often with specialists who have never met before their shift and have only minutes to establish a crucial working relationship. This chapter is all about how you establish that human system and prepare it to meet the unexpected.

My first morning as a flying observer with HEMS started crushingly early, before sunrise, even before my brain was fully awake. I stared sleepily into the darkness outside my kitchen window, forced down some porridge and coffee and made my way to the station.

I caught the first train out of London Bridge, just before half past five, going east into Kent with a handful of commuters spread across the carriages, whose reasons for leaving the city so early must have been at least as bizarre as mine. Over an hour later the train pulled into the deserted and still-dark platform at Marden. It seemed an unlikely location for an air ambulance to be based, a sleepy village with no nearby commercial airports and no aerodrome; and standing there silently, in the mist and orange glow of the sodium lights, I wondered briefly if I might have misread the instructions in the invitation email.

Eventually, though, a tiny red Fiat rolled into the car park and flung open its door. Steph, a friend and fellow anaesthetist flying with the service, had driven from Brighton, blasting over the South Downs and through country roads to collect me in time for our six-thirty start. Together we wound around the lanes and narrow streets to find the service's unlikely headquarters at the back of a nearby industrial estate, where the helicopter was housed.

It was not what I had imagined – the antithesis of a glitzy riverside heliport, little more than a free-standing warehouse next to a modest patch of concrete, with a bold but simple yellow cross painted onto it. A windsock fluttering lazily on the end of a pole at the edge of the compound was about the only feature that began to give away what went on inside.

The modest accommodations were all that a working aircraft needed. And what at first seemed like a faintly bizarre setting, I quickly came to respect as an impressive feat of pragmatism and parsimony. HEMS is a charity-funded service, so being canny with spending is crucial. In the UK there are stringent regulations that govern where you can store and operate a helicopter from – rulebooks that run into tomes. It takes money, but not much imagination, to slap an aircraft on the elevated helideck of a yacht. But it takes proper vision to recognise that you could deploy one here.

Flying a helicopter with HEMS is arguably closer in character to emergency and trauma medical practice than that of long-haul commercial airlines – it's riskier and more unpredictable. Their pilots aren't shuttling between well-lit airports coordinated by air-traffic controllers; they're launching at random grid references, landing in fields and car parks, on hillsides and motorways.

Helicopter emergency medical services are archetypal high-risk, high-reliability organisations. This endeavour – of taking an expert team, flying it to the site of a medical emergency and then deploying the right science and technology against the clock, to improve someone's chances of survival – is a thing of labyrinthine complexity. It is a system of myriad moving parts (literally and metaphorically), from whirling turbines and weather reports to blood transfusions and blast dressings. All of those components interrelate and interact, with one another and with the world outside, and all of it unfolds at more than 150 miles an hour, in circumstances where, often, every second counts. It is the very definition of striving for success in the heat of unpredictability. This is the constant loop of uncertainty that you find yourself in, as a member of the HEMS team: from the moment you start the engines on the aircraft to the moment you finally hand over the care of your patient to the hospital team. What the HEMS teams do is intrinsically dangerous; catastrophic failure lies in wait at every turn, and yet is somehow consistently avoided. How do you build something like that, on an unassuming industrial estate in Kent?

With the warehouse-hangar lit and the kettle on, Steph pointed me at a rack of old flight suits and helmets and told me to find gear in my size. As an observer, this felt a bit like being a six-year-old who'd rummaged around in the dressing-up box – in ill-fitting garb, proudly looking the part, but knowing at heart that you're just pretending.

Steph ordinarily worked in a teaching hospital where, at any time, pretty much anyone of any age in any medical state could turn up in need of resuscitation, anaesthesia, intensive care or, more often than not, all three. The core skills needed to diagnose, rescue and resuscitate people who are badly injured or critically ill are practised by anaesthetists every day. They can render patients safely unconscious, manage their airways, thread breathing tubes into their larynxes, establish them on ventilators, set up drug infusions to support failing hearts and circulation, and – in the face of brisk haemorrhage – can run massive blood transfusions. During their training, anaesthetists learn to fly a patient's physiology in real time, the way a pilot might carefully handle an unreliable aircraft in the worst weather. It is what makes them so ideally suited for their role within the HEMS crew.

'It's not the medicine that makes this job hard,' Steph told me as she showed me around the helicopter, 'it's where you are – when you're out there on the road – and it's the pace of it all.'

As I understood it, most of the patients they cared for were cases of traumatic injury: road accidents, mountain bikers, people falling from rooftops, stabbings and the occasional shooting. But there were complicated cardiac arrests and urgent medical conditions to deal with, too. The goal of the service was not simply to move these patients rapidly from the scene of an incident. Packed on board the helicopter was enough kit and clinical skill to extend something of a hospital's capability forward to the original point of injury or illness, shortening the time before definitive treatment could begin. There was, for obvious reasons, a heavy emphasis on speed and efficiency. The helicopter was supposed to be ready to go by 7 a.m. If a call came in after that, the crew was expected to be on board and launching only a few minutes later.

Overnight the aircraft rested on the concrete floor of the hangar. A couple of aluminium sheets, which looked like oversized baking trays, lay underneath it, collecting the infrequent but constant drip of engine oil; which served to remind me that this meticulously maintained mechanism was nevertheless imperfect.

Steph started my orientation, spending a while – before we even got on board the aircraft – taking me through the locking mechanism on the sliding doors at the rear, where we boarded the helicopter. There was a careful tutorial on how (and how not) to turn the handle. There were some words, too, about not yanking too hard when sliding the door open, for fear of pulling it off its runners and leaving the aircraft in need of expensive attention from an engineer and, more importantly, taking it and the rest of the airborne service offline for the day. Almost nothing seemed too trivial to be worth briefing: from opening the door, sitting down and strapping in, to the subtleties of when (and when not) to speak over the cabin intercom.

The walls around the hangar were decorated with a series of colourful aviation safety posters, which took the form of tragicomic cartoon illustrations of a fictional ruddy-faced pilot who was in the process of getting himself, or his crew, killed through simple oversight. In one set he was colliding with wires; in another his aircraft was getting chopped to bits by a wind farm; in the one facing the aircraft on the hangar door he was seen in silhouette, as a rotating helicopter blade made a wet mess of his head. The not-so-subtle safety messaging was clear.

Once inside the rear cabin of the helicopter, I had to crouch. There was just about room for three seats and a stretcher, along with a pile of medical kit and equipment, and not a lot of Feng Shui going on. A red strip of fabric, with the word 'Emergency' written on it, fluttered tantalisingly in one corner of the door, almost begging to be pulled. But that action, Steph told me, would strip the rubber from the window mount and eject the glass from its frame. All of which would be OK if you were trapped in the aircraft on the ground and on fire, but far less so if you were in flight; a further reminder that you were boarding a working vehicle, not a cosy passenger flight.

Then there was the cabin floor, a sheet of no-nonsense aluminium with rails on which to mount the stretcher and seats, underneath which – a couple of inches away – 950 pounds of fuel was stored. Above us was the rotor head, with blades thirty feet across, whose tips travelled at slightly short of the speed of sound when up and running. It was a marvel, even when stationary.

In a helicopter most of the mass of the vehicle is overhead. The turbines and main gearbox sit on top, with the aluminium fuselage dangling beneath. And that's where the crew sits, in a tin can sandwiched between the rotor blades and the fuel. The seats were bolted into the aluminium sheet. Two of them faced rearwards and were little more than metal frames covered in beige canvas, which folded down the way a deckchair might. Despite their appearance, they were specifically engineered for the task, having what the pilots call 'a stroking property', meaning that their supports would collapse like a stiff telescope upon vertical impact, to take some of the energy out of an unexpected jolt. The remaining seat in the rear of the cabin faced forward. It was cushioned with leather upholstery and far more substantial but, according to the pilots, no better than the rear-facing beige deckchairs in the event of a 'hard landing'.

That was the rear cabin: an aluminium box surrounded by machinery and stuff that might kill you, offset by equipment designed to keep you safe; lined with bags and racks full of equipment and monitors, for paramedics and doctors to grab and carry to the scene. It was a cage full of stuff that either broke the aircraft and killed the crew or tried to stop someone dying in an emergency. That's how it felt to me, at least, as a novice to the service.

Organisations like HEMS are obsessed with failure. It is one of their defining characteristics. They know their systems can fail and they make it their duty to understand how and why. They sweat the small stuff, knowing that a tight rein on the detail forestalls disaster at scale. The graphic posters on the wall of the hangar were part of this, and so was the careful tour of the cabin. And, as I was about to learn, so was the way the team prepared themselves for missions.

This aspect of aviation culture was contagious, bleeding over into the medical side. The teams monitored and measured their performance to an extent that seemed almost absurd: how fast they were airborne after a call came in; whether they sent the right radio calls at the right time; what drugs they used, and why; whether their surgical procedures adhered to protocol; whether their diagnoses on scene matched the later findings from the detailed hospital scans. Where there were deviations from the expected outcomes, those were interrogated, regularly and frequently. To do that in a way that improves your organisation and enhances teamwork, instead of tearing it apart, takes substantial effort.

It is not about stick or carrot, it is about fostering respect for the organisation, the team and the job. For high-reliability systems, God and the Devil reside in the detail. Their attitude to failure is different, too. Failures – for the most part – are not punished; they are explored. If the team is regularly straying outside the rulebook, good systems will first ask why, rather than beginning an immediate search for someone to blame.

When they file incident reports because something has gone awry it is not a pejorative or negative act, but is instead seen as a signal from a frontline sensor, which – if conveyed correctly and acted on appropriately – can build towards something that will improve and protect the organisation and the team.

Gathering feedback always feels like such a simple thing to do. But making sure that you're measuring the right things, receiving the right signals, processing them properly and then providing an effective response takes skill and time. What sets the HEMS crews apart is the amount of time they spend on this process, and the culture they have fostered together, one that encourages reporting – of even the most minor transgressions – in the pursuit of organisational improvement. This is a subject I will return to in Chapter 8.

For now, the important observation is this: all too often there is a personal cost to reporting failure. This makes it easier not to put yourself in that situation, not to leave yourself vulnerable to criticism and judgement. But if the culture has evolved correctly, the risks of making yourself vulnerable in this way are outweighed by the benefits that you and the wider team and system reap in return. For that, reporting needs to be met with an effective response, and the system needs to improve in a way that the team can sense. Above all, it requires the fostering of individual and collective relationships in which respect for and deference to expertise are carefully balanced with the ability to speak up without fear of judgement.

Not long after 7 a.m. we gathered for the pilot's briefing. The crew room was on the first floor, in a room fitted out with desks and telephones, and walls decorated with maps and charts. At the far end, next to the window, there was a corner with sofas where the air crew and medical crew gathered for the briefing.

That first day, to me as an observer, the pilot's briefing came across mostly as jargon delivered at pace: METARs, terminal airfield reports, CAV, occluded fronts, dark o'clock, NOTAMS. The little there was that resembled plain English still seemed like a word salad whose ingredients I could barely make out: there was talk of limits, masts and balloons; of payloads and burn rates; and something about possibly having to kick me off the aircraft at the scene, if they ended up having to carry a heavy patient – I wasn't sure if that was a joke.

The pilot's briefing was, I would later understand, part of the essential ritual of team-building. It was also – more prosaically and crucially – a nod to the unpredictability and potency of that most familiar of all complex systems: the weather. Barometric pressures, wind speeds, precipitation and humidity were measured all over the globe; meteorologists bounced radars and lasers off clouds, while detectors monitored lightning strikes. On the synoptic charts we could see air masses swirling out to sea, slowly turning and heading our way. It took a human on the ground to read those data and translate them into information that the pilots could use to inform their aviation decisions – a complex assessment of a complex system. And as all good pilots knew, the forecast was merely a prediction; what you actually experienced, airborne and vulnerable, was quite another.

There were days when the weather would close in and, despite the capability of the pilots and the state-of-the-art technology that guided our aircraft, it would be folly to fly. It was a reminder that we were hostage to something bigger, that we could only ever fly safely when the clouds parted and the system was prepared to let us in.

At one level all of this felt more than a little familiar to me. It was the truth of all medical practice, too. Whatever expertise, technology or science we brought to bear as doctors, the human body was its own swirling, self-governing system, and when it went wrong – in illness and injury – there was only ever a narrow window of time and opportunity in which to intervene. And sometimes that biological system would shut us out altogether, leaving no chance of rescue or escape.

The briefing was where the day really started, complete with a formal roll call of the crew and an acknowledgement of their experience. It is here that I, as the observer, was gently identified as the 'third man' – a spare part unfamiliar with the aircraft or its procedures and, as such, in need of shepherding by the trained crew.

Nevertheless the pilots tell you that, as an observer, even though you may never have climbed into a helicopter before, your eyes and observations also count. If you should see something that you think nobody else has seen – an approaching aircraft, or something that the helicopter is at risk of clattering into during take-off or landing, or something amiss in the cabin – you shouldn't be afraid to call it out. This was the first critical lesson the service taught me: that no matter your level of experience, everyone counts, and none of us alone could be as good as all of us together.

The pilot's briefing was considered sacred. Nothing, and nobody, was allowed to fly until it was complete. The briefing happened even if an emergency dispatch call came in mid-meeting. This was difficult for me to understand at first: the idea that even if a medical emergency should arise, one urgent enough to warrant calling in an aircraft, the crew would still complete their morning briefing – albeit at pace.

But this was another of the service's counterintuitive doctrines:

where every second counts, it is the seconds invested in careful preparation and prevention that later save minutes and lives. This discipline was part of the fabric that served to reinforce the reliability of the operation. There was a function to these meetings that went beyond knowing the precise meteorology of the day. The briefing is often the first time the crew has assembled with that specific combination of people. And so it provided a structured introduction, which – done properly – broke down barriers to communication and allowed the nucleus of a team to form. It was teamwork, in its embryonic form, prioritised as much as preparing the machinery and the technology. And this attention and focus on the binding together of the human team – one that was explicit about their essential role in defending the safety of the system – was perhaps the best I had seen in any organisation.

After the briefing had finished we lingered for a while over tea, toast and bowls of cereal. It was not long after 7 a.m. and this lull, with the crew eventually straying into retelling stories of medicine and flying from their respective pasts, was also an investment in the machinery of the team.

There was depth to their previous careers. Steve, like many of the pilots working with HEMS units, had previously flown with the military; it was hard otherwise to accumulate the hours and experience necessary to fly in this role. His tales of army aircraft that were less reliable, flown in more marginal conditions – often at the edge of the capabilities of the crew and vehicle – reassured you that whatever challenges the day might offer, they were likely to be well within his comfort zone.

Martin, the paramedic, had been on the road for years before being seconded to this HEMS team. He had flown with the service for more than two years and had, as far as I could tell, seen just about everything you can see, in just about every place it could conceivably happen.

The doctor in this environment is the butt of many affectionately delivered jokes. To people like Martin and Steve, who between them had spent decades understanding how to work out in the field, the physician in the room is at first something of an imposter. Unfamiliar with the territory and unsure of how to behave, the novice doctor, venturing outside the walls of their hospital for the first time, is something of a liability. Steph, having flown with the service for nearly a year, was past that point and was both accepted and well respected. Me, they eyed suspiciously, as though I were a child holding a hammer in a glass palace.

Their casual conversation, over the remnants of breakfast with the day's work still firmly ahead, reminded me somehow of that scene from *Jaws*, when the trio of protagonists sit around a tiny table aboard their all-too-tiny boat, bobbing in the middle of the ocean, showing off their scars and telling each other how they got them, and in the process starting to get to know each other properly.

This was where the beginning of the blending of cultures happened, in these informal moments over coffee and tea; with a crew of four waiting for a terror that lay out there somewhere, lurking unknown and unseen.

When just enough time had passed to make me wonder if anything was going to happen that day, the red telephone on the desk next to us began to ring with a piercing tone. Conversations broke off mid-sentence. There was no running, but everyone was suddenly on their feet and moving. Martin picked up the receiver and scribbled down some details on a notepad, stopping to call out the location of the accident and its accompanying six-figure grid reference as he went. Steve glanced at the huge floor-to-ceiling map pinned on the far wall of the crew room that detailed their flying area across the south-east. Steph and I hastily swallowed the remains of our coffee and fastened our flight helmets.

By the time Martin, Steph and I had gathered by the door, Steve was already aboard the aircraft, with its turbines running and the blades getting up to speed. We ran through another short checklist: radios, blood box, mobile phones all present and correct. And then we were out of the door and on the dispersal, beside the aircraft as it continued to fire up; too loud now for us to speak to one another, waiting to catch the pilot's eye so that he could give us the thumbs-up, telling us that it was safe to move in beneath the disc of rotating blades and board the helicopter.

Steph opened the rear door and ushered me inside, leaving me to plug my helmet into the cabin intercom and fasten my seatbelt. A final checklist followed: equipment stowed, doors closed and locked, harnesses secured, avionics online, engine switches set for flying. Over the radio the pilot talked to local air-traffic control, telling them that we were getting ready to launch. We crept out, reversing on our cushion of air over the cattle grid, half pirouetting gently by a giant oak tree before turning to face a field large enough to let us run.

Steve lined the aircraft up, pausing in a low hover, bobbing gently. 'Anything happens and we're going into that field, just beyond the fence,' he told us, gesturing at a neighbouring patch of less well-manicured grass. By this he meant that should we be visited by mechanical catastrophe while trying to get airborne, he would try to control our descent and aim for the flat and largely unobstructed ground in the distance. Pilots avoid the word 'crash' in the same way thespians recoil from the mention of *Macbeth*. They are all 'landings' in their vernacular: hard or soft. A good landing is one you can walk away from; a great landing is one when you can use the aircraft again afterwards. Despite its carefully engineered mechanisms, this technology – like all others upon which lives depended – was uncertain, and failure was an option.

There is a moment during take-off when it becomes safer to commit and continue with your course of action than abort and turn back; a watershed moment when you trade the accumulated risks of what came before for those that lie in the future, and it was this moment that we now approached.

We should not have been able to survive that instant: riding an absurd contraption into the sky, full of fuel with the turbine furnaces sucking in air and belching fire immediately above us. We should have found ourselves a cartwheeling, pyrotechnic heap in the neighbouring field. And yet somehow the wrapper of technology and science around us maintained sufficient equilibrium from second to second, enabling us to do something that for almost all of human history had been impossible.

The nose dipped a little and we raced across the grass, around fifteen feet off the ground, gathering speed, at this point silent in the cabin, but for a single utterance from the pilot.

'Decision point.'

And then, four minutes after the phone rang, we were airborne.

4.

Horizon-scanning

It takes speed and commitment to get a helicopter flying, with the release of energy sufficient to prove lethal, if suddenly misdirected. But without sprinting across the grass balanced on a bubble of nothing – without launching and exposing yourself to risk and the possibility of mishap – no new possibilities can be created. The cone of uncertainty is at its widest here. The crews launch without knowing where they will land or what they will find there, the whole thing a gigantic leap of faith. But they trust in the system and in each other; because they are one and the same.

If you could somehow see the way air folds and swirls around the aircraft during take-off, you would watch turbulence from the downwash claw at the airframe and vortices forming around the rotor blades sucking still more energy out of the system, as though the airfield understands the perils of what you're trying to do and is reluctant to let you go.

The main rotor has five long blades: shells of carbon and glass fibre, wrapped around a honeycomb of something light and fire-retardant. These rotor blades are part-coated with titanium, protecting their leading edges as they scythe through the air. They are designed to be many incongruous things at the same time: light, strong, flexible, durable.

It takes careful engineering to get an aircraft to endure the many different forces that threaten to tear it apart. It must be adapted continuously to meet the threat of the moment, transforming for each phase of flight, in the same way that its human crew must continue to form and re-form itself as the mission progresses.

When spinning, the main rotor forms a disc as wide as a London bus is long, designed to rotate at a nearly constant rate, turning at around 400 revolutions each minute. That's what keeps us flying – the lift generated by those blades as they rush through the air.

During take-off, as we ascend, the system must be reconfigured, quickly and precisely. To keep us climbing against aerodynamic drag and the force of gravity demands more power from the turbines. The throttle opens, we burn more fuel, the turbines work harder, the disc keeps turning. If the pilots climb too hard, move the controls too violently – if they don't ask for enough power from the engines at the right time – the disc will slow and stall and we will fall out of the sky.

The pilots monitor the aircraft in the way we doctors might monitor a patient. They cast their gaze over the instruments and displays, keeping watch for cautions and warnings on their dashboard that help them spot small anomalies before they have a chance to blossom into something they can no longer control.

Circumstances can change quickly. There is often no buffer of time between cause and effect, few escape options if things go awry, and the potential for small problems to amplify rapidly, if unchecked. Some errors and failures are hard to quarantine; others have the capacity to rip through the system like wildfire. That much, at least, was familiar to me.

And like medical work, these HEMS taskings were more time-pressured and less closely standardised than other walks of life. There was no absolute safety here, no certainty. Instead, the teams were forced to trade risk for risk, in search of something optimal in an imperfect world.

All of that needs careful management. The defence is multi-layered; its foundations lie in the architecture of the system, its engineering and technology. But at the sharp end it depends heavily on the human – social – element, upon teams and the quality of their teamwork, upon their ability to adapt and overcome in real time: to be more than the sum of their component parts.

In the helicopter I could hear the rest of the crew spotting and calling out other aircraft as we cruised along. Closing at hundreds of miles an hour, a speck in the distance could quickly loom so large that it became impossible to avoid. Together the crew scanned the horizon for threats. There was an art to it; you had to know what you were looking for, and then how to pass the information on succinctly and with clarity.

Sometimes all they saw was a glint of sunlight bouncing off the windshield of a glider as it turned lazily on a thermal. More often it was an indistinct dot moving against the landscape. Away from you, towards you? On a path likely to intercept? It wasn't always easy to tell. For the doctor and the paramedic, something awful potentially lay in wait on the ground, but while in flight their focus remained centred on the aircraft. Aviate, Navigate, Communicate, Medicate. In this mission those were our priorities, in strict order.

'Light aircraft, ten o'clock, same level, crossing left to right, range five miles,' called Steph.

'Visual,' replied Steve, acknowledging that he too could see it.

My eyes also searched the sky. The pilot had encouraged me to call out threats if I saw them and I wanted to play my part, but I was never able to see the specks in the distance before anybody else.

After nine minutes of flight we found ourselves above the grid reference we had been given, looking down through the canopy of trees lining the country lanes. We scoured the ground below, looking for the accident scene. Pilot Steve found it first, calling our attention to the ambulance he had spotted – a bright-yellow box starkly neon against the countryside. The scene looked dreadful from the air: a blue transit van had collided with a Nissan Micra, spinning it off the road and pushing it through a dense hedgerow. The van appeared to have continued, coming to rest around a tree stump.

A short flurry of radio calls went to and fro, letting the tasking desk know that we had found the scene, telling them we were in the process of looking for somewhere suitable to land. Steve put the aircraft into a steep bank, bringing the scene into view down the aircraft's right side.

Every one of these landings was a problem that needed to be solved in real time while we orbited. There was plenty to occupy the pilot's attention: handling the aircraft, keeping an eye on the cranes and the taller trees, spotting the wires strung between pylons that lay in wait to tear the vehicle apart. And then decisions about whether the site was large enough to accommodate our helicopter and its blades, whether the ground might be too steeply sloped, how to approach it and from what direction.

Our twin-engine aircraft was engineered with plenty of redundancy. On an airfield, in wide open space, you could approach at a shallow descent with enough spare power and energy that even if one of the engines failed unexpectedly, you would still be able to land safely and softly. But accident scenes aren't airfields. The environment is hostile: space is restricted, obstacles litter the approach. We often have to come in more steeply and more sharply than we would like. A mechanical failure late in those descents would be harder to escape from unscathed. We approach with less spare margin and higher risk. But what we gain in return is the ability to set the aircraft down close to where we are needed. That's the trade-off: risk for opportunity.

The descent began. Steph, in the rear cabin with me, and paramedic Martin, next to the pilot up front, began calling out potential hazards as and when they saw them. A tall tree, a line of wires strung between pylons, some plastic sacks beginning to swirl in the downwash on the field below.

Steve lowered the aircraft into a neighbouring field, sailing gently into the wind before touchdown. I looked out of the port window as we came in to land and noticed a telegraph pole at the edge of the road. I realised suddenly that I didn't have any real sense of quite how far the rotor blades extended. With the helicopter up and running, they were just an invisible blur to me. I hesitated for a moment – wondering if the telegraph pole really was close enough to be worth mentioning – and then decided to call it out over the intercom.

There was a pause as Steve looked around, trying to understand what it was that I was talking about. Eventually he spotted it: a pole so far away that there would have been room to fit another aircraft safely between us and it, so ridiculously out of harm's way that only a novice with no real understanding of the aircraft's operating limits would think it was worth pointing out.

'Visual,' he said, without any note of admonishment.

We bundled out of the aircraft and onto the grass, dragging more than 100 pounds of kit in rucksacks and holdalls. We collected at the nose of the helicopter, waited for Steve's permission to head out from underneath the rotors and then made our way to the scene.

I wondered later why nobody had admonished me, or at least made fun of me, for calling out the telegraph pole. It seemed in retrospect like such a rookie thing to do. But their response was measured and deliberate, and something I would later come to understand as a keystone of the operation and the way it fashioned its teams to become the best possible defence against the risk and uncertainty that surrounded them.

The HEMS team faced too many threats in every part of their jobs. And so varied and unpredictable were these threats that it would be too much for any single individual to manage them alone. In the air, on the descent, on the ground – at every turn there were blind spots, and if you couldn't meet those threats as a team, you had no chance of working at your best.

We were better when everyone was in the loop; better when the information was able to flow; better when we encouraged people to speak up and respected what they had to say, even if we might later rationally discount that input. It's easy when it's easy. But success and survival *in extremis* demand that you squeeze every ounce of performance out of you and your team. For that to happen, you first have to form your team.

This was my first glimpse of psychological safety in action. The idea that individuals feel secure in their membership of the group, and unafraid to play their part. It takes skill to cultivate it, still more to do so successfully.

The term 'psychological safety' was first coined in the 1950s by American psychologist Carl Rogers, who talked and wrote about it in the context of people engaging in therapy. Rogers understood that for therapeutic relationships to work best, individuals had to be able to engage openly and authentically, without fear of judgement or rejection. A non-threatening environment fostered learning and personal growth. Within this lay the idea that people might have the capacity to reflect, learn and later heal themselves and grow, given the right conditions.

In the 1990s leadership scholar Amy Edmondson applied this concept to teams and organisations. Her doctoral research, which included work with hospital nursing teams, showed a curious relationship. The organisations with evidence of the strongest teamwork appeared to report the greatest number of clinical errors in drug administration: wrong dose, wrong drug, wrong timing. This was counterintuitive – the idea that the best teams screwed up most often initially didn't make sense. But Edmondson came to realise that these teams felt safe to report errors and mishaps, secure in the knowledge that they would not be punished and would instead contribute to wider learning and improvement of the organisation as a whole. In her studies of other organisations – from global financial institutions to NASA – she found the same patterns repeated over and over again. The stronger teams weren't failing more. They were reporting more. Organisations thrived and performed best when their teams and team members felt psychologically safe.

A psychologically safe environment is one in which individuals feel safe to take interpersonal risk; one in which people believe that they will not be humiliated or punished for speaking up with questions, ideas and concerns, or for admitting mistakes. Edmondson's seminal book, *The Fearless Organization*, published in 2018, identified psychological safety as the *sine qua non* of successful teams.

There's an arc of progress that leads team members to feel psychologically secure in one another's presence; a scheme described in Timothy R. Clark's 2020 book *The 4 Stages of Psychological Safety*. It starts with a sense of belonging. If you don't feel part of the gang, you will languish on the sidelines, separated from the action in critical moments, even if you have important information to share that might alter, or improve, the outcome.

The second stage is the sense of feeling safe to admit that you don't know, and to ask questions. This helps new joiners get up to speed more quickly, but it also primes the team as a whole to continue to grow and learn through curiosity.

The third stage is the point at which you feel safe enough to contribute. In other organisations you usually have time to develop these relationships and that trust, such that the risk of psychological discomfort feels low. But within HEMS there was a constant turnover of new doctors, pilots and paramedics rotating in and out, along with outsiders like me in the observer's seat. The HEMS crews had to assemble, dissolve and re-form on a daily basis. The breakfast club, the pilot's briefing, the chat over coffee and cereal: they were all part of a fast-track course in bringing people into a team, reducing the chance that they might pose a threat to team safety, and increasing the chance that they might function as an asset. What appeared casual, even a waste of time, was actually a critical and strategic part of teamwork and a vital contribution to the outcome of that day.

That first morning flying with the crew, I knew nothing. And I knew that I knew nothing. But it was possible that at some point on our journey I might stumble across something important. I might notice another aircraft creeping up unseen, out of view of the rest of the crew. I might spot smoke pouring from beneath the rotors on my side, and wonder if it was worth mentioning. I might see a tarpaulin lifted by the downwash, in danger of being sucked into the blades. In each of these scenarios, and many more, it would be better to flag it to the rest of the team rather than hold on to the information, for fear of looking stupid.

The telegraph pole turned out not to be a threat. But the tone of Steve's response – one that welcomed my input – made me more confident to contribute again, because next time it might well be accurate and critical information that could save our lives.

The final stage on the road to psychological safety is arriving at the point where you are confident enough of your place within the team not just to ask questions and contribute, but to challenge decisions directly. This is the trickiest aspect of all. There is usually a deficit of knowledge between you and whoever is leading the team, and a tacit assumption that their experience and expertise should not be questioned. But high-performance teams of this type depend upon people feeling empowered to challenge decisions and strategies, in the moment, if they think they are flawed.

Only four weeks later, I returned to Marden for another observing shift. That day we found ourselves landing on a farm, with dust billowing up around us. And from the back of the aircraft, I glimpsed what looked like a black washing line swaying immediately below us. It was a domestic power line, rigged on a pole about ten feet tall, carrying electricity across the yard where we were planning to land. It hung directly below us, crossing diagonally from beneath where I sat in the rear to emerge on the far-left hand side of the aircraft, hidden temporarily from the pilot's view. I hesitated to speak up for a moment. Surely Steve had seen it, I thought. But the descent continued. And I found myself pushing the foam of the microphone to my lips and saying, very clearly, 'Wire, wire, wire.'

'Visual,' came the reply. 'Repositioning.'

For the team to work in this challenging environment, where the norm was uncertainty and unpredictability, information had to flow freely between everyone. The ingrained culture of psychological safety – which the crew had done so well to cultivate – helped remove inhibitions to that flow. It was the first of many layers of protection wrapped around the crew. Without such close attention to keeping the team connected, feeling open and collaborative, the system could not work.

The HEMS medics who worked alongside the pilots found themselves entrained into their aviation culture. What they learned about psychological safety, building teams and communicating effectively in the aircraft cabin they took into their medical practice on the ground, and with good effect.

But it went further than that. The medical crews had become heavily checklist-driven, and developed a catalogue of standard operating procedures to guide them in their work. I was a little less convinced that this aspect of aviation culture could translate well into the world of medicine. What we did was more complex, more steeped in uncertainty and ambiguity. As doctors, we operated far closer to chaos, and more regularly experienced catastrophic failure and loss.

It was hard to understand how the same approaches might work for us in healthcare or how broadly they might be applied. And as I watched the medical crews at the scene, swept up in the fast flow of events, in a world of endless threat of endless variety as they unpacked their laminated cards and standardised procedures – like pilots on flight decks preparing for take-off – I wondered if those tools were truly fit for purpose here. This wasn't the choreography of an exhaustively rehearsed free kick, it was a goal-line scramble; art, not science. It was this that made me wonder if they might be making a Cargo Cult error. Was it just cosplay? And it was then that I realised it would take more than casual observation to find out.

5.
Adaptive capacity

The thorny challenge, which plagues all those who try to study, design or lead teams and organisations, is how to close the gap between what you imagine the people at the sharp end are doing and what they are *actually* doing.

That gulf is hard to close. But it is a challenge that all organisations face as they grow in size and complexity. The solution, in part, lies in getting up close to where the work is being done, where the real-time decisions are being made and where their consequences are most keenly felt. For the HEMS crews, these scenes were dynamic, chaotic and time-pressured. Often the team's first rehearsal of an action was their last opportunity to get things right. But that was precisely why it was impossible to fully comprehend what was running through their heads without being on the job and responsible for the outcomes yourself.

I flew in the observer's seat for weeks watching the HEMS teams work, trying to understand how they did what they did. And then one day, while I was sitting in the kitchen at Redhill Aerodrome, talking with the director of HEMS operations about the service and how they kept all the plates spinning, he remarked that they were hiring for the spring.

The invitation to apply was too good to refuse.

The training was quick and difficult: success in the interview was followed by an intensive week-long residential medical course in a disused hospital somewhere near Folkestone. There were four new recruits in the intake: me, two emergency-medicine doctors and another anaesthetist. We spent the mornings in a seminar room behind desks, with the faculty of instructors and assessors lining the edges of the space, watching us intently; there was more than a shade of tribal initiation about it.

We had equipment to learn, an aircraft to understand, procedures and protocols to memorise. The operational elements of the service were guided by a leash of Standard Operating Procedures (SOPs): didactic guides covering everything from the conduct of anaesthesia in the pre-hospital setting to the rescue of casualties from train tracks. We were expected to know them intimately and to adhere to their rigidity, wherever possible. Deviation from the SOPs was tolerated, but only if absolutely necessary and only if it could later be defended in front of your peers. At times the training felt neither like art nor science, but instead more akin to a drill for dismantling and reassembling a rifle repeatedly, and so thoroughly, that eventually you could do it with your eyes closed. But this was how you began to fold a new line of doctors into the system and blend them with its other components. In growing this team, this was where the first new connections were made.

In the afternoon they ran the *moulages* – medical scenarios simulated with as much fidelity as the training team could muster, with professional make-up and actors and latex prostheses, all of which injected an uncomfortable sense of realism into the exercises. Whether the aim was to put us off our stride more than we already were, or to begin the process of desensitisation that we were going to need, wasn't clear. But the casualties lay there, wet and red, shouting and screaming, occasionally waiting with a mouthful of cold chicken soup to spit at the unwary candidate, as an all-too-convincing simulation of vomited stomach contents.

The *moulages* felt never-ending. The training team would throw mannequins into basements, and then you in after them. They would get you to run the case as though it were the real thing, throwing in curve ball after curve ball, heaping so much simulated stress upon you that you almost ceased to be able to distinguish it from reality. They forced errors out of you and studied how you dealt with the aftermath.

*

We run downhill towards the scene, weighed down by backpacks stuffed with medical equipment. A paramedic from one of the ground crews runs alongside us, delivering a precis of the case as he understands it.

The situation is still evolving, and he is short on detail. We know there has been an incident at a warehouse; that someone called the ambulance service with a garbled message asking for help, describing injuries bad enough to consider sending for us and our helicopter. There's a lot of confusion. The crew already at the scene thinks someone might have fallen from, or even through, the roof. They think there's at least one injured person inside, but there may be more. What starts as grey only gets greyer.

We arrive outside the warehouse a little breathless, throw our packs onto the ground and look up at the wall above, which is maybe thirty or forty feet high. A fire officer in full protective garb greets us and we manage cursory introductions. He is working with a Hazardous Area Response Team (HART), called out because the building looks as if it might be unstable. The rest of the fire crew are already inside, searching for casualties.

In the background there is the overwhelming sound of generators and compressors running in an enclosed space. The fire officer has to shout to make himself heard. He tells me they have just discovered a man who, apparently, in the process of trying to steal some lead from the roof, has fallen through it, all the way to the ground, and is now lying trapped inside. The warehouse is old and disused. The only access to the patient they have found is through a tunnel barely wide enough to accommodate one person at a time. None of this is ideal. He stops talking, having given me all the information that he has. I look at the forbidding opening on the ground. There has to be a better way in.

'Is that all there is?' I ask him.

'I'm afraid so,' he replies.

We leave our packs behind – depriving us of most of our medical kit – and crawl on our bellies through the hole into the darkness of the warehouse beyond. We scuff our elbows on the cold concrete floor, finally emerging, to be helped to our feet by one of the firemen inside. Our first impression is of commotion, of the fire crew trying to break something down. In the gloom I can't quite make out what.

The man in the corner is combative and shouting, illuminated only by red headlamps. I can barely see him.

'Is there any better light?'

'No.'

This is it. It's not going to get any better. There is a lot of chatter, and the fire crew tell me again that they're worried the walls might not be structurally sound.

It's cold, dark and noisy. I've lost some of my kit, and just making my voice heard above the din of machinery is going to be a challenge. All of that has to be broached before I even get to my patient. This is unfamiliar turf – it feels like a million miles from the well-lit warmth of the hospital. I'm getting maxed out. There are too many distracting details; too many variables to consider. This is what the psychologists refer to as 'cognitive tunnelling': a rabbit hole of the mind, into which we all are prone to fall in high-stress situations.

I know the theory, I know the consequences of falling victim to that trap. I know it's happening here, right now, but I still can't do anything about it. My perception is narrowing; I'm losing sight of the wider picture. I try to slow it down, but it's no use. There is the uncomfortable realisation that whatever there is in my mind – moving me forward and making decisions – I am barely in control of it.

I approach the casualty. His pelvis is a mess, as is his left leg. He's in agony – I can barely get any sense out of him. I try to provide some reassurance, but to no avail. I ask him what happened. He's vague on detail. Between expletives, he snarls something about not wanting to go back to prison. That's the least of his worries. He has fallen perhaps thirty feet into the darkness of this basement; more than far enough for there to be life-threatening injuries. Now, bathed only in the red glow of a fireman's head-torch, he is bleeding and in pain. To him, this must feel like hell itself. Words alone won't get me out of this spot.

Ayesha, the paramedic working with me, has somehow managed to site a drip in the patient's left arm. Through that, I give him some pain relief. Ketamine is the drug of choice: an anaesthetic agent and a potent painkiller. I dribble a tiny dose in, not wanting to risk an overdose here in this awful place, far away from any hospital.

'Time is ticking by,' comes an impatient, disembodied voice from somewhere in the darkness.

I can feel myself getting lost here; muddled about what my priorities are. I trickle in some more ketamine to help settle the patient.

'What do you want us to do?' asks the man leading the fire crew.

I'm not sure I know the answer to that question.

Leadership. That's what they're looking for. They're looking to me for a plan of action. But there are too many possibilities. This man is badly injured. Possibly bleeding briskly to death. If his pelvis and left leg have been shattered in the fall, there may be other injuries. What about his spinal column? What if there are fractures there? If I move him, I risk making the whole thing worse.

I try to get a grip. I answer the fireman's question with a couple of my own.

'It's bloody loud, isn't it? Can you turn the generator off? And do you need to do all that banging?'

'Can't turn the generator off; and yes, we do need to do all the banging – the rest of the crew are trying to shore up the walls and gain better access to the warehouse.'

That exchange got me nowhere. The crew is waiting for me to put something into motion. They must by now have questions about my competence. I try not to feel the glare of the four of them looking at me, wondering why I'm not moving things on.

I ignore the fire crew and turn my attention to the patient. Perhaps that will help me make a decision. His leg is badly broken, his pelvis probably also smashed. This is something I can do: address the injuries. And here something is better than nothing. I announce that I want to bind the pelvis and splint the broken leg.

They hand me a folding splint in a bag; one that I don't know how to use, because I haven't studied the HEMS team's SOPs closely enough. I fumble around in the dark. Out of nowhere, someone leans in and hisses, 'Bandwidth!' close to my ear before unfurling the splint for me.

'Bandwidth' is a term the service uses to describe someone's ability to process parallel streams of information and act upon them. It is the secret to coping with these scenes. Lots of bandwidth equals lots of spare capability, in their book. Getting stuck – distracted by the detail – narrows bandwidth and increases the risk of failure. This I know, but I still can't help myself.

I stare at the splint. It is a mess of straps and coloured tabs; like a pole from a tent with bunting on it. It doesn't come with instructions, and this is no time to learn by trial and error. More wasted time. Finally I wrestle the splint on. I give the patient some more ketamine to settle him down.

Things feel a bit better now; we're moving in the right direction. I try and get a stretcher underneath him, finally organising the fire crew into a team, giving them a role and something to think about other than my earlier impression of being a muppet. The stretcher is split into two halves, allowing us to assemble it around and underneath the patient, causing as little disturbance to him as possible as we prepare for the move. I begin to think ahead, to where this is all going. Once the patient is packaged up properly, we'll get out into the daylight and have a proper look at him. We're in good shape, I think.

Then, just as I'm struggling with the stretcher assembly, an alarm whistle sounds. It comes from outside: shrill and louder than any of the equipment noisily chugging away in the background. The fire crew all turn their heads at its first blast. It sounds again, repeating every two seconds or so. By the time of the third whistle blast they are all on their feet and heading for the exit.

'Do you know what that is?' shouts their chief.

'No,' I reply.

'It's the evacuation signal! We have to get out. Now!' he says.

The fire crew don't panic. Now really does mean *now*. I get to my feet.

'Should we take him with us?' shouts Ayesha, gesturing at the patient on the half-assembled stretcher.

I give it a second's thought. It's all the time I have. The fire chief is pulling at my shoulder. The stretcher isn't ready. I can't close the clasp at the top. I make my decision, 'No,' I say, looking around me at the fire crew and my own team.

We leave in a hurry, with the fire crew bundling us through the gloom. The whistle is still blasting away, heralding – as far as I can tell – impending catastrophe. I leave my patient behind. A large opening has appeared in the far wall, presumably created by the rest of the fire crew smashing through the warehouse doors, providing a fast escape route. We break out into the bright sunlight.

The building collapses behind us. My patient dies. The story ends.

'End ex,' someone says.

The exercise is over. Simulated disaster not averted. The exercise director – the owner of the unhelpful voice that snarled in the darkness – creeps out from among the bemused fire crew. He looks at me and half sniggers, scribbling on his scorecard. 'How do you think that went?'

The fire crew smirk, knowing that I've not made the mark.

It is hard not to beat yourself up. I know the theory. I know the traps that I shouldn't fall into. But in the moment, even with that knowledge, I fell into all of them. And that's the problem. The theories are all well and good. But what you carry into those complex scenarios is the mess in your head. All the academic papers you can quote don't provide armour against that.

The service knows this, through long, hard experience. This type of simulation is the mainstay of a training regime that is designed to stop you falling into the usual traps: confirmation bias, fixation error, failure to act . . . the list goes on. The pressure is manufactured, but the paramedics, the fire crews and the buildings are real. The stories are all based on cases they have encountered. And this scenario – down the tunnel into the gloom – is in many ways the perfect metaphor for what they hope to do with us, their new trainee doctors. They chuck you into a dark hole, beat you up and drag you out again. They keep sending you back in until one day you emerge a changed person.

It is necessary. This is more than training; it's an attempt to undo the lessons I've learned through five years of medical school and twelve years of postgraduate training; an attempt to divorce me from a culture that simply won't work aboard the helicopter, or out there in the messy, unpredictable real world.

This version of professional simulation was a far cry from the training for the HEMS pilots. They would regularly retreat to Italy to spend time running nightmare scenarios inside a full-motion simulator; an all-singing, all-dancing state-of-the-art video-game-cum-fairground ride. Their version of training made use of a convincing computer-generated virtual reality: engine failures and fires, avionics glitches, tail-rotor malfunctions, inadvertent flight into low cloud. We, on the other hand, were reduced to using latex mannequins, pantomime costumes and some make-up – there is no way to simulate the complexity of a human body and the myriad ways it can fail.

The disaster in the warehouse occurred almost halfway through the HEMS induction course; I was still finding it hard to get used to the rhythm and pace that my new role demanded. The simulations were deliberately absurd; designed to push you to your limits when the stakes were low, hammering home the importance of knowing your kit and your SOPs. But there was always something unexpected in the scenario, something that forced you to improvise. You were expected to have committed the kit and procedures to memory. The decision-making was what they were assessing, and a sense of how you would cope when your carefully laid plans had fractured away.

In modern, digital communication we use the term 'bandwidth' to describe a system's data capacity: how much information it can send and receive. It is possible to saturate a system's bandwidth, such that no further useful information can be sent or received. And when the instructors talked about bandwidth, they were partly using it in that way. But bandwidth here is about more than raw data capacity. There is information to process, decisions to make, actions to deliver. Bandwidth, in the HEMS vernacular, is actually a measure of a team member's capacity to *adapt* to an unfolding scenario.

In the simulated warehouse scene, the instructor was chiding me for *not preserving that capacity*. When your bandwidth is exhausted, so is your ability to adapt, and when you are facing fast-moving, fast-evolving threats, that can be fatal. I got distracted because I didn't know how to use the splint, and that in turn forced me to commit head-space – what psychologists would call 'cognitive resource' – to solving a minor procedural problem that I should have made standard long before.

The SOPs – a set of core tasks that can be performed almost reflexively, when required – make sense because they help to preserve this capacity. Prioritising tasks, and recognising those that you – and you alone – must do, against those that can be farmed out to other members of your team, is similarly essential. This is why skilful delegation is also vital: it enables tasks to unfold in parallel and thus conserves cognitive capacity. In the uncertainty of these scenes, preserving your ability to adapt, improve and overcome in real time is the key.

So what exactly is adaptive capacity?

Progress is not made by reasonable people, and John Boyd led a life of spectacular progress. Born in 1927, the youngest of five children, he grew up in Erie, Pennsylvania, a boom-town emblematic of the optimism and industrial renewal of the Roaring Twenties. But the American economy was already perched on a precipice, and hard times lay ahead. His father, Harold, died of pneumonia shortly after the stock-market crash of 1929, leaving his mother, Grace, to see the family through the depths of the Great Depression alone. In the years that followed, jostling for priority with his older siblings, competing in a world where resources were suddenly scarce, Boyd learned his earliest and hardest lessons about life and survival.

As a teenager he enlisted in the Army Air Corps, though too late to experience combat during the Second World War. He found himself honourably discharged after the war, but took advantage of the GI Bill to fund a place at university, studying economics at Iowa State. Shortly after gaining his degree he joined the US Air Force, commissioned as a fighter pilot, and was summarily deployed to serve in the Korean War.

Boyd flew twenty-two combat sorties in Korea without ever firing his guns or downing an enemy aircraft. Nevertheless, he was highly regarded as a pilot and, on his return to the United States, attended the elite Fighter Weapons School at Nellis Air Force Base. He graduated at the top of his class and later returned as an instructor.

In simulated combat – as on the ground – he had a fearsome reputation. Impossible to defeat in the air, and confident to the point of arrogance, he challenged all-comers, offering any pilot who survived more than forty seconds in a dogfight with him the prize of $40. It was a bet he never lost.

For fighter pilots engaged in a dogfight, success isn't simply about having superior firepower or a faster plane. Instead it is about being able of outmanoeuvre an opponent who is – at the same time – trying to outmanoeuvre and defeat you. Boyd's invincibility in the air was a product of his unique and calculating approach to aerial combat.

Until this point in history, dogfights had been regarded as more art than science, guided by gut feelings and instinct. But Boyd came to see these duels objectively, as a matter of physics and mathematics, coining a powerful new concept called 'Energy–Manoeuvrability Theory'. In this framing, dogfights boiled down to a pilot's ability to manage the trade between a fighter plane's potential and kinetic energy; an understanding of how its altitude, power and speed could be translated into action, allowing a pilot to out-turn, out-run or out-gun their opponent. If you had awareness of an aircraft's thrust, drag, velocity and weight, you could estimate how fast it could change its state: speed up, slow down, gain or lose altitude or shift direction. Boyd called this the aircraft's specific energy. To him, it was a physical measure of the system's adaptive capacity.

This is an important concept. If you face a simple, predictable challenge, you can meet it with a specific, well-rehearsed response.

But few real-world challenges are of this type. When confronted by threat, complexity and uncertainty, the ease and speed with which you can alter your response, and the extent to which you are able to do so, are core determinants of success or failure.

In a dogfight the faster a pilot can turn and bring their weapons to bear on their enemy, the more likely it is that they will defeat that opponent. In Boyd's theory, this meant preserving your capacity to adapt and overcome, storing the aircraft's specific energy until the time came to spend it on attack or escape. 'He who can handle the quickest rate of change,' Boyd said, 'survives.'

He later applied this philosophy to military strategy more broadly, describing decision-making in the face of complex, fast-moving threats as a deliberate and continuous process, something that he famously came to call the 'OODA Loop'.

The OODA Loop is disarmingly simple. In fighting an opponent, you have to Observe and Orient yourself around them, then using that information you have to Decide how to attack and, finally, Act. Actions without decisions are reckless, Boyd said, but decisions without actions are useless. OODA is a framework for rapidly cycling through a series of actions designed to force you to perpetually gather and respond to new information, and make the adaptive corrections necessary to defeat your opponent. It is designed to be brief and simple enough to use in the time-pressured, life-critical arena of aerial combat. And it assumes that your opponent, or whatever threat you are facing, is engaged in a similar process. Because that is the nature of complex threats: they adapt to whatever you throw at them. Your job is to outmatch their pace.

Boyd generalised this concept, applying it to scenarios that extended well beyond the cockpit of a fighter jet. He used it to redesign the United States' fighter aircraft, trading brute force for agility and adaptability – a doctrine that survives in the US Air Force today. OODA was also central to the US military strategy during the first Gulf War; later it was taught in business schools around the world.

Two key aspects are worth noting. First, it is deliberately designed to be an aggressive approach, characteristic of Boyd himself. The reason being that the rigid, immovable defence will survive the threat of the moment, but it is unlikely to prove impervious to the next or successive variants. It is why modern organisations are better served by moving away from the apparent comfort of absolute security and positioning themselves instead close to the edge of chaos. This is where HEMS teams operate, by default.

Second, implicit in the concept of the OODA Loop is the idea of continuous, and sometimes rapid, adjustment to stay ahead of a threat. The HEMS teams run a version of that loop repeatedly in any and all missions that they face. It takes energy and effort to do so, constantly re-orientating yourself, gathering or refining observations, making new decisions, discarding earlier ones and then committing to new action. Of course it is not a combat opponent that they face, but something just as unpredictable and dangerous: a rapidly changing set of circumstances and unstable physiology, which together can conspire to serve up a steady stream of unexpected events, demanding repeated innovation.

Where Boyd's fighter planes had specific energy, the HEMS crew members had their cognitive bandwidth. You didn't want to spend that adaptive capacity on cognitively trivial tasks that you had failed to master in training – as I had in the simulated warehouse, wrestling with the splint. And so the SOPs and protocols did not exist because the job was thought to be machine-like and predictable; they were there in large part to protect your capacity to respond to uncertainty. It was why reverence for them among the HEMS teams was near total.

The first standard operating procedure in the file talked about safety at the scene. The first lives you were expected to protect were your own. It read a bit like a 1970s public-health safety pamphlet: don't get run over, don't stand on the live rail, don't fall down holes on building sites, don't play with fire.

This may all have seemed obvious, but railway stations in particular presented a plethora of problems for teams trying to stick to the rules. We were taught how to spot the live rail and overhead power lines, and how to avoid being caught in the high-voltage circuit. The key to approaching incidents on the railway network, the SOP explained, was to be sure that the power was off, which you did by making a call to the responding Rail Incident Officer (RIO). But that was never straightforward. When called, the RIO would travel in an ordinary car, without a blue light, through the traffic; he or she could be miles away, and because of that was rarely present at the scene when you arrived. In his or her absence, it was harder to be certain that current wasn't running.

Even with the power off, hazards remained. We were taught that trains could coast for miles under their own momentum, creating an automatic time pressure, urgency and anxiety about working on railways.

The railways crystallised an important lesson. The assessment of real-time risk wasn't a single question; it was dynamic, shifting second by second, shaped by the scene and its circumstances. It was the familiar merry-go-round of feedback: set a goal, gather data from your surroundings, update your expectations of reality, effect a change that gets you closer to your goal and then go again.

The message from the training and the SOPs was clear: the things that killed, injured and maimed the patients we attended could do the same to us, if we were not vigilant. We were often still at the scene where the accident had happened. These risks had to be assessed, navigated and avoided; ambulance crews did this effortlessly, as this was their world and to them its myriad threats were well understood. We physicians, on the other hand, were used to the cotton-wool environment of our hospitals, where the most lethal environmental hazard was that which we created ourselves.

After the procedures that taught you how not to get killed came those that gave you the opportunity to save lives. They were like a series of well-honed recipes. One spelt out how to pack a badly fractured face and stop it bleeding; another how to bind a pelvis, splint broken limbs and assemble a portable stretcher. There was a detailed section covering the conduct and substantial hazards of pre-hospital anaesthesia, shortly followed by a page that taught you how to stab and twist a scalpel into the front of someone's neck to form a makeshift surgical airway, should your anaesthetic endeavours go awry. There was little apparent grace to any of this. The processes described appeared crude in character – none more so than those that detailed the invasive surgical procedures.

I say 'surgery' here, but it is not of the type that any respectable modern surgeon would recognise. The procedures we were taught to do at the roadside bore a greater resemblance to the sort of intervention a barber-surgeon might have performed centuries ago, made barely respectable in our hands only by the anaesthesia that we were also able to provide. *In extremis* we could – theoretically – amputate limbs, open chests, even carry out something that looked like a Caesarean section. In practice, most of these skills were rarely tested, and none but the most foolhardy physician relished the prospect of having to perform them.

It was important for us to recognise what being a physician in a HEMS crew really meant: we were not emergency physicians, surgeons or anaesthetists, but some mongrel combination of the three, crudely adapted to deliver decisive intervention at a speed that wouldn't otherwise be possible.

By the end of the week-long residential medical course, having played through dozens of scenarios and endured the feedback, I felt as if I had worked out how to approach each scene and what I needed to say, and do, to get myself into a position where I could deliver the right medical care.

I had memorised all of the procedures and I could almost make them appear like drop-down menus in my head. I had an answer for every scenario that the training team could throw at me. This was medicine borrowing from the aviators and their checklists and standardisation. The system was crude in parts, but it had many virtues: everyone knew what to expect. It had been honed over years and had been proved to work. You were a component part, feeling temporarily more like a technical than a social part of the system. The paramedics joked that, to them, the new doctor was just another item of equipment on the rack, which they would pull out of the aircraft and deploy at the scene. Everyone always laughed at that – the doctors perhaps more nervously than the paras.

The HEMS medical-crew course was an ordeal. A week of being constantly scrutinised by the people who would soon be working alongside you. They were looking for more than mere technical competence. They wanted to know if you might come apart in a tight moment, to see if you could manage the team of strangers – paramedics, fire service and police officers – that would assemble around you at the scene. More importantly, they wanted to know if you could manage yourself. While you were trying to learn how to operate as a member of a HEMS crew, the instructors were taking careful note and learning plenty about you.

The week-long crew course did its job. It gave you the confidence to think that you might actually be up to the task. The standard operating procedures – once digested and mastered – were a suit of armour against uncertainty and, by the end of the course, we had played through and debriefed so many scenarios that we were all raring to go. But it wouldn't take long to learn that SOPs, exhaustive simulation and rehearsal can only get you so far.

6.
Decision point

We arrived at the railway station soon after the accident had happened, and commuters were still flooding out through the ticket gates away from the platform. The story wasn't clear. Nobody was sure how or why he'd fallen. A lone police officer greeted us, telling us the little she knew and that a land-ambulance crew was already with our patient and working on the tracks beneath the train.

The standard operating procedure here couldn't be clearer: you don't get onto the tracks until the RIO has confirmed it is safe to do so. But it felt wrong to wait when there was a team already working on the patient and at risk, and even more so to pull that team out while they were delivering care.

In the ambulance control room the HEMS dispatchers had been working hard in the background to get hold of the RIO – who was still on his way in his car – to confirm that the power to the tracks had been cut. We radioed them again, trying to get reassurance that it was safe to proceed, but they were still waiting to hear. Unsure of what to do, I caught the eye of what I assumed was a rail worker wearing a hi-vis jacket marching along the line in a hurry, away from the scene, looking a little distressed. I shouted after him, asking if the power was off. 'Yes,' he replied without breaking his stride.

In trains that run on electrified rails there is a set of conducting bars in the driver's cab that can be laid down in front of and behind the carriages to short-circuit the flow of electricity, providing added protection. 'Are the bars down?' I asked. He half turned, raised his thumb weakly and nodded.

We climbed into the trench and followed the rails on the track next to the stationary carriages, eventually finding the paramedics and their patient. They handed over to me, telling me what they'd found and what they thought they could see. Our patient was trapped underneath the train between the sleepers; it was hard to know how badly he was hurt, but he lay quiet, motionless and in need of the kind of help that none of us could administer to him there.

I should – at this point – have been listening intently to the all-important briefing from the ambulance paramedics. But instead I was now wondering who the guy in the hi-vis jacket really was; there had been no time for introductions in that exchange. He wasn't the RIO, I knew that for sure. I had assumed he was a rail worker. I had assumed he was qualified to tell us whether the power was off and that the short-circuiting bars were down. Was I willing to bet my life, and that of my team, on a stack of hasty assumptions?

I found myself absently glancing up and down the track on which we were standing; at the heat haze that shimmered above the hot rails far into the distance, from which I was partly expecting an oncoming train to come roaring at any instant. I was distracted too by the potentially live rail stretched out before me – a strip of steel through which enough current to kill any and all of us instantly might run. It all felt wrong: us, there on the tracks, next to something ordinarily so lethal. Perhaps 200 feet away, on a parallel line, a through train thundered past behind the platform, creating enough of a racket to make it difficult to hear the ambulance crew.

And then the handover was finished and everyone waited expectantly for a plan – one that I didn't have. We stood in the trench, on the tracks, by the rail that might or might not be live, in the path of trains that might or might not be oncoming. And the rumbling in my head was not another fast train on the distant line, but the sound of cowardice rising to a crescendo.

I could adhere strictly to protocol. I could wait for the RIO to arrive. But that would mean pulling the whole team out of the rail trench and onto the platform, abandoning our patient. I radioed the dispatcher again. Still no word. And as I continued to stall, Ellie, the air-ambulance paramedic working with me, appeared at my side having jogged, unnoticed by me, to both ends of the train while I was still procrastinating.

'Right,' she said, 'the short-circuiting bars are down. Both ends. I've seen them myself. Let's get him out.'

What guided us now was not the RIO's official confirmation that we were safe, but Ellie's dynamic assessment of the risk. We were off-protocol and improvising, but this was a necessary and justified deviance by one of our most experienced paramedics. Unlike me, this wasn't Ellie's first job on a rail track.

We eased our patient out from underneath the train as best we could, and with plenty of pace. We weren't complacent about the risks and continued to assume that the middle rail might be live, working carefully around that hazard. The goal here was to get out of this trench and onto the safety of the platform as fast as we could, however we could. This was the real world – one that forced us to choose between bad and worse.

The SOPs were a necessary imagining of the scenarios that we would face, but there was a gulf between those idealised flowcharts and the way they actually played out. I had got stuck, unable to make a decision, because I was searching for a perfect solution when 'good enough' was what we needed. The SOP asked us to halt and wait for certainty. But the paramedic team was already committed. If we followed our protocols to the letter here, no progress could be made: both our team and the patient would remain in danger and bound by the restrictions of the narrow space, the potentially electrified rail, and the splitting of our attention between how best to deliver care and the safety of the crew.

Trying to provide the right care for a trapped, injured patient felt like a race to build a ship in a bottle. And the realisation I had yet to develop was that sometimes the fastest and best method was first to smash the surrounding glass.

In medical practice there has always been a strong desire to standardise our performance as far as possible. For years after the publication of 'To Err is Human' it made sense to try and iron out the variation, to both our managers working at the blunt end and us operating at the sharp end. We had seized upon SOPs as a way of creating structure where there was little otherwise to be found. This was the behaviour of other safety-critical organisations, such as the commercial airlines, and something that it made sense for us to emulate.

We borrowed the concept of checklists too. Unlike the SOPs, these were not recipes to be learned off by heart so that actions could be delivered urgently and precisely when required, almost on automatic. Our checklists were sheets of laminated card that you would read through, in the midst of action, line by line, to make sure that no critical steps had been missed.

In 2008 the World Health Organization (WHO) introduced the Surgical Safety Checklist, akin to the pre-take-off checks that we sometimes see commercial airline pilots running through. It was among the first clear examples of medicine borrowing from aviation. In a surgical setting, the checklists similarly serve as an aide-memoire, to make sure that the essential equipment is available, that prophylactic antibiotics have been given, that blood is available for transfusion and that everyone is on the same page: what we're doing, how difficult it's likely to be, how long we'll be doing it and how much blood loss we're expecting in the process.

In the decade that followed, checklists started popping up everywhere in medicine. In places they proved useful, improved care and were proven to save lives; the WHO Surgical Safety Checklist is a good example. But part of my motivation for joining HEMS was that I wasn't convinced we had gained a proper understanding of this technology: how the airline industry generated its checklists, how it made use of them and what they were actually for.

In our HEMS practice there was an orgy of checklists: one to help us check the helicopters and the response cars; one for every bag that we carried; one to run through before you even left the hangar; one to guide emergency anaesthesia at the scene; one for us to go through before we took off again. But the scenarios and emergencies that we faced were often fast and densely uncertain. And so the key question in my mind revolved around this paradox:

what value is there to this kind of standardisation when so much of what you do borders chaos?

I would find the answer – not from HEMS, but in the detail of a particularly high-profile airline accident and from the first-hand experience of someone who had reached for a checklist, and the shield of standardisation, in the most extreme circumstances the aviation industry has ever seen.

On 15 January 2009, US Airways Flight 1549 was taxiing on the runway at New York City's LaGuardia airport, waiting to depart for Charlotte, North Carolina. In the pilot's seat was Captain Chesley Sullenberger – or 'Sully' as his colleagues and friends know him – and to his right was First Officer Jeff Skiles. What would follow has become a celebrated example of performance under pressure: the 'Miracle on the Hudson'. But I want to introduce it to better understand what place standardisation has, when the threat you're facing is emergent and the correct course of action is largely uncharted.

During the climb out of LaGuardia, just short of five miles north-west of the airport and below 3,000 feet, a flock of Canada geese crossed the aircraft's path. The windshield turned brown as the birds smashed into it. Their plane, an Airbus A320, had twin turbofan jet engines whose principle of operation was to suck in air, compress it, mix it with fuel and then burn it to produce enough thrust to keep the 70-ton vehicle in flight. The geese were sizeable, each weighing an estimated nine pounds. As the flock slammed into the turbine blades of the aeroplane, birds were sucked into the core of both engines. On the flight deck the whine of the turbines dropped in pitch and the aircraft shuddered. The engines, now clogged with the feathers and carcasses of geese, ground almost to a halt. Their thrust disappeared.

When you lose power in the jet engines on an A320 you lose more than propulsion alone. Normally the engines drive the electrical generator in flight. But with their turbines jammed, Sullenberger and Skiles were about to lose much of their electrical power. This in turn would deprive them of enough current to run the avionic suite of controls in the cockpit that helped keep the aircraft stable. But Sully has instinctively anticipated this, and almost reflexively started the Auxiliary Power Unit (APU) – a separate, turbine-driven generator that can maintain the electrical supply in such an emergency. This does more than keep the cabin lights on. It powers the avionics and their feedback control loops, preserving the assistance, trim and protection that they bring, keeping much of the system intact.

By all accounts, Sullenberger could have landed without the assistance of those sub-systems, but it would have proved much harder, and when your chances of survival are marginal, every advantage counts. That single action – starting the APU – helped him to delegate some tasks to the automated flight-control system, preserving his attention and cognitive bandwidth for what was to follow.

US Airways, like all commercial airlines, had a strict programme of simulator training to help pilots prepare for a range of rarely encountered emergencies. But while there was training for contingencies involving the failure of both engines, those scenarios played out with the aircraft starting high in the sky, at 25,000 feet or more, and focused on a long, shallow descent over many minutes, during which there was enough time to try and relight both engines. In all cases, the simulations ended with the successful restart of at least one engine.

Flight 1549 is at this point at 3,000 feet and travelling at just over 180 knots. Sully knows that there is a checklist in the Quick Reference Handbook that covers loss of thrust on both engines, and he asks Skiles to fetch it. Skiles is ahead of him – the book is already in his hands. The checklist is three pages long. Sully would have known there wasn't enough time to complete it, so why did he even try?

In the pause while the First Officer finds the right page, Sully puts out his distress call. 'Mayday, mayday, mayday, uh, this is, uh, Cactus 1539. Hit birds. We've lost thrust on both engines. We're turning back towards LaGuardia.'

In the air-traffic control centre Patrick Harten acknowledges and instructs them to turn left, to a heading of 220. Within seconds, all departures from the airport are halted.

The checklist begins; Skiles reading, Sully responding.

Skiles: 'If fuel remains, engine mode selector ignition.'

Sullenberger: 'Ignition.'

Energy management is something pilots pride themselves on. Sully – as an accomplished glider pilot – more than most. For aviators, this is about their feel for the perpetual trade between kinetic and gravitational potential energy as their aircraft dives and soars.

Skiles dutifully reads through the procedures in the checklist line by line. Time is running out and they are slowly losing altitude.

'Cactus 1529, if we can get it for you, do you want to land on runway one-three?' comes the call from Harten.

Sullenberger keys the radio. 'We're unable,' comes the reply, 'we may end up in the Hudson.'

Notice that in these early exchanges both Sullenberger and Harten get Flight 1549's callsign wrong. Sully calls it 'Flight 1539' in his mayday; Harten replies with 'Flight 1529'. These are basic mistakes that neither Harten nor Sullenberger would ordinarily have made. And yet, under intense pressure, errors begin to creep in.

Sully and Skiles are now at 1,600 feet, travelling at 200 miles per hour. They have made the beginnings of a U-turn over Van Cortlandt Park, but they know already that there is insufficient altitude and forward speed to get them back to LaGuardia.

The checklist continues.

Skiles: 'Emergency Electrical Power.'

Sullenberger: 'It's online.'

Skiles: 'Distress message; we did.'

Over the radio, air-traffic control offers another runway, on a heading of 310. Sullenberger replies with a single word: 'Unable.' He knows that the more he turns the plane, the more energy his aircraft will bleed. They are at 1,400 feet. It is seventy-one seconds since they first hit the flock of geese. They are now heading southwest over the banks of the Hudson River.

Harten switches strategy and asks the crew what they need from him to be able to land. Sullenberger asks him to explore options in New Jersey, at Teterboro airport. There is so much at play in these moments. Sullenberger is the handling pilot, at the controls of the aircraft, while talking to Harten in air-traffic control and running the checklist with Skiles. The tasks begin to pile up. They are now below 1,200 feet.

It is a masterclass in Crew Resource Management (CRM). Sullenberger and Skiles together are making the best use of the resources at hand and are folding Harten neatly into that scheme: the best information, decisions and actions. Responsibility for preparing the rear passenger cabin for a forced landing is automatically delegated to the flight attendants, who are already working through their own well-rehearsed procedures. It is Sullenberger, the airline captain, whom we see most prominently, but he cannot solve this problem on his own; this is the essence of CRM.

Skiles: 'No relight after thirty seconds. Engine master one and two confirm off.'

The radio crackles before Sully can respond to Skiles. 'You wanna go to Teterboro?' asks Harten.

'Yes,' Sully replies before returning to the checklist.

Sullenberger: 'Off.'

Harten has spent time working in Teterboro and knows that runway one is an arrivals runway and can be cleared quickly. He also knows that the runway is facing into the day's prevailing winds, which would further assist Sullenberger and his crew with their abortive flight. He takes only fifteen seconds to make these judgements, communicate with his counterpart at Teterboro airport and offer the option to Flight 1549.

Teterboro was a good thought. Seven miles roughly west of their position at that moment, it offered perhaps the best chance of getting the crippled aircraft to a hard-surfaced runway.

Sullenberger keys his mic. 'We can't do it.' They are at 682 feet, travelling at 190 knots. It has been 136 seconds since loss of engine thrust. 'We're gonna be in the Hudson.'

'I'm sorry, say again, Cactus?' says an incredulous Harten.

US Airways 1549 disappears from the flight radar at 557 feet.

Harten was certain, at that moment, that the aircraft had come down into the water and that all 155 lives had been lost. As the air-traffic controller responsible for that flight, the effect on him was devastating. In an emotional testimony later, Harten described the experience as being 'the lowest of all lows'.

But Sullenberger and Skiles are, of course, still very much alive, continuing to wrestle with their plane. They know now that they will have to ditch the plane: bring it down onto the surface of the Hudson River. The aircraft is designed to be able to survive this – in theory – but only if they hit the water at just the right speed, in just the right way.

At 300 feet and with the waters of the Hudson right below them, the Ground Proximity Warning System (GPWS) in the cabin sounds, with a recorded voice chiming, '*Too Low. Terrain. Too Low. Terrain.*' Over and over again.

They abandon what remain of their procedures and prepare to ditch in the Hudson, gliding now, well below the height of the bridges that span the river.

'*Caution. Terrain,*' insists the GPWS. And then finally, with its electronic sense of the impending impact, '*Terrain. Terrain. Pull up. Pull up.*'

Sullenberger levels the wings and bleeds off a little speed, trying to find the right balance between stalling and hitting the water too fast. Skiles checks the position of the flaps, asking Sully if they need to extend them more, but Sully asks him to leave them as set.

'Got any ideas?' Sully asks Skiles, a last attempt to recruit his first officer's expertise.

'*Caution. Terrain. Caution. Terrain.*'

'Actually not,' comes the reply.

That exchange is a notable example of good practice in the heat of the moment. At the last moment, seconds before they're due to hit the water, Sully continues to practise Crew Resource Management, casting out to Skiles for anything that he might have missed or a contribution that might still give them an edge, making the most of the resources around him. The fact that Skiles has nothing more to offer is beside the point. This is a hallmark of high-performance behaviour under pressure: that ability to draw out the best information, to use your team and inform the best decisions, and thereby the best actions.

The final moments of Flight 1549 are caught on a riverside surveillance camera as the airliner slides onto the water, intact and afloat.

Later the same year Sullenberger's story was retold – largely from second-hand reports – at a number of medical conferences. Papers were published in medical journals, searching for lessons that doctors might learn from Sullenberger and Skiles's remarkable tale of survival. To the medical community, this was an exemplar par excellence of a small team of individuals managing to stay cool under fire and, in so doing, save their lives and those of their 150 passengers. As a community, we were quick to see similarities. The story appealed to us as clinicians – one of superlative performance in the life-saving moment – and it begged the question, 'Why aren't doctors more like pilots?'

But Sullenberger's success, and that of his crew, takes a lot of deconstructing, and it isn't altogether what you might think. Sullenberger is without doubt a superlatively good pilot, whose expertise had been shaped through his military career as well as his love of gliding. But he admits to having been less than calm, at least in the initial moments, as the cockpit window turned brown with the blood and bodies of geese thudding into it, smearing across the aircraft's whole windshield and obscuring their view. Sully experienced what he described to me as 'an extreme physiological response'.

'There were noises I've never heard, in any aircraft, *ever*,' he told me. 'I could feel my blood pressure spike; my vision became tunnelled, interfering with my ability to process information . . . I could hear the raspiness in my own voice, the stress . . .'

To me this was a refreshingly honest – and reassuringly recognisable – account of the experience of those opening moments, which sees you torn from a nearly automatic routine and leaves you instead preparing to face something you have never faced before. In our conversation Sully never used the word 'fear', but even if he wasn't actually afraid, he was experiencing all the physiological features that go with it: his blood pressure spiking, his tunnel vision.

There's a name for this; it's called the 'startle response', your body's reflexive reaction to an extreme threat; an activation of your fight-or-flight reflexes. It makes your heart beat faster, increases your rate and depth of breathing and constricts your blood vessels, increasing the blood supply to your muscles in the process, setting you up to do battle or to run away. But all of that can have negative impacts on your cognition: narrowing your perception, impairing your working memory and slowing your capacity for decision-making. Managing that initial response – emotional and physiological – becomes the first challenge, and that, says Sullenberger, is a product of preparation. Sufficient training to have confidence in your abilities is fundamental.

Beyond the performance of the checklist, this underlines the importance of pre-rehearsed standard operating procedures – of the type that the HEMS induction course had hammered into me. These are actions that you can perform almost without thinking while your brain is caught in the moment, trying to reboot.

For pilots like Sully, the procedures start with a simple mantra: Aviate, Navigate, Communicate. This prompts them to make sure the plane is pointed in the right direction, with the right power and within safe parameters, before plotting a sensible course and radioing your concerns. For doctors, caught in the headlights of a medical emergency, the mantra is: Airway, Breathing, Circulation – a rapid assessment followed by definitive actions. These critical responses are how you deal with the first assault on your senses that surprise brings, how you overcome your hardwired responses, force a restart and keep going.

Before the procedures, before you try to regain control of the situation, you first have to regain control of yourself. And what the airlines train their pilots to do is something that works for all of us, whatever we're facing, as you feel that startle-response kicking in: Pause, Breathe, Think, Act.

This is the truth of the opening moments of any crisis: you are trying to manipulate the scene and bend it towards your will, while the scene is at the same time manipulating you and your performance. In those moments you are an integral part of this beleaguered system, connected to it, interacting with it, part of its complexity.

Interestingly, Sully told me that it never entered his head that they might not survive. 'I never thought I was going to die that day. I knew that based upon my training and experience I could deliver the craft to the surface intact and, if I could do that, I was confident [the aircraft] would float long enough for us to be rescued.'

This is a recurrent theme among survivors of this type of event. Rarely do they ever admit to contemplating their likely demise. And this is more than braggadocio. Humans have a very limited cognitive capacity at the best of times and, in the face of events that play out so quickly, you cannot afford to allocate any of that precious resource to contemplating your mortality. To do so only makes death more likely. It's a trick that Captain Sullenberger has mastered. And it's one that we can learn from. In those decisive high-consequence moments, whatever the threat and whatever your goal, it helps to muster a degree of mindfulness. You need to stay in the moment, avoid ruminating on the price of failure and focus on what you are doing, and on doing that well.

But let's return to the role of the checklist here, which was centrally important in the successful landing of Flight 1549. The flight crew's Emergency Action Checklist draws our attention because it feels like a counterintuitive step in a moment of time and life-critical crisis; choosing to perform an apparently prosaic task when there is no time to spare. When I asked Sully why he turned to the Quick Reference Handbook in that rarest of split-second scenarios, he told me this.

'Everything we know in aviation, every rule in the rulebook, every procedure we have, we know because somewhere someone died – often many people – so we have purchased with great cost, lessons literally bought with blood, that we have to preserve as institutional knowledge and pass on to the succeeding generations. We cannot have the moral failure of forgetting these lessons and having to relearn them.'

And in these words lies the truth of what a checklist is supposed to be and how it should be crafted. The checklist is a technology in its own right. A means of capturing the lessons learned from past tragedies and making them available for retrieval, to those operating at the sharp end, facing the immediacy of real-time crisis.

Like so much in this world of risk and uncertainty, the checklist is designed *with change in mind*. The pilots tell us that their checklists are never done, that they are always being revised as new lessons come to light. It is why the most important items – those most likely to save your life – rise to the top of the list; and why, for Sully, the checklist was worth the time-investment, even though he knew he would never get to the end of it.

And that is crucial: for Sully, when the usefulness of those carefully laid emergency action plans came to an end, improvisation became necessary. His decision to glide powerless onto the surface of the Hudson River is regarded as the one of best, and most creative, solutions that was left available to him and his crew. But the question for them wasn't whether or not one should improvise during an emergency unfolding in real time; it was about *when* they should begin that process.

The trick here lies in having the discipline to reach for the checklist – despite the urgency – to standardise your response *until the time comes when you have no choice but to improvise*. The true skill lies in having the judgement to know when that point has arrived, and the confidence to strike out on your own.

This is very different from the way we have come to use standard operating procedures, protocols and checklists in the world of medicine. The focus for medics is standardisation of the response in an attempt to iron out variation. Very little attention is paid to the inevitable deviation from protocols, and almost none to what follows when the pre-formed responses have to end.

Complex systems tend to operate at the edge of chaos. In medicine the system that is the human body is more complex and more unknowable than almost all others, and the chaos is often closer than we would like. This means that the departure from agreed protocol has to happen sooner, and more often, than we would prefer.

The mistake to make, when examining the story of Flight 1549, is the one that Sullenberger – in what at first sight appears to be a tremendous display of modesty – urges you not to. Sully knows what all pilots know: that the success of this story is not about him alone, or his crew, or the air-traffic controllers. Its roots aren't to be found in the 208 seconds that followed the bird strike or in the hours of rescue that followed, or even in Sullenberger's long and illustrious career. Nor is it down to the checklist itself: that on its own doesn't make the team safe. Rather, their success is owed to what lies behind the checklist. It isn't simply a list of emergency actions that someone dreamed up. It is a document that has evolved over decades. And it is emblematic of the wider system, one that has *evolved over time* – in this case, decades of accumulated experience.

After the Miracle on the Hudson, one of the initiatives taken following the investigation was to revise the A320 Quick Reference Handbook checklist for double engine failure. Sully's improvised action – to start the APU – was *not* mandated by the procedures that were then in place. Instead he did it from experience and instinct; an action that played a significant part in their survival. It kept the aircraft's electrical power online and, importantly, left the avionics suite and the fly-by-wire systems fully operational. And this served to further stabilise the aircraft, free up Sully's cognitive bandwidth and preserve his adaptive capacity.

And this is perhaps the most important lesson from the rescue of Flight 1549: how, in the wake of catastrophe or near-catastrophe, these experiences and the learnings that came from them were preserved and carried forward, so that the knowledge is immediately available for all those who face comparable crises in the future.

7. *The leadership ball*

What should leadership look like in a system set up to deal with the unexpected? How do you corral and coordinate teams when the scope of the operation is so vast and so unknowable? Within the HEMS teams I learned that to meet this challenge – of complexity, uncertainty and volatility – you had to redesign everything about your system, right down to the way you lead and the idea of what leadership is. To be maximally responsive, to preserve your ability to adapt, leadership ceased to be the exclusive role of any single member of the team. Instead it had to become a property that was woven across the fabric of the team as a whole, something that every team member was capable of and could be expected to deliver. And the best way to explain what that looks like, and why it works, is to turn for a moment to human space exploration. Much of what we know about working in complex, volatile systems and facing down uncertainty in real time finds its roots in NASA's human spaceflight operations and Project Apollo, which sent the first humans to the Moon in the 1960s – and this new concept of leadership and teamwork is one of them.

After Yuri Gagarin became the first person to fly in space on 12 April 1961, sending greetings from orbit around the Earth on behalf of the Soviet Union, the United States found itself scrambling to catch up. There was desperation among the politicians: the space race was a surrogate battlefield for nuclear conflict, and the US couldn't afford to fall behind. A little over a month later, President John F. Kennedy was standing before the US Congress outlining his new plan to send a man to the Moon and return him safely to Earth, all before the decade was out.

The pace of technological advance in the decade that followed was outrageous. There are few engineering programmes in history whose speed of progress or scale of investment are comparable. In today's money, many hundreds of billions of US dollars were spent on what became known as Project Apollo. In all, 400,000 people across the US are thought to have been involved, along with tens of thousands of companies and universities. In the eight years after Gagarin's flight, the United States went from building small rockets that could send a solitary astronaut a few hundred miles high, to hurling crews a quarter of a million miles across the void of space between Earth and the Moon.

The architecture of these missions was vast. The giant Saturn V launcher that NASA would use to send their astronauts and spacecraft to the Moon between 1968 and 1972 was described by NASA aerospace engineer Christopher Kraft as 'the single most intricate and unforgiving machine we ever tried to make work first time'.

This was no overstatement. Project Apollo forced an explosion in complexity. NASA invented new materials, built the most powerful rockets ever seen, fielded the first compact, integrated-circuit digital computers, devised techniques to rendezvous spacecraft in lunar orbit and developed techniques for navigation in deep space.

At the sharp end of this, NASA had to form an interface between the vehicles and crew flying in space and the teams working on the ground back on Earth. It was Kraft who recognised that to process the scale of the uncertainty and complexity this endeavour demanded would take a new kind of team. He established NASA's human spaceflight operations headquarters at the Manned Spacecraft Center in Houston, Texas, where he set up the Mission Operations Control Room (MOCR) – the place we've come to call 'Mission Control'.

The flight-control team that ran it was sub-specialised and largely compartmentalised, but their systems overlapped and a failure in one could have a domino effect on all the others. Nobody could know everybody's job. Most flight controllers were limited to their own narrow sphere of expertise: power systems, guidance and navigation, life support, propulsion, and so on. All of that needed a new approach to leadership and teamwork. Above all, they needed new people.

In the early 1960s, when NASA was setting up what would become the iconic MOCR from which the first missions to the Moon were guided, they found themselves short of suitable candidates to sit behind the consoles. Human spaceflight was in its infancy and there was a dearth of available rocket scientists and aerospace engineers. But with the president's challenge laid down and the decade already well on its way, NASA began hiring hard and fast nonetheless.

For those who had somehow found their way to the Manned Spacecraft Center in the 1960s, with a background in engineering or science, opportunities were rife. Flight controller Jerry Bostick, who was part of the team that famously rescued the *Apollo 13* mission, told me the story of how – fresh out of college – he had managed to get a job with NASA. Wanting to get closer to the business end of human spaceflight, he worked his way around the maze of corridors at the Manned Spacecraft Center, knocked on Chris Kraft's office door and sheepishly asked if there might be a role for him in mission operations.

Kraft looked him in the eye. 'Have you got any engineering, son?'

Bostick stared at his feet. 'Only civil engineering, sir,' he replied ruefully.

Kraft paused, thought for a moment. 'Well, who knows, we might need to build roads on the Moon one day – you're hired.'

Out of this frenzy of appointments came a new cadre of Apollo flight controllers making life- and mission-critical decisions, whose average age was a mere twenty-six years old. For the flight directors of that era, who led the flight-control teams, that lack of years and experience wasn't in itself a problem. Indeed, it came with its own advantages. This cohort, fresh out of college, had a confidence and optimism that they found less common in their older and more experienced flight controllers.

As revered Apollo flight director Gerry Griffin once told me, 'It's not that they didn't understand risk, they just weren't afraid of it the same way we were.'

NASA became comfortable with delegating authority to and deferring to the expertise of some of the youngest people in the organisation. This wasn't simply advantageous; it was mission-critical. Project Apollo was a programme of exploration like no other before it. Much of the technology that the agency was grappling with had only recently been invented – the propulsion units, the navigational instruments and prototype digital computers incorporating integrated circuit boards – and it was very possible that the newbie twenty-something computer engineer knew more about it than their highly experienced flight director.

Young flight controllers were given enormous responsibility, told to own it, encouraged to ask for help if they needed it, but made to understand in no uncertain terms that on the day, in the moment, the calls would come down to them, and them alone. This wasn't a case of recklessly assigning responsibility to rookies. NASA hired hastily, but it worked its young flight controllers hard, steadily exposing them to more risk and furnishing them with more authority as they went. Importantly, there was a refusal to infantilise its junior team. On the contrary, there was a concerted effort to accelerate them through, maximising their potential as quickly as possible. This is how NASA assembled a cadre of energetic, proficient experts from scratch: a crew capable of sailing the hazardous new ocean of space.

This balance of trust, responsibility and support represents a perfect example of deference to expertise and delegation of authority – concepts that could usefully be put to work in boardrooms and organisations throughout the world, if only we were more open to understanding that complex endeavour demands that we view leadership as a distributed property within our high-performance systems.

Whenever I tell people how old the average flight controller was during the Apollo programme there is generally a sharp intake of breath, followed by some disbelief. Surely someone, somewhere, was supervising their actions. But that was not how the missions worked. Problems had to be solved immediately, as and when they arose. There was no time to consult a senior team member – just the reflex of the unfolding instant. And if you think that's an exaggeration, consider for a moment the story of John Arran and the rescue of *Apollo 12*.

On 14 November 1969, NASA dispatched its second mission to the Moon. Commander and spaceflight veteran Pete Conrad was joined by Dick Gordon and Alan Bean – a rookie astronaut and former US Navy test pilot, who had until this point never flown in space. The weather at Cape Canaveral in Florida had been predictably unpredictable. A cold front had been moving through, pelting the launch site with thunderstorms and showers.

The three astronauts sat suited, with their helmets on, crammed into their seats and sealed inside their *Apollo* command module. The trio were still unsure if the launch-control team at Cape Canaveral would postpone their flight because of the inclement weather. But by mid-morning conditions had improved just enough to launch. They blasted off into rain and cloud at 11.23 Eastern Standard Time. As soon as they cleared the tower at Kennedy Space Center in Florida, the launch-control team handed over to their colleagues in mission control at Houston, Texas.

A little over thirty-six seconds after lift-off *Apollo 12* was struck by a bolt of lightning, triggering the vehicle's master alarm. Strapped into their seats, the astronauts couldn't see or feel the strike, but the display on the console in front of Dick Gordon lit up. Of the sixteen caution and warning lights on the grid in front of him, more than half of them were now illuminated.

'What the hell was that?' Gordon exclaimed. 'I just lost a whole bunch of stuff.'

The Saturn V rocket continued its ascent. To the astronaut crew, the launch still felt stable. But the instrument panel protested furiously, showing a slew of impending failures across the board. Only one minute into their flight, they were now a mile and half above the ground and travelling at more than 1,000 miles an hour. Conrad began to worry that they might reach orbit only to find themselves at the helm of a dead spacecraft. Less than twenty seconds later the rocket was struck by a second bolt of lightning, again unseen by the crew.

More alarms flared. A red warning light now told them that their guidance and navigation platform was no longer working. Without it, the rocket would soon begin to tumble out of control.

Pete Conrad radioed down to mission control, 'OK, we just lost the platform, gang. I don't know what happened here; we had everything in the world drop out.'

Over the next thirty seconds the astronauts tried to trace the fault without success, running what checks they could while the rocket engines continued to rattle them violently. Back in mission control, the team was no wiser. The flight dynamics officer, twenty-five-year-old Jay Greene, responsible for tracking the spacecraft's path through the sky, reported that the Saturn V was still on track and ascending as expected. But that intelligence conflicted with what the crew aboard the vehicle was reporting. The gap between the state of the system and the team's understanding of it was opening up. On the ground, flight director Gerry Griffin tried in vain to close this gap.

There were mere seconds left in which to make the call. If the spacecraft's internal guidance mechanisms were truly malfunctioning, then the rocket was about to cartwheel through the sky, destroying the vehicle and its crew. Griffin was now sure they would have to abort the mission.

On top of the capsule was a single, powerful solid rocket – about twelve feet high – packed with enough punch to accelerate the capsule away from the rest of the stack and lift it high enough to let the astronauts parachute safely to the ground. Inside the capsule, Pete Conrad's hand rested on the T-shaped handle that would trigger the abort.

And then, seemingly out of nowhere, John Aaron, another twenty-five-year-old flight controller, piped up. Aaron was the Electrical, Environmental and Consumables Management (EECOM) officer, letters that NASA smeared together, giving him the mission-control callsign '*ee-com*'.

'Flight, EECOM,' he says, announcing his entry into the comms loop. 'Try SCE to AUX.'

I have spoken to both Gerry Griffin and John Aaron more than once about this pivotal moment, partly because in hindsight it is so incredible. Griffin always tells me that he, as flight director, heard the words, but didn't have the first clue what they meant.

'Say again?' he replies. 'SCE to AUX?'

'AUX,' repeats John Aaron, in his thick Oklahoma accent.

'AUX,' echoes Griffin, less convincingly and none the wiser.

Gerry Griffin faced a dilemma here. The mission has departed from any recognisable plan, for reasons that were unclear to the flight-control team or the astronaut crew. If the instruments were to be believed, they were mere seconds from catastrophe. Griffin was the flight director, notionally in charge of the flight-control team. But here was his young EECOM serving up a solution that Griffin didn't understand.

It was Griffin's call. Should he command the abort, sacrificing the mission and the vehicle, while potentially saving his crew? Or should he trust the youthful John Aaron and his obscure suggestion? It is one thing to believe in delegation of authority and deference to expertise, quite another to be willing to bet the lives of an astronaut crew on it. But in mission control the trust was absolute. Griffin's decision took little more than a heartbeat.

'SCE to AUX. CAPCOM,' he says clearly and deliberately, delivering an order to the CAPCOM, or capsule communicator, to instruct the crew to implement John Aaron's mystery action.

In mission control, sitting alongside Griffin, is astronaut Gerry Carr, callsign CAPCOM – the only individual allowed to speak with the crew directly: a measure designed to ensure crystal-clear lines of communication. Carr keys his mic and sends the radio transmission to the *Apollo 12* crew.

'*Apollo 12*, Houston. Try SCE to Auxiliary. Over.'

Conrad, like Griffin, doesn't understand the command, but attempts to repeat it, 'Try FCE to Auxiliary.' Off the radio, talking to his crewmates over the capsule intercom, Conrad turns and says, 'What the hell is that?'

Carr sends again, 'SCE to AUX.'

Neither flight director Griffin, leading the team on the ground, nor the mission commander Conrad understands the command. But in the capsule rookie Alan Bean also hears the calls and remembers a little-known switch tucked out of the way, whose position can be toggled between two states. There are two sets of letters printed in white font above and below it: SCE and AUX. He reaches down and flicks it from the SCE position over to AUX, just as Aaron has suggested. And inside the cabin everything magically returns to normal.

Later Aaron would explain that he had watched his readouts 'turn to garbage' immediately after the lightning strike. The strings of numbers scrolling on his display looked like gibberish, but it was a gibberish that Aaron recognised. In earlier testing he had seen the same pattern of numbers rolling up the screen when the voltage in the circuits had transiently fallen because of an electrical failure. And he had learned, from this experience, that if you bypassed the Signal Conditioning Equipment (or SCE) and switched over to the Auxiliary circuit instead, the problem would go away.

For NASA, the flight-control team served as its defence in depth against emergent threats. When the plan was going off the rails, it was this empowerment and deference to expertise that saved lives and missions. NASA had created a team of teams. To cater for fast-moving crises, it had chosen to decentralise decision-making. Real-time decisions were made on the shop floor, closest to where their consequences would play out and be most keenly felt. Even within the Mission Operations Control Room, the style of leadership departed from our conventional idea of Command and Control. Yes, there was a flight director, along with an astronaut serving as commander in the *Apollo* capsule, but they delegated their decisions, deferring to expertise wherever it lay, because no individual could hold all the knowledge and experience necessary for total control. And the maturity and insight to understand this is what made NASA so successful in this period.

This concept of leadership in complex systems as a *distributed property* – the idea that different people must be prepared and enabled to take the lead at different times – is important. For the Apollo flight-control teams no single person had enough specialist knowledge to be able to command all aspects of the mission. And so NASA's approach of delegation and deference to expertise fostered the best outcomes by allowing the right person to lead at the right time.

In this scheme, leadership is a fluid role that shifts between members of the team, depending on the circumstances of the mission. And this idea – of leadership as a ball that can be passed from person to person – is something that our HEMS teams have adopted to great effect.

In the hangar, when the bell goes and we rush out to the aircraft, it is the pilots who are leading the team; they are in charge of the technology needed to get us to the scene, and are responsible for keeping us alive while in transit aboard the helicopter. When the crew lands at the scene and the helicopter engine shuts down, the ball of leadership passes to the paramedics, whose experience in entering and managing chaotic accident scenes now comes to the fore. They know this place better than any doctor. This is the environment in which they have trained and worked for years; they understand how best to navigate through it, how to marshal the teams already present, and how to safely rescue and retrieve the patient from wherever they are, so that the care and treatment can begin. More than that, the paramedics' first impressions of the scene and of the patient, and their overall situational awareness, are almost invariably better than that of the doctors: a product of their specific training, coupled with well-honed pattern recognition.

In a HEMS scene, the leadership role does eventually pass to the doctor in the team, but only briefly and very specifically. Our job is to bring our detailed diagnostic training to bear along with a handful of interventions and drugs that only we are authorised to administer. None of that is easy, of course; we're there holding stethoscopes and wielding ultrasound probes, straining the limits of our senses to recognise when something doesn't fit the usual patterns. But that is what we bring: the skill to tease apart the signs and clues, which help us recognise those rare occasions when the neighing and the braying, and the drumming of hooves on soil in the darkness, herald the arrival not of horses, but a herd of zebra.

The resuscitation phase – when it begins – is a tight partnership, with the doctor and paramedic leading the wider team, in a race against the clock. The goal is to build sufficient stability in our patient for the next phase, knowing that it might not last, but recognising when 'perfect' is the enemy of 'good enough'. And once we're done, the leadership ball goes back to the paramedic, who navigates us out of the scene, gets us back to the aircraft, where we hand over once more to our pilots.

There's a rhythm to the passing of that mantle of leadership back and forth. It's not always a simple circular flow. Sometimes the leadership has to be gently wrestled away. Early in my time with HEMS, when I would sometimes find myself overwhelmed by the enormity of the challenge and in danger of stalling, the paramedics would step in and take over, to keep momentum going in the scene while giving me some respite to think. Good teams understand the fluidity of leadership. In complex systems there is no single point of control.

This is a core strategy in dealing with complex challenges. You have to set aside your conventional idea of who, and what, a leader is. In these frontline teams the leader is more than one person, and leadership is something that more than one person is capable of. That is how you leverage and realise the potential of the team as a whole, and how you set up to adapt to novel threats.

There is a last essential element to this approach. To be able to lead in this way you also have to learn how to follow. In corporate training programmes we tend to talk a lot about leadership and what it takes to be a leader, but we spend very little time considering what good followership looks like, even though that is an essential piece of the puzzle.

Good followers understand their role in the team and support the leader of the moment in achieving the goal; they are competent and conscientious in the tasks that fall to them. Some of it is about humility: recognising that there are limits to your knowledge and capability and that, at times, you must rely on others to drive the team forward and set the course. But it is not a passive role, and it isn't about blind obedience. Good followers contribute ideas and challenge authority, when necessary and appropriate. And there is power and deep value in good followership. You are there to help make sure the team becomes greater than the sum of its parts, that the group is working with the best and most up-to-date information and insight, and that the leader of the moment has access to that information.

As followers, you are expected to contribute to the mission and to create solutions when the team faces challenges; to have the courage to speak up when you think the direction may be wrong. Above all, you have to be adaptable. In volatile environments when things are changing quickly, followers need to accept that the plan might have to alter suddenly. When that happens, their role is to play their part, helping to reconfigure themselves, their actions and the system as a whole.

Goals can be met in the absence of good followership, but the solutions will rarely be optimal. And worse still, teams of this type are vulnerable: to the literal and metaphorical blind spots in the task, and to novel threats. The speed and completeness with which you as a team can detect a threat, adapt and turn to face an emerging problem depends upon a model of leadership that is distributed across the team, with the ball constantly going back and forth.

8.
Go again

Every other week all of the doctors, paramedics and dispatchers working for HEMS, the air-ambulance service, gather in a small seminar room and offer up their most difficult cases for scrutiny. We call these 'Death and Disability' meetings, or 'D and D' for short. Here we are stripped of all our paraphernalia: out of our fireproof flight suits, absent our piles of bags, our pharmacopeia, the aircraft and its avionic sophistry. It is just us, in a room with a laptop and a projector. Nevertheless, this is one of the organisation's most potent and important technologies – a device for taking our experience and failures and using them to forge an armour against the future.

As I mentioned in Chapter 3, one of the defining characteristics of HEMS and organisations like it is their obsession with failure and their insistence on understanding how and why it happens. It takes courage to do this, as an individual or as an organisation. And it's daunting at first, revisiting cases in which people died or suffered life-changing injuries, asking whether things could, or should, have gone differently. These meetings happen days or weeks after the hot debrief: that conversation we have in the immediate aftermath, as adrenaline is still coursing through us. D and D meetings, by contrast, are most useful when the dust has settled a little. That's important, because the critique is relentless. Often we come to the realisation that in the moment there might have been better approaches than those we chose, even if they wouldn't ultimately have changed the outcome. Whatever the conclusions, you grow, individually, as a result and learn to be a better and more effective doctor and team member, but you have to allow yourself to be partly deconstructed first.

The exchanges are occasionally brusque; but it's light, and not heat, that you want, and the doctor chairing the meeting reins all of that in. As a general rule, if you are running a debrief in search of learning and it begins to feel like a scene from *Fight Club*, then you're doing it wrong. For the most part, though, the meetings are self-regulating, with everyone understanding that this is not about finger-pointing or shaming individuals. It is about 'how' we might improve, rather than 'who'. That's all-important. The question is: 'What can we learn here?' We go at it, asking if and how we might change the system to be better – both the social and the technical components.

Today it is the turn of my crew. We are debriefing the case that this book opened with: the traumatic motorway crash. I am sitting alongside the rest of my medical team – three of us in a row, in the spotlight – as the wider HEMS audience begins their interrogation and we account for our actions.

I tell them the story as clearly as I can, projecting us back to that day on the motorway, amid the wreckage and the dying. I explain what I did, and why – at the time – I thought those were the right decisions. With the lights low and dust flickering in the beam of a projector, the meeting chair now brings up a table showing a list of events and recorded times: when the 999 call came in, how long it took our crew to get airborne, where and when we landed, how many minutes we spent at the scene, tracking every time-stamp all the way to the moment when we arrived in the hospital resuscitation bay. We resist the construction of lazy, storybook narrative. There is no 'once upon a time', and often no 'happily ever after'. And because of that, there is no search for a root cause, only an attempt to understand the myriad contributing factors.

For these meetings to work, all of the same tenets of psychological safety that we use in the aircraft must operate here. There has to be a sense of belonging and a willingness to admit ignorance. Furthermore, it is crucial that there is enough of a sense of safety for anyone to feel able to contribute and, where necessary, challenge. It isn't always gentle, however. That's one of the misnomers about psychologically safe debriefs. It's not – in the main – a thing of sunbeams and rainbows, or teammates stroking your brow and telling you it was all OK. There is room for contrition, sometimes without accompanying absolution. But there is always learning.

There's a sense of reassurance, too, that the people present understand what it's like to be where you have been – in these scenes, amid the chaos and confusion, trying to claw your way in and gain purchase. And that fosters openness. Everyone knows that seated here, in the warmth of a seminar room, beyond the flow of real time and the terror of the moment, things can look as if they had a structure, a narrative, a logic, when we all know that was never present at the time. Everyone in the room has sat where we now sit, facing an inquisition, wondering if there was a chance to do better. But this is about the system rather than the individual. None of it is personal. That's the key.

It sounds simple in principle – learning from your mistakes with your peers in this way – but it takes time and great skill to create a culture in which everyone understands how essential this feedback is to the continual improvement of the organisation.

My boss and fellow doctor, Alex, describes the scene on the motorway, stretched out over a couple of hundred yards, and how long it took us to move through it and make our first assessment of the casualties. He talks about how strange it felt to have to walk past the dead and injured patients, some of whom needed urgent help, and not immediately run to their aid.

The questions are searching, often direct, particularly where we have departed from the standard operating procedures. Improvisation is almost always needed, and there's a mutual understanding that this is an inevitable part of the surprises that HEMS work brings. But it's still useful to understand why we made the choices we did and where we deviated for no good reason, and in a way that made us more dangerous or less effective, and we take the expected verbal hiding from our peers. But they in turn learn from the departures that *were* necessary, those that allowed us to continue to treat our patients where the protocols would otherwise have brought us to a standstill.

Sometimes there is the realisation that the carefully laid-out SOPs don't work in the way the system architects intended, and the procedures – not the crew – are found wanting. Sociologists would regard SOPs as technologies in their own right; a sort of interface between the human and the physical elements of the system, a way of tuning one to the needs of the other. They encode the organisational memory of the system. And as such, they can only work if they themselves are mutable. Sometimes the result of a case review is a consideration of actions that might have resulted in a better outcome. But sometimes it is about rewriting procedures that are no longer fit for purpose, for the benefit of future crews and future patients – or adding to them, as was the case after Sully's landing on the Hudson.

Alex explains our innovation of using the bonnets of broken vehicles and the side of the crashed van as makeshift whiteboards, where we listed the casualties and triage categories, and how that helped create a shared mental picture of the scene. From that, we could divide the accident into three distinct zones, enabling Alex to assign the right paramedic expertise and fire crews to each one.

The challenge with this accident, put simply, was the scale: there were too many seriously injured people for us to attend to, at the speed they all needed. More than a few patients needed advanced medical intervention. We could have tried to keep them on scene and treated them in turn. Instead we called in another aircraft and HEMS crew. But even that wasn't enough. And so we found ourselves dispatching two of the casualties in ambulances to nearby hospitals with critical-care paramedics, who could do most of what we doctors might have done. It was the best we could do with what we had. Not ideal, but optimal in the moment. These are the adaptations that help us to go again, time after time. This is how the delegation of authority and deference to expertise work in practice. There is no good outcome to this scene. Sometimes you need to choose between bad or worse.

Conversation turns, inevitably, to the surgery on the helipad. Until now the questions and interruptions have been incisive and occasional. But this subject brooks the dam. A torrent follows. The first cardiac arrest happened early in flight. Did we consider aborting and landing? Should we have done the surgery earlier? Could we have landed in a field somewhere between the accident scene and the hospital? Should we have started cutting in the cabin of the aircraft? Should we have done it at all?

Everyone knows how this case ended. And so there is an obvious outcome bias. There's a difference in the way that you interrogate something, depending on whether your patient survived in the end, even though there are many cases in which no action would have made any difference to the result, no matter how timely or how deftly executed. And still the questions come.

Alex responds. In the aircraft the blood transfusions seemed to be working; we managed to restore our patient's circulation, we were less than ten minutes out from the helipad, we could feel a weak pulse, so we continued. We thought it might hold. We were wrong. It is right that they go at us this hard. Controversy has always dogged this procedure. Nobody should do it lightly, or expect it to avoid forensic scrutiny. But the decision to do the surgery was the consequence of the failure of all other plans: one last hope. One that requires that most difficult of all combinations: careful consideration and immediate action.

Montgomery, Alabama, 1902. It is late in the evening as Dr Luther Leonardis Hill Jr and two fellow physicians make their way to a small shack on the edge of town, lanterns lighting their way, to the bedside of a thirteen-year-old boy, Henry, who was stabbed in the heart some eight hours earlier. Henry is able to speak in broken sentences, but is barely conscious. His hands and nose are cold, his pulse thready, rapid and weak, his breathing difficult and shallow. He is on the verge of death.

The team of doctors carry Henry to the kitchen table, telling his parents that there is no time to lose, they must operate here and now. They begin the anaesthetic: sweet-smelling chloroform is dripped onto a cloth mask held over Henry's face. As he lapses into unconsciousness, Hill begins his surgery. The stab wound is one-eighth of an inch wide at the apex of the heart, just below Henry's left nipple. A dribble of blood spurts from it with every heartbeat.

Hill opens a flap of muscle and skin over the wound, before cutting through the ribs below and exposing the heart. He opens the pericardium, the sac surrounding the beating heart, which is engorged with blood. He shells out the clot inside, leaving it free to beat, and then finds a small wound in the wall of the heart, which he skilfully closes with a run of sutures. The surgery takes the best part of an hour.

They withdraw the anaesthetic, leaving Henry to breathe the ordinary air of the room once again as his consciousness returns. In 1902 chloroform-induced unconsciousness would have been hazardous enough; it was a drug loaded with its own potentially lethal consequences. This is a procedure that Henry would be lucky to survive today in a hospital, on a properly lit operating table, in the hands of a cardiothoracic specialist, a skilled anaesthetist and a full scrub team with access to a modern suite of medical monitoring and drugs. But this is the risk that the moment requires: anaesthesia with nothing more than a mask and a bottle of vapours; heart surgery, by lamp light, on a kitchen table. To do nothing would have meant certain death.

Against the odds, young Henry Myrick survived the night and made a full recovery – the first known survivor of an out-of-hospital thoracotomy. But despite this remarkable outcome, and a slew of similar hospital case reports from the late nineteenth century, surgeons continued to regard this practice as a thing of folly. In fact, cardiac surgery as a whole was considered untenable. It wasn't until the Second World War that surgeons were forced to revisit the possibility at scale, with US military surgeon Dwight Harken pioneering new techniques to treat shrapnel and bullet wounds in the hearts of dozens of casualties evacuated after D-Day and the Battle of the Bulge in 1944–5.

Doubt nevertheless remained, well beyond the middle of the

twentieth century, even after the first successful open-heart surgeries and transplants. It wasn't until the 1980s that cardiac surgery began to gain broad respectability. Advances in blood transfusions and antibiosis, coupled with new, safer anaesthetic drugs and improved bypass machines, together transformed the practice from a maverick indulgence to a revered discipline. It was only at this point that a team of emergency physicians, working at the Royal London Hospital in Whitechapel, began to wonder if the art had advanced far enough to be taken, once again, out of the hospital and into the community.

The Royal London Helicopter Emergency Medical Service was the first of its kind in the UK, carrying a physician and paramedic team with advanced anaesthetic, surgical and resuscitation capabilities. Faced with a growing number of patients across London suffering penetrating injuries from knives and handguns, they decided to revisit the procedure first pioneered by Luther Leonardis Hill: the pre-hospital thoracotomy.

The initial attempts were made in the late 1980s and drew sharp criticism, with echoes of the controversies that had always dogged the field. This was not surgery the way anyone else understood it. And it was decidedly not medicine. It was considered irresponsible, futile, bordering on an act of vandalism. And even today, with many thousands of these procedures performed and hundreds of new survivors, we still ask our questions. Should we have opened that patient's chest? We know that for patients who have suffered traumatic cardiac arrest from penetrating injuries of the chest, a well-executed thoracotomy within the first ten minutes after the pulse initially disappears confers a survival advantage of somewhere between 5 and 15 per cent.

The picture is less clear-cut for those who have experienced blunt trauma – injuries from falls or road-traffic collisions – like our patient. In these cases the survival rate is much lower, maybe as low as 3–7 per cent. And this approaches zero if there are no signs of life upon the team's arrival at the scene. But we were there with her, in the cabin of the aircraft, when her pulse first faded. We made the decision as a team, although in retrospect the chances of success were marginal at best. Would I do it again in the same circumstances? I honestly don't know.

These case discussions, at their best, are about having the courage to tear apart a sequence of poorly understood events, to try and make sense of something that doesn't resolve in any simple way, understanding that most of it will remain unknown, but knowing also that this attempt to understand might somehow better prepare you for that rare moment in the future when you might have the chance to make the difference between death and survival.

The crucial point is this: safety is central to all that we do in medicine, and incidents and accidents must be investigated and understood as thoroughly as possible in its pursuit, but the goal of those investigations is not to *guarantee* that those accidents can never happen again. It can't be. Not every risk can be avoided, not every outcome is avoidable. And to act in the best interests of our patients we are constantly forced to choose something other than *absolute* safety. All interventions carry their own risks, every decision has its uncertainties.

What we should be striving for is a culture of continual improvement, within which safety is a part; one that progressively *reduces risk* – even though it cannot eliminate it – through the ensemble of research, innovation and education, which together serve to augment our capability, giving all of us more and better choices in the decisive moment.

In medicine, the road to progress and the future that we all hope for come from a proper understanding of the risks and benefits that go with everything we do. An understanding of the risks we take on behalf of others, an appreciation of the sometimes profound consequences of those risks, and a commitment to managing that risk in the best way we can.

We must meet failure with infinite curiosity. But we should greet success in the same way. And when we ask ourselves the hardest questions – trying to tease out which events were and weren't within our conscious control, what we might have done differently or better – we must recognise that no line of enquiry is perfect, and that we might never know for sure. But none of that should stop us from searching; not in a way that fashions our recollections of the past into an instrument of torture, but in service of the future and something better for ourselves and the people that we care for.

Medicine is *about* risk – it always will be. It is about the mitigation of that risk, to the best of our ability, understanding that despite our best efforts, real risk and tragic consequence always remain.

It's odd to be in a profession where so much joy can sit next to so much sadness; where the transitions between the two can be so rapid. There is no single way of dealing with this, no protocol, no checklist, no standard operating procedure.

Some practitioners construct carefully maintained fences, rather than walls, to weather the emotional headwinds of the career; barriers that you can see through, that you need to repair and reinforce every now and again, but which at the same time let you see through to the other side from both directions. For others, it is about professional distance.

The crews are perhaps self-selecting. No one chooses to expose themselves to this, repeatedly, over months and years, if it truly gets under their skin. And yet everyone has a threshold. The jobs that involve children are harder for almost everyone. But there are other elements that catch you off-guard, like something in the patient that reminds you of someone close: your mother, your father or a friend. In that moment fences fall and have to be hastily re-erected.

After the worst job I ever attended, when I confided in my colleague about how hard I had found it – indeed, was finding it – he in return shared with me his story of standing in a field in the middle of a scene so tragic and awful that afterwards he had to take himself away and vomit quietly. There are things that I think you simply can't understand, or make understood, unless you've been there as well.

It affects us all differently. It's hard not to become risk-averse, which is weird given what we do. It's something to guard against, and at times I find myself left wanting. For every scene we go to, there is someone who thought this could never happen to them. For any given activity – horse-riding, motorcycling, hang gliding, drunken skinny-dipping, you name it – we've seen the worst possible thing happen.

And when my children were little, shortly after a particularly difficult job, I found myself compulsively fastening and refastening their seatbelts as they wriggled underneath me in their car seats in the back of the car, trying to make sure they were absolutely secure. I could hear them giggling at me, complaining that we were going to be late, echoing their mother (who was by this time not laughing). It made me smile and want to cry, all at the same time, because I couldn't explain to them why it had taken me ten minutes to strap them in for a quick drive down to Granny's house.

And when I was finally done and I took my seat next to my wife, studiously avoiding her gaze, because by now I really had made us late. There was a frisson of irritation – until our five-year-old chimed, 'Daddy, you are a man of safety!' from his well-reinforced position in the back seat. And we all laughed.

PART TWO

9.
Edge of chaos

We spent the first part of this book looking at the sharp end of practice, examining how individuals form themselves into teams and how, through the connections they build between one another, they become part of a wider, more capable system, able to monitor for emergent threats and adapt to them in real time.

In Part 2 we're going to shift our attention to look at some of the principles and strategies that organisations adopt to support these frontline staff in dealing with volatility, uncertainty and complexity, as well as at the role that technology plays. We can think of this as being about the 'blunt end' of operations – the elements shaped by the people who design and manage these systems.

It is traditional for the sharp-end teams to malign their blunt-end counterparts, casting them as distant and out of touch. But when we talk about the blunt end, it is not a pejorative term. Rather, it is about the tier of leadership and management responsible for establishing the foundations from which sharp-end operations must be launched. The planning and structure they provide are absolutely necessary; the infrastructure that they choose to build, the hierarchies they configure, the culture they set and the principles they adopt are decisive in determining how well placed and how well equipped the frontline teams are to manage the uncertain world they are confronted by.

Part of the challenge here lies in striking the right balance between *structure* and *improvisation*. We have seen various shades of this in the way that small teams operate. But those principles also apply at an organisational scale. Getting this balance right is what gives an organisation its competitive advantage, enabling it to grow and adapt, creating opportunity through innovation and change. When your best-laid plans inevitably disintegrate, it is this that enables you to persist and survive without being torn apart. This state is neither easily reached or held, and it requires deliberate effort to achieve and maintain it. But to deal with uncertainty, this is where you have to be: on the edge of chaos.

We are mostly raised to think of order as an unlimited virtue. Tidy your room, organise your work, write neatly, conform to the rules, et cetera. When we describe someone or something as chaotic, it is invariably a pejorative statement. There is comfort in the idea of stability, and we fear that feeling of being on the point of toppling over and only barely staying steady. But there's a reason why for many, if not most, of us there will always be a little bit of anarchy in our lives, and why that's not entirely a bad thing.

It is understandable that we fear chaos. Chaos is about the practical impossibility of prediction; it describes a system in which – beyond all but the shortest timescales – we do not know, and cannot guess, what will happen next. American mathematician and meteorologist Edward Norton Lorenz, widely regarded as the father of modern chaos theory, once described chaos as a state in which 'the approximate present does not approximately determine the future'. For those of us who spend our lives making ballpark estimates of the present, hoping that it can guide decisions and actions that will guard us against the threats that loom ahead, that definition of chaos is uniquely terrifying. But in the management of uncertainty, it turns out that it pays to stick close to what we fear the most.

Faced with deep uncertainty and impending chaos, it is tempting to retreat into the fortress of rigid protocol; I have thrown myself behind its walls more than a few times. It is not a wasted gesture. Standard operating procedures, as we have seen, preserve your adaptive capacity and keep you moving when you are at risk of grinding to a halt. But that is only a temporary refuge. Sooner or later you have to emerge and face the challenge that is threatening to overwhelm you, with improvisation and innovation.

We saw this at the motorway crash scene, in the railway trench and on Flight 1549, where in each case it was the actions taken after the plan had disintegrated that prevented catastrophe. There is a balance to be struck between the security of the fortress and the need for an agile, adaptive response crafted outside its walls.

That sweet spot – giving you the freedom to shed the bonds of standardisation while hovering on the verge of loss of control – can feel deeply uncomfortable. But here, where the system is at its most complex and most responsive, is the Goldilocks zone where you are most creative, have the greatest agility and are most able to adapt.

The 'edge of chaos' is more than a casual metaphor; the concept finds its roots in computer science and mathematics and emerged from complexity theory. Chris Langton, the computer scientist who first explored and popularised the concept, wrote and published his seminal PhD thesis on the subject while at the University of Michigan in 1991. He devised a kind of primitive, self-playing video game. The program explored what happened to a colony of artificial cells – what scientists refer to as 'cellular automata' – as they grew and reproduced on a grid, and the conditions under which they would collectively thrive. As modern video games go, it was underwhelming: a grid of pixels, flashing on and off, to signify life or death, as they marched across the screen. But this simple scheme enabled Langton to look at what happened as you moved the system away from rigid order and towards chaos.

Langton's game had a parameter that he could adjust, which determined how excitable his artificial universes were. He called this variable lamda, and it could be set to zero, one or anything in between. Setting it to zero led to a stone-cold barren landscape. Nothing was born, nothing lived: no life. Setting lamda to a value close to one gave you a universe that was boiling over with live pixels, flickering like static on the screen without form or pattern: the very definition of chaos. But it was what happened between these extremes that caught Langton's eye.

At low values of lamda, not much more than zero, his virtual universe would generate a few stable structures – long lines of pixels that repeated again and again, for ever without change. And higher values of lamda gave you a system that quickly descended into chaos. But with just the right amount of excitability – the correct balance between the dull, enduring structures and the fizz of chaos – there was a burst of wonderfully complex forms, sometimes stable for long periods of time, sometimes shifting around the grid, occasionally seeming to pass information back and forth.

This knife edge, between rigidity and anarchy, he came to call 'The Edge of Chaos', a realm in which complex structures could form, adapt and change continuously, without being destroyed by the chaos or regressing to something simpler; the place where something that looked akin to artificial life could thrive.

Edward Lorenz's work with weather systems in the 1960s had shown us the natural world's propensity to chaotic behaviours, but Christopher Langton had noticed something wonderful happening at the fringes of that chaos. It led him to establish the field of Artificial Life, or A-Life: experts from across the full spectrum of scientific disciplines would later gather at workshops hosted by Langton to try and understand his work in relation to their own area of expertise. Langton's work generated fierce discussion: maybe the features dancing on the screen in Chris's lab were alive in some philosophical sense. Maybe life was about the process rather than the substrate it formed from. Maybe his algorithm was as alive as the bacteria growing on an agar plate. The implications ran far and wide, in fields ranging from philosophy and biology to computer science, and they continue in today's discussions about Artificial Intelligence. But there were implications, too, for teams operating in complex and uncertain environments, and lessons on how best to organise a system to cope with the unexpected.

When I first flew with the HEMS teams, watching them as an observer, I initially jumped to the wrong conclusions. Checklists, SOPs and protocols were everywhere you looked. They appeared to rule the roost. And I thought that perhaps I was looking at a stripped-back version of medicine – something urgent, but in which there was precious little complexity or art, and which could therefore be practised as though you were painting by numbers. That wasn't it at all.

The medicine the teams practised out there was as difficult as anything I had ever seen, and the scenes were formally chaotic: the sparse information we gathered, and the guesses we were forced to make, often didn't lead us to the future we expected. Surprises lurked around every corner. I realised later that the checklists and standardisation were a beginning and not an end, and that as an organisation, what HEMS had created was something much more impressive than rigid standardisation. Setting up the teams to function in the way they did – with their protocols, tight teamwork and forensic debriefs – was how they married the structure of the blunt end to the near-anarchy of the sharp end, tuning the entire endeavour to sit at the edge of chaos. It was how they built a foundation firm enough to support an identity, a shared purpose and a means of capturing and storing useful organisational memory, but flexible enough in its frontline operations to be responsive to the unpredictable and unknowable challenges that the teams face every day.

Recent history abounds with examples of the need to get this balance right, especially when the world around us is transforming at speed. The first one that we'll look at happens to be particularly close to home.

In the 1980s, Wealdstone on the outskirts of north-west London was doing well enough. It had a busy high street with a supermarket called Victor Value, where you could buy a can of bargain-basement cola for twelve-and-a-half pence; there were banks, a railway station, bric-a-brac shops and a leisure centre nearby. The engine of the local economy was the Kodak factory, tucked away from the main road, which employed thousands of people. At the north end of the high street was a Roman Catholic comprehensive school – the Salvatorian College – whose pupils wore bright-green blazers. And in the 1980s I was among their number.

The school had no sixth form; more than a few boys left education at sixteen, and some of them found their way into good and long careers locally at the Kodak factory. It felt like a safe bet, a secure job in a long-lived industry; a good place to do some growing up and to learn some skills. By that point the factory had stood for nearly a hundred years, expanding steadily as the photographic business had grown. It had opened its gates in 1891, becoming Kodak's first headquarters outside the United States. We thought it would last for ever.

Kodak was in the business of selling cameras, photographic film and paper. For decades it had led the field without obvious competition, holding contracts far and wide. In the early part of the twentieth century people used the term 'kodaking' to describe the act of taking a photograph, in much the same way we might talk about googling something today.

From Ansel Adams to Henri Cartier-Bresson, from Spielberg to Kubrick: all of them shot on Kodak's film stock. And it wasn't just the artists. When the US military launched their first spy satellites in the 1960s they carried Kodak film; when astronauts walked on the Moon, it was Kodak in the magazines of their Hasselblad cameras. By the 1980s Kodak had a virtual monopoly on high-quality cinematographic film; it's easier to list blockbusters of that decade that weren't filmed using their stock than those that were.

But all of that changed rapidly. In the 1990s digital photography entered the market. The first retail cameras produced fuzzy images that didn't come close to rivalling the quality of film. But that technology rode Moore's Law all the way, and as processing power increased sharply, so too did the clarity and capability of digital cameras. The number of photographs taken on hard film fell precipitously, while the number of digital images soared. By the mid-1990s Kodak's sales were faltering and its profits flattening. At the height of its success in the 1950s the Kodak factory in Wealdstone had employed more than 6,000 people. At one point it had served as the company's research centre in Europe. But by 2005 Kodak had decided to stop manufacturing film in the UK, and after a failed attempt at launching a spin-off company in 2013, the factory gates finally closed in 2016.

Kodak's is a well-worn tale in business circles, but what is often overlooked is that this was not simply a case of a legacy model being disrupted by new technology. It's not, in fact, that Kodak didn't have the right substrate with which to meet the future. Alongside its film and paper product lines, it had developed a rich expertise in chemical processes, as well as a vast distribution network. And it made more than token efforts at diversification. At one point it spawned a photocopier business, producing reprographics of a quality that threatened Xerox, the market leader of the time. Later it sought to leverage its expertise in chemical processes, acquiring a pharmaceutical company.

But it displayed what some analysts later described as 'cognitive inertia'. Kodak's executives were reluctant to stray too far from their core business: selling paper, film and chemical processes to dealerships, who would then sell them on. But the photocopier market didn't work like that, depending instead on leasing units to consumers and running service contracts to support them. Kodak later shed both its photocopier arm and its pharmaceutical businesses. They were reluctant to commit wholesale to innovations and revolutions that appeared to sit far from their comfort zone, despite the fact that they had ample evidence to inform the need for a more radical strategy.

In 1975 one of Kodak's own employees, Steve Sasson, invented the first digital camera. It looks almost laughable now: a box with a lens, mounted on top of something that resembled a short filing cabinet, with a cassette recorder bolted to the side of the contraption. But it worked, and it showed Kodak where the world was headed.

In the 1980s Vincent Barabba ran Kodak's market-intelligence division. His assessment of the trend in digital imaging threw up some uncomfortable insights. It was clear that digital imaging would one day surpass the quality and capability of traditional film; Kodak was safe for the moment (that being defined as the rest of the 1980s), but his team projected the arrival of technologies that would be comparable to film sometime in the 1990s. Kodak, whose business was making devices that captured and stored images, now had an opportunity to make the necessary pivot.

But while the dalliances with photocopying and pharmaceuticals represented an acknowledgement that the company's future lay in something different from its existing business model, it was far from a firm commitment to resculpting its strategy and operation as a whole. In Barabba's book *The Decision Loom* he cites this as being central to Kodak's declining fortunes. They had gathered the right information, made the right analysis and had the right expertise to respond, but they were unable to make good use of that information and failed to transform themselves with enough speed and confidence to head off the looming threats.

Kodak's behaviour here is a textbook example of a loss of situational awareness. As an organisation, Kodak had failed to understand what had happened, what was happening and what was about to happen. The right information was present, good people were in the loop, but they had not been able to collate those resources and use them to make the right decisions. The whole was becoming substantially less than the sum of its parts.

All of this was compounded by a general inertia that held back the pace and agility with which Kodak could effect change. It wasn't simply Kodak's failure to see the future coming that hurt them. It was the way it dealt with the pace of change, and the cloud of ambiguity that hovered over what lay ahead. In truth, there was great uncertainty in the unfolding of the digital-photography market: how soon would the right technology arrive, how quickly would customers adopt it and how completely? Faced with this uncertainty, Kodak – instead of innovating – chose to stick close to what it knew best.

The company started with cautious innovation, choosing new retail models that assumed their customers would continue to favour old materials and habits. They married existing camera bodies with digital sensors and created the photo CD, on which high-resolution images could be captured and displayed on a monitor. They invented devices that could scan photographic negatives, too. All of this cleaved to the underlying assumption that people would continue to want what they had always wanted: hard prints on photographic paper.

This was a hybridised business model: old-fashioned film and paper, combined with the advantages of modern digital technology. It was, in retrospect, spectacularly cautious. Financial disaster lay ahead.

In 1986, the year that Tony Scott filmed *Top Gun*, Kodak had been at the peak of its profitability and power, worth tens of billions of dollars worldwide. The decade that followed would prove punishing: Kodak's sales slowed, as did its profits. With the arrival of the millennium, the company was firmly in negative growth.

In 2012 director Sam Mendes released *Skyfall*, the latest blockbuster in the James Bond franchise, which saw the ageing and diminished secret agent grappling with themes of obsolescence and reinvention. It was the first film of the Bond franchise to be shot entirely with digital cameras. That same year Kodak, a company that had endured for more than a century, filed for bankruptcy.

The lessons we are learning here – about how to deal with dense uncertainty and volatility – apply over all timescales. It would be a mistake to think that just because you're not in the middle of some life-threatening, blue-light emergency, those rules don't apply. The time we live in is unique in all of history. What slayed Kodak was the rapid onset of change, brought about by the digital transformation of its industry. That rate of change has only intensified since.

Innovation, adaptability and agility do not stem from order and stability. If you fashion yourself into a monolith, you may survive the threat of the moment, but you won't be able to reshape yourself quickly, or effectively enough, to meet whatever threat comes next.

The alternative, as practised by our HEMS teams, can feel uncomfortable. For them, constant reappraisal unearths new information, forcing them to abandon old plans and commit to new ones. In difficult scenes, they often find themselves having to change direction more than once in the space of minutes. But that is their competitive edge – their ability to operate at the edge of chaos.

In this changeable world, that is where we all need to be. And that frisson of discomfort that you sometimes feel – it is just a sign that you're probably in the right place.

10.

An ocean of risk

How do you design an organisation that is capable of existing at the edge of chaos?

Until the 1980s there was a broad assumption that all an organisation needed in order to be successful was rational planning and standardisation, coupled with strong leadership and hierarchical control. But waves of technological revolution brought a raft of new industries and capabilities that were more complex, more lethal and needed to play by different rules.

By 1986 the twentieth century had seen twenty-eight major industrial accidents – disasters in which fifty or more people had been killed. Half of these had happened in the previous decade. In February 1984 the rupture of a pipeline carrying petroleum gas in Cubatão, Brazil, flooded a swamp over which sat a favela of wooden dwellings, built on stilts. Fire broke out less than two hours later, killing hundreds, families and young children among them. In November 1984, in San Juanico, Mexico, the leakage of a fuel line carrying petroleum gas caused an explosion that is thought to have killed up to 600 people. And before the year was out, in December 1984, the infamous accidental release of the highly toxic gas methyl isocyanate, from the Union Carbide pesticide plant in Bhopal, India, killed many thousands of people and seriously injured hundreds of thousands more.

According to some, this was just the price of progress; the other edge of the sword of technology. Despite the capability and advantage these organisations brought, their complex character meant that small anomalies could sometimes emerge undetected and, rippling outwards, cause a cascade of failures as they went, making disasters of this type and scale essentially unavoidable. Academics in the field coined the term Normal Accident Theory (NAT) to describe the problem.

But there was an alternative, less pessimistic school of thought. One that suggested it was possible to evolve ways of working that could forestall catastrophic mishap, even in complex, high consequence, state-of-the-art endeavours.

Aboard aircraft carriers in the 1950s and 1960s you could expect around seventeen serious aircraft accidents per 100,000 hours of flight operations. There were several notorious incidents, among them a catastrophic fire aboard the USS *Enterprise* in January 1969 – the same year that Neil Armstrong and Buzz Aldrin walked on the surface of the Moon.

In that incident a 'huffer' – a mobile auxiliary power unit, used on aircraft carrier decks to start jet engines – was parked too close to an F4 Phantom fighter-bomber. The Phantom was loaded with Zuni missiles, and the hot exhaust from the huffer heated one of the five-kilogram warheads to more than 300 degrees Celsius, enough to trigger its explosion.

The Zuni warhead was part of a small, inexpensive weapon system, designed to destroy lightly armoured vehicles. Alone, it should have posed little hazard to the massive aircraft carrier. But this was only the beginning of a more lethal chain of events. Fragments from the detonated missile punched holes in the deck and ruptured the Phantom jet fighter's fuel tank. The resulting fire triggered the explosives in the remaining missiles beneath its wing, leading in turn to the detonation of a Mark 82 bomb, a weapon loaded with nearly 100 kilos of high explosive.

This damaged a fuel bowser, which spilt its contents, driving fires above and below decks. But the explosions had also severed fire hoses, hampering effective firefighting. With the inferno of jet fuel raging and temperatures rising dangerously, bombs mounted on racks elsewhere in the ship now began to detonate. In all, eighteen explosions ripped through the flight deck, destroying fifteen aircraft, killing twenty-seven servicemen and injuring 300 more. All of this was the consequence of a mobile auxiliary power unit that had been parked in the wrong place.

In the wake of the USS *Enterprise* fire, the US Navy undertook a radical redesign of its flight-deck procedures and systems for handling and disarming weapons. It reinforced fire-suppression systems, firefighting equipment and training, and redesigned the huffers so that their exhaust was directed vertically, making it harder for servicemen to repeat the same mistakes that caused the fire aboard the *Enterprise*. Ordnance magazines were hardened against thermal and blast threats. And there was a wider legacy. The United States' Naval Safety Center was established, which would later become the Naval Safety Command, with a stronger culture of risk assessment and hazard-reporting engendered throughout the fleet.

All of this helped deliver an organisational culture that would reduce the occurrence of serious accidents aboard aircraft carriers tenfold over the next decade; a culture that also drove a hunger for learning, and the acceptance of the need to turn to outsiders in search of ways to improve.

In the late 1980s Rear Admiral Thomas Mercer, then captain of the United States aircraft carrier USS *Carl Vinson*, invited a team of social scientists – psychologists, sociologists and academics in the field of management theory – to embed themselves aboard ship with his crew. Mercer hoped that fresh, analytical eyes might help further improve the performance of this team.

To the researchers, the *Carl Vinson* was an enigma: a 1,000-foot-long floating city with an airport stuck on top, powered by a nuclear reactor, with a crew of more than 5,000, who together maintained and operated the ship and its complement of seventy-five aircraft.

The crowded flight deck was littered with aircraft, loaded with missiles and bombs; throttling turbines that could suck someone in or blow them off the deck; steam catapults with force enough to accelerate twenty-ton planes from nought to 165 miles an hour in two seconds; arresting wires to catch the same aircraft when they landed; and an intensity of operation that allowed take-offs and landings at intervals of less than sixty seconds. On the bridge and below decks, there was the business of propelling and sailing 100,000 tons of warship and carefully maintaining its multi-megawatt nuclear reactor. On the face of it, it was an accident waiting to happen. But here was the curious thing: it was an accident that, for the most part, almost never happened.

By the 1980s the USS *Carl Vinson* – and the rest of the US carrier fleet – had somehow cut the expected serious accident rate by an order of magnitude, from seventeen to just one accident per 100,000 hours of flight operations. The investigating academic team – led by Gene Rochlin, Todd La Porte and Karlene Roberts from the University of California, Berkeley – studied carrier operations for three years, shadowing the rank and file, night and day.

Between them they had spent their careers trying to understand how teams, businesses and industries handled the challenges of the modern world. La Porte had explored how the public sector managed hazardous technologies in the aviation and nuclear domains. Roberts was similarly interested in organisational behaviour and culture, and in how teams went about making decisions in pressured environments. Rochlin meanwhile had a background in physics, but had transitioned to studying science and technology policy. The team's multi-disciplinary background provided many lenses through which to inspect the inner workings of the USS *Carl Vinson* and its crew. But they soon came to realise that they were looking at a new kind of organisation, operating in a way that none of them had ever seen before.

The behaviours and structures aboard ship were so different – so at odds with managerial convention – that they treated the USS *Carl Vinson* as though it were the first sighting of a newly discovered species. Taxonomy followed. They gave their new creature a name, calling it a High Reliability Organisation (HRO); one that should be visited regularly by failure at scale, but which largely managed to avoid it. British comedian Spike Milligan once remarked that going on a cruise was 'like being sent to prison with an outside chance of drowning'. But here, at sea aboard the USS *Carl Vinson*, was confinement with an outside chance of many things far worse: exploding munitions, aeronautical disaster, all the way to nuclear catastrophe. And the question, for the research team, was how those threats were avoided.

The instinctive response to an environment so filled with danger is to seek safety. The safest thing to do, in terms of protection of the vessel and its crew, would be not to put to sea at all. But safe harbour is not where the work of a carrier group is done. The teams must set sail and accept the risks that come with deployment. More than that, they have to find ways to survive it, even under conditions of war; to make progress despite the adversity of the conditions in which they operate. Like the HEMS crews, after the moment of launch what they are left with is not safety, but the dynamic management of risk and the burden of eternal vigilance.

Reliability is not safety. This is an important but often poorly understood point. HROs make mistakes, get things wrong and experience failure. What sets them apart is their ability to adapt and learn, and to *create mechanisms that anticipate and contain errors*, in a manner that severely limits the number of ways in which catastrophe can occur in the future.

There is no suite of key performance indicators that qualify you as an HRO; this is not something that an organisation suddenly becomes, or a club that it gains membership of. For HROs, reliability is instead *a state that is pursued, continuously*. Being an HRO is about embracing complexity rather than cowering from it; about recognising that the roots of failure and success are multifarious and difficult to understand. But failure itself presents an opportunity to learn and improve. And it's about the process of continuously training and developing a highly skilled team, who can configure and reconfigure the system, over time and in the moment, to meet the demands of the ever-changing world in which they operate.

When describing a new species, the first order of business is to list all of its observable traits that differ from existing creatures. For HROs there were five broad, distinguishing features. They were obsessed with failure; they were sensitive to their own operations, meaning they were highly attuned to what exactly it was that they were doing at any one moment; they refused to simplify; they deferred to expertise; and they cultivated resilience. These are easy to say, but they are not straightforward to understand and are hard to achieve. We're going to try and unpack them a little here, with the help of Professor Kathleen Sutcliffe, whose book *Managing the Unexpected* (which she co-authored with fellow organisational theorist Professor Karl Weick) first popularised HRO theory.

Kathleen's academic background is eclectic, with separate Bachelor's degrees in arts and sciences, a Master's degree in nursing and, later, a PhD spent studying organisational behaviour and theory. She spent time on US Navy aircraft carriers, furthering early work in HRO theory, but her exposure to sharp-end practice and real-time risk started much earlier in her career. Long before her academic research began, Kathleen had taken jobs as a pipeline construction worker in her native Alaska, and had served as a crew member aboard crab boats in the Aleutian Islands, an occupation widely regarded as being one of the most dangerous jobs in the world.

I had long been fascinated with the way in which she and her colleagues described safety as something that people and organisations must strive to create day by day and in every moment. Kathleen told me that she wishes now that they had called the field 'High Reliability Organising theory' to underline the idea that reliability stems from active processes. Nevertheless, Professor Sutcliffe unpacked the five key principles that appear common to all HROs, as follows.

HROs' preoccupation with failure is a cornerstone of their success. They try to anticipate in advance as much as possible of what might go wrong and, in doing so, design an environment and develop standard operating procedures that reduce the likelihood of failure during the mission itself. HEMS is a great example of this, with its rigid SOPs and checklists; similarly, the USS *Carl*

Vinson separates, by time and space, hazardous processes such as the loading of munitions and the fuelling of aircraft. The flight deck is carefully marshalled, strictly divided into three zones, with crew wearing colour-coded uniforms that designate their role, and this deck itself is divided into three operational areas. No one is permitted to stray beyond their assigned area, or to take on tasks outside their specialist role. Training to prepare the crew to manage unexpected emergencies is a core activity. Fires are among the most destructive emergencies that a carrier could face: the whole crew is taught how to prevent, manage and fight fires, and that training occurs on a near-continuous basis.

The second principle for HROs is 'sensitivity to operations', which means that they monitor events as they unfold in the moment, to give them the best and most up-to-date information, which can be used to recalibrate the teams and system as a whole. This fosters a kind of organisational situational awareness – an understanding of what has just happened, what is happening and what is going to happen. It enables small anomalies to be identified, tracked and contained before they have a chance to mushroom into something unmanageable.

But this characteristic also allows system leaders to monitor the state of the organisation over longer timescales. On the USS *Carl Vinson* the reporting of incidents and mishaps is expected and rewarded. Junior ranks are encouraged to contribute and challenge, if they believe the safety of the operation to be at risk. Naturally there is a well-established military hierarchy, but at the same time mechanisms are in place – formal and informal – which enable information to flow, encouraging people at all levels in the organisation to contribute to the perpetual pursuit of reliability. This has the effect of closing the gap between the system's architects and leaders and the experience of the frontline teams, trying to avoid the problem of creating a disconnected management tier that is out of touch with the realities of day-to-day operation.

The third characteristic is a refusal to simplify. HROs know that what they are able to do arises out of their willingness to embrace complexity, and their ability to fashion an organisation that is truly greater than the sum of its parts. They understand that their successes and their failures are caused by complex interactions and chains of events. When they search for answers, they look beyond the surface detail and try to challenge assumptions, drawing in information from a wide range of sources, embracing diversity of opinion.

Team leaders encourage their team to contribute to solutions and to challenge ideas, providing a way of scanning the cloud of uncertainty for hidden threats, and giving themselves and their crews greater opportunity to act in a timely fashion. People operating in these environments expect to be surprised, but find ways to equip their teams to deal with that surprise.

Fourth is the powerful concept of deference to expertise. HROs also recognise that complexity demands that leaders defer to expertise wherever it lies in the organisation. NASA was fond of this practice – as previously mentioned, in the 1960s the average age of the flight controller was just twenty-six (of which more later, in fact) – and chose to delegate authority and decision-making to those with the greatest expertise, working where the consequence of those decisions was most keenly felt.

Finally, HROs foster resilience. This shouldn't be confused with ideas of personal fortitude. Resilience here is the property of the system that – as far as possible – prepares for error, surprise and failure and is able to restore in its wake, and recover most (if not all) of its function thereafter. As Professor Sutcliffe describes, the pursuit of resilience is not about making your organisation error-free. It is about preventing it from being disabled by error and discrete failures.

Let's walk back through the HEMS breakfast-club meeting again to find behaviours that echo HRO principles. The preventative strategy begins with the equipment checks before we sit down to brief. The pilots do their external walkaround: inspecting the helicopter airframe for damage, studying the rotors for cracks, the gearboxes for defects and undue wear and tear, along with the oil and fluid levels in the engine and hydraulics. They move the flight controls through their full range of motion; making sure it all feels right, and then fire up the avionics, radios and transponders. The assumption is that sooner or later some vital component will fail, and that it is best to find out on the ground rather than while you are hurtling through the air.

The doctor and the paramedic, meanwhile, perform the same checks on their medical kit. It takes around half an hour for them to comb over the contents of the helicopter and the response cars, leaving them sure that the many systems that contribute to the team's reliability are intact and functioning. This rigour and attention to detail are an expression of their preoccupation with failure: something that you also see in the garish safety posters on the walls in the hangar, and then later in the crew briefing – everything putting them in the best position to respond, should something unexpected happen later.

Bringing me into the crew on that first day, acknowledging my status as a novice and an outsider, but empowering me to contribute to the safety of the crew in flight, is an expression of their refusal to simplify. It is borne of a recognition that the threats ahead are so numerous and difficult to forecast that you need to set up a multi-pronged defence, making best use of all the resources available to you. Folding me into the team, making me a safety sensor of sorts, improved everyone's chances.

Resilience is a combined product of individual training, team performance, the engineered system and a rehearsal of the many ways in which the sortie might go wrong. We anticipate the unexpected and, should it arise, we configure the crew to scan for and detect those errors and failures and to respond competently. All of this lays the foundations of operational resilience – of a team that knows it will experience mishaps and failures, but one that is less likely to be disabled by those encounters.

As Professor Sutcliffe is at pains to underline, the 'reliability' component of HROs isn't a discrete state, but rather a continuous pursuit, a process. The process itself is akin to evolution. Put another way, for an organisation to persist in the world over any significant period of time, it needs by definition to have evolved ways to deal with and survive perturbations, uncertainty and complexity. Those that continue to persist and prevail, despite these many challenges, must have at least some strands of High Reliability Organisation DNA.

We see this parallel evolution across a range of organisations and industries that sprang up in the mid to late twentieth century. Remember that the USS *Carl Vinson*, the archetypal HRO, was not assembled according to some pre-formed blueprint. Rather it emerged over time, the product of lessons hard-won through war and peacetime cataclysm.

The question then arises whether or not these systems can be created or whether they have to be left to design themselves. For Professor Sutcliffe and researchers in the field, this is something of a billion-dollar question. When I asked her, she laughed out loud. 'You might as well ask me something easy, like if I think there's a God!'

In truth, the answer is likely to be a bit of both. All extant organisations have developed their own strategies for coping in the real world; the form they take is an expression of what it took to survive this far. So even without knowing the detailed taxonomy of High Reliability Organisation theory, you and your teams may already be part of the way there. But whether you can survive the uncertainty of the oncoming storm requires something other than more of the same, as Kodak found, to their great cost.

One of the US Navy flight-deck officers that Karl Weick's team interviewed in the course of their research memorably described the reality of carrier operations as follows:

> Imagine that it's a busy day, and you shrink San Francisco Airport to only one short runway and one ramp and one gate. Make planes take off and land at the same time, at half the present time interval, rock the runway from side to side, and require that everyone who leaves in the morning returns that same day. Make sure the

> equipment is so close to the edge of the envelope that it's fragile. Then turn off the radar to avoid detection, impose strict controls on radios, fuel the aircraft in place with their engines running, put an enemy in the air and scatter live bombs and rockets around. Now wet the whole thing down with sea water and oil, and man it with twenty-year-olds, half of whom have never seen an airplane close-up. Oh, and by the way, try not to kill anyone.

The USS *Carl Vinson* is clearly a warship operating at the edge of chaos. That core competency – of being able to hold position there so constantly and so reliably – is what gives it the best chance of surviving. And that is why it presents such an exemplary anatomy of a High Reliability Organisation; the features of the animal as observed in the wild. But on its own, it doesn't fully explain how organisms of this type continue to be alive when so many forces are ranged against them.

For that we need a different lesson, this time in the physiology of feedback.

11.
Feedback

Let's take a little time to think about *you* for a moment, sitting there reading this book, feeling like you're in standby mode, with not much going on. Nothing could be further from the truth. Your body holds a frenetic soup of biochemistry divided into trillions of discrete compartments, each one running its own set of reactions, shoving ions back and forth across cell membranes, generating electricity, burning fuels, building proteins, demolishing cells, shedding waste, constantly taking on oxygen, water and food, all in a necessary effort to keep alive.

What you get for that is something very fragile, but very beautiful. Life – of the rarest kind – with the potential to hurl itself down a running track, invent the wheel, design cities, engineer rocket ships, build economies, compose 'Purple Haze', write the collected works of Iain M. Banks or fall in love. But you exist far from equilibrium, out on a ledge: on the edge of chaos. And something has to work to keep you there, in that precarious state, so that the stuff of wonder can happen.

The human body sits closer to the edge of chaos than most other systems, even when it's in rude health. And like many complex systems, it is robust within limits, and fragile thereafter. Of course, it is the thereafter that medicine deals with: the chaos that accompanies illness and injury.

Scientists were late to arrive at this realisation. Until well into the nineteenth century they assumed that the body's internal state was inherently fixed and resilient, rather than something that had to be actively and constantly defended; they made many of the same assumptions we continue to make about the apparently stable organisations in which we work.

It was the French physician and physiologist Claude Bernard who first began to understand that the body was not quiescent, that there was a perpetual, internal battle going on, even in healthy individuals, to prevent it from being disrupted by the outside world. Our biology was more fragile and more vulnerable to injury, illness and disturbance than scientists had previously thought. And all of the remarkable feats that the human body was capable of could only unfold if its inner environment – what Bernard called the *milieu intérieur* – could be regulated within fine limits.

We started this book amid chaos, with a patient in our care bleeding torrentially, fine limits thoroughly breached, and my team unable to see this until it was too late, or do enough to prevent the death that followed. The problem of haemorrhage, its consequences and how best to address it is ancient. Despite centuries of effort, the phenomenon remained poorly understood even as the First World War broke out. 'Wound shock' – as the clinicians of the time called it – was something of an enigma.

The term 'shock' had been borrowed from French military surgeons who, as early as the eighteenth century, had noticed how bleeding patients could hold their own up until a point, but then suddenly fade and die. Their term, *choc* – the French word for 'impact' or 'blow' – was an attempt to capture the suddenness of that collapse. But while they were all too aware of the consequences of haemorrhage, they didn't understand what they were seeing in their casualties, or why it was happening.

Among those who attempted to unravel the mystery of shock during the First World War was the physiologist Walter Bradford Cannon, an American scientist from Harvard who joined the conflict in 1917 as part of the United States' war effort. Cannon journeyed to Europe, hoping to get close to the fighting, to better understand how wound shock evolved.

His first posting in May 1917 was in Camiers in France, at a facility with the capacity for 2,000 patients. It was a busy field hospital. In the month after Cannon arrived, it treated 3,000 Allied casualties, in rows of tents pitched on sodden fields, which eventually became infested with rats. The quickly multiplying rodents were vectors for disease, further threatening the health of already-wounded soldiers, and had to be controlled with a carefully deployed business of ferrets: one complex system set upon another.

Cannon could not pursue his ambitions here. It was a less-than-ideal place for scientific work and left him far from the battle lines. Short of equipment, he abandoned his laboratory research and instead chose to assist the military surgeons in their operating theatres. But Cannon soon realised that to get to the truth he would have to get even closer – in time and space – to the point of injury.

Cannon cut an unusual figure in the arena of war. A bespectacled Harvard academic in his mid-thirties, opposed to the idea of military conflict, he had initially resisted calls to join the fight; 'mother had never intended that I be a soldier,' he once confided. So it seems unlikely that he should have found himself in 1917 on the battlefields of France, repeatedly begging to get closer to the combat. But Cannon felt the need to find something that he might set against the tidal wave of suffering and loss.

The American Expeditionary Force (AEF) accepted Cannon's petitions and he got his wish. He would end the war on the Western Front, in field hospitals on the frontline during the Second Battle of the Marne. In July 1918, during the last major German offensive of the war, Cannon served with a shock unit, from where he could hear the constant rattle of guns and rumble of artillery; close enough that the hospital unit itself was shelled, and shrapnel ripped through his ward.

Here Cannon found hellish scenes: casualties with gaping wounds; heads blasted by munitions; eviscerated livers protruding from beneath bandaged abdomens. At night in the darkness he would hear the anguished cries of soldiers and witness the delirium that heralded death. He did what he could on the shock ward – continuing to trial therapies: drugs to constrict vessels and neutralise blood acidity, infusions of saline – but nothing proved effective.

It was only later, after the Armistice and in the wake of conflict, that Walter Cannon was able to gather and reflect with scientists with whom he had worked during the war. Among them were William Bayliss, John Scott Haldane, Nobel Laureate Henry Dale, Charles Sherrington and Ernest Starling – giants in the field of physiology – who had spent the conflict focused on the same problems. It was the synthesis of their joint studies of wound shock, and an approach to the problem that considered the human body as a complex whole, that finally crystallised their combined understanding of the phenomenon.

Let me explain briefly why people bleed to death, because it is a good illustration of how a complex yet integrated system works and why a deep understanding of the relationships between the component parts of that system is required to unpick it.

The circulatory system is not like a petrol tank. Death doesn't occur simply because there is no blood left. In brisk haemorrhage, your heart will stop beating long before that happens. The average adult has around five litres of circulating blood, which is pumped continuously by the heart through the body via its system of blood vessels. The sudden loss of 40 per cent of that volume – enough to fill just a couple of tall milk cartons – will bring the body to the edge of cardiac arrest. The circulating blood should also be thought of as a component of a vital physiological system; even its partial removal from that system sets in motion a cascade of failures, which, without immediate remedy, will quickly prove lethal.

We think of the heart as being akin to a mechanical pump, but that metaphor – though useful – doesn't do it justice. It's not an isolated mechanism of pistons and plungers, sucking and pushing the body of fluid that it is tasked with moving. It doesn't stand separately from the rest of the cardiovascular system, and it is impossible to properly understand its function without also comprehending the network of veins from which it fills, the arterial tree into which it empties or the litres of blood coursing through it.

The heart is woven from dynamic contractile tissue and is powered by biochemical reactions, which in turn drive molecular machines operating at a sub-microscopic scale – far more sophisticated than any comparable mechanical device. It is infiltrated by spontaneously beating pacemaker cells and a network of biological electrical circuits, and it depends upon the volume of blood entering its chambers to generate its driving force.

As the heart fills with blood returning from the veins, the muscle fibres in its walls stretch. This has the effect of loading the heart, the way you might load an arrow onto a bow and tension its string, priming it for action. Electrical impulses from specialised pacemaker cells within the heart then start a wave of contraction that spreads through the heart's muscle walls, triggering a coordinated release, generating a single heartbeat. The heart resets, the pacemaker cells keep time and the cycle begins again.

If, as a result of haemorrhage, blood leaks quickly from the circulation, then less volume returns to the heart. Less volume means less stretch of the muscle fibres – in our analogy, less tension in the bow string – and in turn a heart that beats less forcefully until, if the bleeding continues, the heart is unable to beat at all. The pacemaker cells continue to keep time, but the band is no longer marching behind them.

The story of haemorrhage doesn't stop there. We are of course able to stop ourselves from bleeding if the blood loss is not too brisk or the wound too extensive. We've all watched that happen, after a careless moment with a kitchen knife or a tumble and a grazed knee. Blood flows, but soon stops and forms a sticky plug, closing the wound.

We take the spontaneous arrest of modest bleeding, and the closure and healing of the wound that follows, for granted. But this, too, is the product of an intricate and carefully orchestrated mechanism. Once severed or torn, a blood vessel's walls will spasm, constricting and reducing the local flow of blood. The tissues lining the vessel wall will go on to release chemicals signposting the damage – the biochemical equivalent of a row of traffic cones encircling a hole in the road. That's enough to slow blood flow down and signpost the injury, but not enough to seal it reliably.

Next the body moves to close the gap. Platelets – fragments of old red blood cells that also circulate in the bloodstream – sense the signals sent by the damaged vessel wall and respond by accumulating at the site of injury. The gathering platelets then send chemical signals of their own, which summon still more platelets, amplifying their response. This temporary plug is consolidated by the activation of something called the 'coagulation cascade'. This sets off a small avalanche of chemical reactions, laying down a biological mesh called fibrin, a dense web that sits across the platelets and begins the task of pulling the edges of the wound together.

And so we see that the complexity of the body's response to wounding is fractal: there is detail at every level, and the more you look, the more you find. The beating of your heart and the formation of a blood clot are by no means the only facets involved in the human body's response to wounding. But this hint at their sophistication hopefully begins to give a sense of just how interconnected and layered are the mechanisms of the body, and helps to explain why some of history's greatest physiologists took so long to understand the problem. And why medical teams sometimes still continue to struggle in the face of that threat today.

At the start of twentieth century, physiology and medicine were still shifting away from a broadly Cartesian and mechanistic view of the human body – one that considered it machine-like in form and function, with components whose operation could be fully understood in isolation from the mechanism as a whole; in the same way one might remove and understand the gear mechanism of a grandfather clock.

But the challenges Cannon and his colleagues had faced in solving the problem of haemorrhage and shock had shown them the limitations of that approach. Physiology and medicine moved from the study of loosely connected, separable parts to a discipline that embraced the concept of the body as an intricate weave of mutually dependent systems.

Like Claude Bernard before him, Cannon realised that for the body to be able to hold itself separate from the chaos of the outside world, it needed a means of creating balance; something that enabled human physiology to sit perched at what we would now recognise as the edge of chaos. So many parameters have to be kept within tight limits just for us to stay alive from moment to moment: blood pressure, the levels of oxygen and carbon dioxide in our bodies, the volume of water they hold, the concentrations of glucose and ions in our bloodstream, our core temperature – to name but a few.

The tolerances are thin: only a few degrees Celsius separate significant hypothermia from high fever; differences in the concentration of ions in your bloodstream in the order of a few per cent are enough to interfere with the function of muscles, nerves and the heart; modest falls in blood pressure are enough to drive your body into shock. Humans, Cannon once wrote, are 'made of sensitive and unstable stuff'. What he was coming to realise was that the precipice on which life balances was far narrower and sharper than he had first imagined, and that there had to be something working constantly in the background that stopped the body from falling off that edge.

He came to understand that biological systems achieved this feat – of holding steady despite the turbulence of the outside world – through a specific mechanism: by sensing their environment, gathering and processing information and then triggering actions designed to return the system to its original state. This would become his most enduring and important contribution to science, the coining of the concept of homeostasis; from the Greek roots *homeo* – meaning 'similar to' – and *stasis* – meaning 'stability' or 'standing still'.

Homeostasis described the biological feedback loops that created enough order, in an otherwise hostile and mostly chaotic universe, for life to find a way. And in this scheme lies the answer to our question about how any system manages to cling to the edge of chaos.

We're all familiar with the principles of feedback. Consider for a moment the thermostat that controls the central heating in a house during winter. You set the desired temperature – let's say an environmentally friendly nineteen degrees Celsius – and this becomes the so-called 'set-point' after which the system moves to either warm up or cool down the room to try and achieve, and then maintain, that goal.

To create a feedback loop like this you need four key components: a set-point – a desired value – for the system to aim for; a sensor that can detect and measure the variable that you're trying to control; a control centre that can decide how to respond when there's a difference between the set-point and the actual level; and finally an effector that can adjust the variable you're trying to control. So for the heating system in your house, you have a human user setting the temperature, an electronic thermometer which measures that variable, a control centre in the form of a digital processor that works out whether it needs to heat or cool the room, and then a boiler that can be switched on if the room is too cold or switched off if the temperature is too hot.

This is a so-called 'negative feedback loop'. Negative because when something changes, it attempts to move the system back towards its set-point. Feedback loops of this type resist change and, in so doing, help to maintain stability. But they do more than keep your house warm.

Negative feedback keeps you where you want to be; it fights against perturbation. Feedback loops are an essential feature of complex systems, necessary to allow the whole to continue in its exotic state, at the edge of chaos and far from equilibrium, and prevent it from being reduced to something simpler and altogether less dynamic.

The homeostasis that Cannon described is not a mechanism that drives a system to its most secure configuration. It is instead about stability within limits, allowing a system to maintain a precarious state indefinitely that it would otherwise be impossible to hold. It creates balance while preserving the system's agility and adaptability.

Let's now consider a biological negative feedback loop – one designed to regulate blood pressure, for example. The control of blood pressure within tight limits is essential. If it's too low, you can't perfuse your vital organs – your heart, brain, liver, lungs, and so on. If it's too high, the pressure will inexorably damage those same organs, which is why your general practitioner is constantly asking you to do a little more exercise and cut down on the salt.

From day to day, the body has its own feedback mechanism for maintaining blood pressure at the correct value. It kicks in to adjust for prosaic changes – such as a change in posture from lying to standing – but can also compensate for injury and illness, and in particular for blood loss. It is part of the reason why haemorrhage is so difficult to detect. Feedback loops compensate for the loss of blood volume, maintaining blood pressure up to a point, despite the loss.

Here the same four core components of a negative feedback loop are present. The main sensors for blood pressure reside in the carotid artery in the neck and in the walls of the atria in your heart. They comprise a cluster of specialised cells that can sense the stretch of those tissues as the blood pressure rises and falls. Nerve fibres carry that signal to a control centre located in the brain; specifically, to the nucleus tractus solitarius and other cardiovascular centres in the brainstem.

Next comes the effector. For the human body, this involves signals sent from the brainstem to the heart and the blood vessels. If you're bleeding and your blood pressure is falling, the brainstem will trigger responses that instruct the heart to beat harder and faster and force blood vessels throughout the body to constrict. This is part of your fight-or-flight response. Together, these responses increase blood pressure, pushing it back towards the desired set-point.

I should point out that this is an accurate but very simplified description of that system. People have spent their entire careers trying to understand and unpick its nuances; I can already sense the professors of physiology who once taught me its finer details wincing on reading the previous paragraphs. Suffice to say, even this apparently uncomplicated system of a negative feedback loop – among the most basic examples that we teach our undergraduate medical students – is many orders of magnitude more complex than the way the thermostats in our houses work.

It is feedback that keeps us healthy and alive from moment to moment, and the disruption of those loops that is responsible for almost all disease. Cancer, for example, arises because cells divide uncontrollably, breaking free of the feedback processes that regulate their replication. Diabetes is a condition in which the body finds itself unable to maintain the levels of glucose in the bloodstream within sufficiently tight limits – either because it becomes insensitive to the changing levels of glucose (a fault in the sensor) or because the body can't secrete enough insulin of its own (a failure of the effector).

Even dementia can be traced to faulty homeostasis. The brain is mostly made up of neurons: cells that are responsible for forming connections and transmitting nerve signals. These are highly active, manufacturing many proteins to maintain and remodel themselves. These proteins are constantly produced and cleared – a balance between creation and destruction. But in Alzheimer's that balance is lost, and proteins (specifically a protein called beta-amyloid) accumulates, damaging the neurons and eventually causing them to malfunction and die.

What is true of the human body is also true of our modern organisations. If something is going wrong, it can usually be traced back to faulty feedback mechanisms: you're not hearing what you should be hearing, or you're not processing the evidence at hand properly, or you're not equipped to make the necessary changes. Indeed, feedback loops of this kind are a core feature of most, if not all, complex systems. They are key to adaptation and survival.

Cannon understood their fundamental importance and how central this idea of homeostasis was to human health. He wondered further whether those ideas might be extrapolated to other systems beyond biology; whether indeed political, social and mechanical systems could be considered to be depending upon the same scheme, sensing their environments, processing the signals, triggering effectors over and over again, thereby maintaining or returning their systems to stability.

Cannon's insights later influenced the thinking of others from the fields of sociology, philosophy and psychology. The Austrian biologist Ludwig von Bertalanffy would later propose his General Systems Theory (GST), in an attempt to look at the modern world the way a biologist might look at an organism or colony of organisms.

There is a price to pay for sitting too close to chaos, for too long. Cannon returned from war a changed man, haunted by what he had seen, and in the summer of 1919 he collapsed with exhaustion. He would later describe attempting to form a set of parentheses in his mind, to lock those events away from the rest of his life. But the experience continued to bleed beyond that confinement long afterwards.

Thirty years later, when writing his memoirs, it was clear that the memories of his time in the shock units on the Western Front continued to intrude. Wound shock had been a mystery disease, claiming the lives of many thousands of people each day of the war. In the accounts that detail his efforts at resuscitating his patients, the feeling of despair is palpable. Of his work in understanding the cause and treatment of shock in wounded soldiers, he wrote, 'We grasp at any gains that can be set against the appalling loss of war. Here is one.' But in truth there were many.

Cannon and his colleagues together built the substantial foundations of trauma care today: the importance of early transfer to definitive care; the replacement of lost blood volume with blood rather than other fluids; the need to avoid hypothermia; and the use of tourniquets to stem limb haemorrhage.

That knowledge endures, guiding the work of the HEMS teams in their own efforts to treat haemorrhagic shock; all of it wrapped in a hybridised system, whose technology and human teams are held steady by the mechanisms of feedback that Cannon first identified.

Let's consider again the USS *Carl Vinson* and see it as a complex system hovering on the edge of chaos. Some organisations sit closer to that precipice than others – aircraft carrier operations among them; medical practice sits closer still.

The reason that the *Carl Vinson* doesn't burst into flames and limp back to port a smoking wreck on every sortie is because it has developed tools to deal with uncertainty and the disturbance that might bring, by creating feedback mechanisms that stabilise it against surprise.

Their principal sensor array consists of the hundreds of sailors engaged in the task of operating the ship. Captains don't succeed by knowing the vessel's myriad systems intimately; they do so by knowing their people. The flattened hierarchy encourages the flow of information – in the same way that the culture of psychological safety does on our HEMS aircraft. Incidents are reported without fear of retribution, and with an appreciation for the contribution.

And so the sensors are able to transmit their signal. And while it's true that some of the processing and necessary corrective action can only be achieved and delivered by the senior leadership, the ship is a team of teams, each one running its own version of a feedback loop, each one holding its own patch of chaos at bay – from the shooters on the flight deck to the chef in the galley. The *Carl Vinson*, like the human body, has many cells, each one engaged in a process of tight regulation, each one able to flex and adapt to meet the needs of the moment. All of them working together to create an organisation of a type we rarely see in the wild.

12.

Humans in the loop

On 20 July 1969, Neil Armstrong and Buzz Aldrin, crammed into the cabin of their lunar module *Eagle*, began their perilous final descent. At 50,000 feet above the Moon they had fired their engine, braking their speed and their path through space, arcing their vehicle's trajectory towards the lunar surface. This was the beginning of their powered descent – the mission's unique thirteen minutes. Michael Collins, the third member of the *Apollo 11* crew, was now alone in orbit around the Moon aboard the command module *Columbia*, keeping careful vigil from above. If the landing didn't go to plan, he was to be their last and best hope for rescue.

Up until this point everything they were doing had been rehearsed by other crews during earlier flights. Their vehicles had been flown and tested in orbit around the Earth and the Moon. Two months earlier *Apollo 10* had approached within ten miles of the lunar surface. But for the *Apollo 11* crew, this was a true leap of faith. Armstrong would later describe it as being 'rampant with unknowns', and with good reason: the descent would test the technology – and the people who operated it – to their very limits.

How then did NASA deal with this most unpredictable concluding chapter in their attempt to land on the Moon? The first mistake, with any grand sociotechnical endeavour, is to see only the humans at the centre of it all; the second is to fail to see them altogether. To push back the frontiers at the edge of possibility, and to deal with the glut of unknowns that accompany those pioneering moments, demands a partnership between humans and state-of-the-art technology and a new kind of teamwork.

The lunar module was a craft designed to fly in an unfamiliar landscape. Fractional gravity; no weather; no air: it was fragile. It was built this way to be as light as possible; to enable it to be carried to the Moon. If you threw a rock at it, you would tear the delicate mylar foil wrapped around its lower half. The thin wall of the cabin that housed the crew bulged like the skin of a tent if you leaned on it and could be punctured with nothing more than a sharpened pencil.

With its spidery legs below and the crew compartment on top, it looked like a climbing frame in a playground with a cluster of cardboard boxes unceremoniously piled on top. More space than substance. Nevertheless, it weighed almost fifteen tons – most of which was fuel. If it were standing on Earth, in denser gravity, it would have collapsed under its own weight. But out here, in the vacuum, glittering like a jewel in the uninterrupted sunlight, it was perfect.

Everything about this journey was strange – even the way the astronauts flew. You might have imagined that throughout their descent the crew would be sitting up and facing forwards, as though they were at the controls of an aeroplane or helicopter. But there were no seats, and the crew were lying feet-first and face-down – like a superhero flying backwards across the lunar surface – looking down at the lunar landscape below through a pair of small triangular windows.

The first burst from the descent engine was tentative, with the throttle deliberately set at only 10 per cent of its maximum. The jolt was sensed by the vehicle's guidance platform, enabling it to steer a stream of propellant and to aim its force accurately through the lunar module's centre of mass. All of this was the work of *Apollo*'s onboard guidance computer and the instruments connected to it. The braking phase was controlled exclusively by a program called P63, which gathered information about the spacecraft's position and then set the throttle power, steered its thrust and determined how long the engine would be allowed to burn. A state-of-the-art automatic system of feedback and control, holding the module steady at the edge of chaos.

Just short of thirty seconds later, *Eagle*'s onboard computer commanded the engine to throttle up. We tend to imagine these *Apollo* manoeuvres as balletic, thanks to television clips showing the spacecraft twisting gracefully and gently. But more than a hint of violence was necessary to get them out of the black sky above the Moon. *Eagle* had arrived in lunar orbit travelling at nearly 4,000 miles per hour across its surface. Its engine was now generating considerable thrust, beginning a silent screeching halt in the void of space. The lunar module decelerated sharply, all the while losing altitude.

To keep them out there in this outrageous place, on the limits of imagination, took more than the crew alone was capable of. The flight controllers in mission control, keeping watch from a gallery on Earth a quarter of a million miles away, were all essential. There was so much to monitor, so much that might still go wrong. Throughout the early descent Armstrong and Aldrin were plagued with communication problems. Bursts of static swamped the radio signal, intermittently cutting the crew off from mission control and depriving the team on the ground in Houston of vital telemetry. The faltering communications link created more uncertainty, more risk. Yet still they continued.

Armstrong could see familiar features of the Moon's surface passing by, some 40,000 feet below. The unmistakable outline of Boot Hill, a towering lunar mountain, followed by the solitary Maskelyne crater, more than thirteen miles in diameter. He used these as ready reckoners, timing their appearance in his field of view and, from that, estimating the lunar module's ground speed. But the landmarks were appearing too quickly, which could only mean that *Eagle* was travelling too fast and was in danger of overshooting its planned landing site.

In Houston the flight controllers shifted uncomfortably in their seats. The onboard computer was built for reliability and could be counted on to do its job precisely as instructed; and so unaccounted-for discrepancies were a worry. The computer had a childlike view of the universe, one that was simple and pure. The mathematical models it held in its memory didn't deviate from the rigid laws that Isaac Newton had laid down more than three centuries earlier. No friction to slow it down, no wind resistance to blow it off-course, a journey of infinite length at constant velocity, unless otherwise acted upon; the vehicle and its computer were designed to fly in a clockwork universe in which everything worked precisely in the way it was supposed to.

But the Moon was an unknown quantity. Earlier missions had shown it to be irregularly assembled, with areas of concentrated matter, or 'mascons', that had the potential to throw off a lander's trajectory. If the distribution of the Moon's mass was substantially irregular, then it followed that the gravitational field would be, too. The fear, at this point, was that a hitherto-uncharted mascon might be accelerating the vehicle or, even worse, that the *Eagle*'s onboard guidance computer might be malfunctioning.

Four minutes into the descent, with the engine still firing, Armstrong rolled *Eagle*, rotating the vehicle so that its windows now faced the blackness of space above, leaving them on their backs, riding an invisible celestial slide, still plummeting towards the Moon.

The change in orientation caused more communication problems. Aldrin and Armstrong tried to manoeuvre *Eagle* and its antennae into more favourable positions, attempting to get a better line of sight to Earth; like a couple seated in their living room around an old analogue television set, trying to twist their aerial to get a better picture. The mission was slowly but surely diverging from the plan. The judgement now centred on exactly how much divergence to tolerate.

And then, at around 33,000 feet above the Moon, more than five minutes into their descent, a caution sounded in their headsets, buzzing angrily for attention. The red master alarm flicked on and a small white light on their console labelled 'PROG' illuminated. Armstrong called it out over the radio: 'Program Alarm'.

Let's look past Armstrong and Aldrin for a moment, and think about the system of automatic control at the heart of this mission. *Eagle* boasted a guidance computer to assist them in the complex and uncertain task of landing on the surface of another world. Navigating this new ocean was far from trivial: in the void of space there are no maps, no landmarks to recognise or set your course by, and no magnetic field with which you can point a compass of any kind.

Instead the *Apollo* vehicles used an ingenious guidance system, which could sense the spacecraft's orientation and acceleration and then use that information to track its own position and guide its propulsion and progress: an automatic feedback loop of unparalleled complexity and precision, upon which the mission and the lives of the crew depended.

Any object, once spinning, stubbornly holds its orientation – a consequence of the laws of physics. The faster it spins, the more stable it becomes. This is why it's easier to hold your balance on a bicycle when you're moving than when you're at a standstill, and why a spinning top remains upright until it slows.

Apollo's inertial guidance system exploited the stability of three rapidly spinning gyroscopes; one for each axis. These were precision-engineered wheels, each about the diameter of a golf ball, driven by electric motors and made to spin at 24,000 revolutions each minute. They were held in a platform, suspended within a cage of three concentric rings, which could rotate independently and freely around it. In crude terms, this provided a constant reference in three dimensions – the stable gyroscopes – around which the surrounding cage (and hence the spacecraft attached to it) could rotate. From this, the *Apollo* spacecraft 'knew' which way it was pointing. This arrangement, coupled with simpler devices that could measure acceleration, formed the bones of an inertial guidance system.

Using this information, and the time elapsed since the mission started, the spacecraft's systems – specifically the Apollo Guidance Computer, or AGC – could calculate where it was in space relative to its point of origin, how far it had travelled, how fast it was travelling, which way it was pointed and, crucially, where it was headed. The AGC could calculate the changes needed to correct the course of the vehicle: precisely how much thrust was required, and on which heading it should be vectored. And having made those calculations, it was capable of commanding the engines and thrusters to make those changes. Neil Armstrong was the mission commander,

Aldrin his lunar-module pilot, but for much of the flight the AGC was firmly at the helm.

The AGC was the first of its kind in 1969: a portable, digital, general-purpose computer of the type that we have come to take for granted in everyday life in the twenty-first century. But in terms of form and function, this machine bore no resemblance to the svelte laptops that grace cafes and offices across the world today, and certainly not to the palm-sized mobile phones that we have in our pockets. All told, the AGC weighed around sixty-six pounds, with its bulky components hidden away in the body of the lunar lander, in a bay the size of a suitcase.

Yes, it was slow and – compared to the microchips available to us today – laughably short of processing power, but those descriptions grossly underplay the AGC's critical importance to the mission. This was a prototype computing device upon which the lives of the astronauts depended; a system that distilled the knowledge and expertise of thousands of individuals and brought it to bear in the moment. Without the AGC and the augmentation provided by it, the task of landing on the Moon would have been impossible. This digital tool, which the astronauts had carried with them from Earth, was the product of nearly a decade of design, engineering and integration, and was very nearly a miracle of its age: a machine capable of flying the vehicle and her crew all the way from Earth to the surface of the Moon and – in theory at least – all the way to touchdown.

The AGC's primitive appearance belied this capability. The elements of the Apollo Guidance Computer visible to the astronauts looked like little more than an oversized calculator. The so-called Display and Keyboard Assembly, or DSKY, was an all-too-grandiose title for a number pad linked to a screen, not much larger than the palm of your hand, which could display only a few rows of luminous green numbers. But that was the limit of the interface between the astronauts and their digital device; theirs was a dialogue drummed out in numbers.

Now, well into the final few minutes of descent from lunar orbit – the phase of the mission during which Armstrong and Aldrin were most dependent upon the AGC – their computer began to flash warnings at them repeatedly. The master alarm and its angry buzzing pleaded for their attention. Aldrin, whose job it was to monitor the systems, tried to diagnose the problem. The digits 1202 flashed up on their display.

'It's a twelve-o-two,' Armstrong called out.

'Twelve-o-two,' repeated Aldrin.

Neither had ever seen that type of alarm before.

Their digital partner had spotted trouble and was calling it out. It was left to the astronauts and mission-control team to interrogate the problem. Digital sensor, digital signal. Human decisions and actions. Real world, real time, real consequences.

Armstrong called down to mission control for clarification. 'Give me a reading on the twelve-o-two,' he gabbled through his microphone. It was one of the few times that anyone can recall noticing a hint of stress in his voice. The alarm could have meant just about anything, but Armstrong understood how heavily they depended on their AGC. If it was about to crash, then so would they.

The call for a read on the 1202 alarm came down from Armstrong to fellow astronaut Charlie Duke on CapCom – the capsule communicator – the only person allowed to speak directly with Armstrong and Aldrin during critical mission phases. That call was also heard by the flight director, Gene Kranz. He in turn looked to his array of flight controllers – whose average age, let us remember, was only twenty-six years old – for answers.

The question fell to the youthful Stephen Bales. Bales was from Iowa and had come to Houston a handful of years earlier looking for adventure. He had started out at NASA merely giving tours to visiting dignitaries who passed through the space centre, before finagling his way into a job in mission control; indeed, the process that got him hired as a flight controller – and noticed as someone who might be up to the task – was, to Bales, as mysterious as it was swift. His superiors gave him an early opportunity and then proceeded to layer responsibility upon responsibility on him, thick and fast. Every new layer was an unspoken test, with real power and steadily escalating consequences.

It seems odd to have given such a mission-critical decision to someone in their twenties, not long out of college. Bizarre that you would construct a system upon which people's lives depended in that way. But Apollo flight director Gerry Griffin saw this delegation of authority as essential to the creation of an agile, responsive and reactive team. The junior flight controllers understood that too. 'We gave them that responsibility, even though they were young,' Griffin told me. 'They accepted it, *they owned it*.' And so on 20 July 1969 there was Stephen Bales, twenty-six years old, with the weight of Armstrong's question resting on his shoulders, and the world watching.

There was no other way to run a team like this. There were three possible outcomes: the crew could abort to the safety of lunar orbit; they could land successfully; or they could die trying. That drama would play out over the course of a handful of minutes.

For the flight-control team there was little room for self-doubt. They were trained to own their risk, deliver their decisions and commit to their actions. For real-time operations, where the mission hinged on decisions that needed to be made almost immediately, NASA believed firmly in delegation of authority and deference to expertise, wherever it lay in the system. With so much at stake, decisions were best made by the people closest to the centre of the operation. And if that happened to be the youthful engineering graduate from Iowa sitting at the guidance officer's desk, then so be it.

Bales knew the guidance systems inside-out, but his team of engineers, sequestered in a back room somewhere in the recesses of the mission-control building, knew the deep detail of every single component, including how and where each one had been built and, in some cases, even who had built it.

The Apollo Guidance Computer's capacity for processing tasks was narrow. The 1202 alarm was a message from the AGC telling them that too much was being asked of it and that, at this critical point in the mission, it would prioritise only the tasks absolutely necessary to keep them flying. It signalled a caution, rather than a crash, a code through which the computer whispered, 'I am close to the limits of my capacity. I can do this, but not much more.'

In the back room Jack Garman, a twenty-three-year-old engineer, had been logging the alarms as he heard them called out; he had anticipated the request from Armstrong and called the answer forward to Bales, even before the request had been uttered: they could continue so long as the alarms did not recur continuously.

Neither Garman nor Bales had arrived at this knowledge by chance. In the weeks leading up to the launch date they had drilled endlessly, in simulations designed to feel as close to the real mission as possible. The instructor teams had thrown the kitchen sink at them: every conceivable error had been explored. During one of these earlier simulations, a similar alert had been triggered. On that occasion Bales – unable to interpret it – had instructed an abort, which, retrospectively, Garman thought to have been unnecessary.

After that debacle, Garman and Bales had been set the arduous task of combing through and listing all of the possible program alarm codes and the appropriate course of action for each. When they heard the 1202 alarm mentioned over the communications loop, Bales and Garman recognised it immediately.

Only five seconds after Armstrong's strained plea for the team to give him a reading on the 1202 alarm, Bales had an answer.

'We're go on that alarm, Flight,' came his reply, affirming that the mission could continue.

The astronauts were gifted pilots, arguably among the best in all of civilian or military aviation at the time. But they did not – and could not – have understood every facet of this vast and uniquely complex endeavour. So expertise had to be distributed across many thousands of people and distilled into the technology at their fingertips and into the flight controllers in mission control. There was no room in the lunar module for the thirty desks in the Mission Operations Control Room or the people who sat behind them, but they were as present in the mission – and as essential to its success – as Armstrong, Aldrin and command-module pilot Michael Collins.

The audio-loop recordings of the chatter between the astronauts and their flight-control team in those final minutes of descent are near indecipherable, with acronym layered on acronym as the team troubleshoot one problem after another. And while the endeavour bore some resemblance to aviation, it represented something very different. The system was too vast and too complicated to be operated by any individual alone; nobody could see all the moving parts. There were too many tasks to attend to, too much complexity to resolve.

When problems arose, with time and fuel running out, mission control behaved like a hive-mind, processing tasks in parallel and feeding solutions back to the astronaut crew. What you are listening to, as the radio calls go back and forth, is not a human team taking the reins from a failing computer, but a partnership between a social system – the flight controllers – and a technical system – the lunar module and its AGC.

The Apollo Guidance Computer system was designed, in the same manner as all plans are, to operate in an ideal universe, one that conformed perfectly to the rules. But no real universe does. And so this was a system that could never entirely replace the human in the loop with digital automation. Nor was it the vainglorious story of the triumph of man over a fallible machine in the moment. Instead what we see in the terminal phases of the *Apollo 11* landing is a hybrid of these two; a partnership that took a task that existed only at the skinny edge of possibility and enabled it to be forged into reality.

The last minutes of descent to the lunar surface were a true voyage into the unknown. In every second the system threatened to stumble over into anarchy. As we now know, functioning feedback loops are necessary to stabilise a system in this state. But in the *Apollo 11* landing we have two overarching feedback loops working in parallel: the AGC, sensing accelerations and trajectories, adjusting the descent engine and manoeuvring thrusters to keep the vehicle on track, and the human flight controllers who were monitoring the performance of the system as a whole, processing what they could see, stepping in to adjust and rebalance it where necessary.

The computer is precise and capable, but has no internal representation of reality; it doesn't know what the real world is truly like.

The human controllers are agile and adaptable, understanding when justified deviation from the operating rules becomes necessary for the mission to continue and for the astronaut crew to survive.

When you design systems, you have to start with an idealised representation of the world. Without that, you have nothing that you can begin to build a system around. But as we have seen time and again, reality regularly parts company with that expectation. In the gap between what the system thinks is happening and what is actually happening lies the capacity for catastrophe. The essential role of the human operator then is to help close that gap. The key is to design a system such that the humans in the loop have the ability to sense it opening, the autonomy to adjust and the agency to intervene.

Eight and a half minutes into the descent, 7,000 feet above the Moon and less than five miles from their landing site, they reach the point of switchover. The braking phase is over, slowing the spacecraft from nearly 4,000 miles an hour to just short of 400.

In the circuits of the AGC a new program called P64 starts running: a sequence of instructions designed to begin the phase of approach and landing. The lunar module, which until this point has been arcing out of the sky, sliding feet-first on its back, pivots halfway to vertical, with its windows – and astronaut crew – finally facing the direction of travel and able to see the landing site for the first time.

David Mindell, author of *Digital Apollo: Human and Machine in Spaceflight*, the first book to properly celebrate the nascent technology that lay at the heart of the Apollo programme, likened this moment to a resurrection; as though the astronauts had been spirited all the way from Earth to this point by the AGC, to be revived for their role in this, the mission's last act.

This was where the plan made final contact with reality, where the clockwork universe dissolved, to be replaced by a scarred lunar terrain, churned into desolation by aeons of meteorite bombardment. The technology recedes, a little, and the humans prepare to take centre-stage.

The AGC was still running, and P64 continued to guide them. But there was an understanding that this close to contact with reality, the models' fine mathematics might break down and the imperfect universe might serve up something unexpected – something that hardwired algorithms alone might not be able to handle.

The 1202 alarm continued to flare intermittently throughout. But guidance officer Stephen Bales was confident they could continue.

The lunar module continued to drop from 7,000 feet above the Moon, with the AGC still driving. It slowed to a forward speed of around 100 miles an hour. Armstrong and Aldrin studied the vista ahead. The hardest feats in all of space exploration are starting and stopping. And this was no ordinary stop.

In mission control, flight director Gene Kranz polls his flight-control team, asking for a simple decision: Go/No-Go for landing. He calls out each position in turn: Retro, Fido, Guidance, Control, Telcom, GNC, EECOM, Surgeon. All of them reply with a single word: 'Go.'

They radio up to Armstrong and Aldrin, '*Eagle*. Houston. You are go for landing. Over.'

'Roger. Understand. Go for landing,' Aldrin copies back.

They approach the Low Gate, not much more than 500 feet above the lunar surface. *Eagle* is now cruising at forty miles an hour, not much faster than a car in the suburbs, with the crew easing their descent and hunting earnestly for their landing site.

Master alarm and buzzing in their headsets once more: another program alarm. Aldrin interrogates it. They call it down to mission control. Bales bats it away without consequence.

Inside the lunar module the challenges are beginning to stack up in this, the most dynamic phase of the flight. All of this draws the astronauts' attention inside the module, to focus on the problems with their computer, at a time when it should have been outside the vehicle, searching for a place to land.

Left to its own devices, P64 would have taken the crew all the way down, flicking over automatically to a terminal-phase program called P65 that would have taken them to touchdown. But in the final few seconds of *Eagle*'s descent, with only a few hundred feet to go, Armstrong recognises that the AGC is going to land them in a boulder field, strewn with rocks the size of cars. On the Moon, the pilot's old adage that any landing you get to walk away from is a good landing doesn't hold true. A hard collision during touchdown might damage their fragile spacecraft – and their means of return – irreparably.

Armstrong selects program P66, a setting that gives him more direct control of the spacecraft, making himself a component part of the feedback loop. This mode allows him to rotate the vehicle and direct its thrust so that he could move across the surface and directly control its rate of descent.

The lunar module's cabin had the trappings of an aircraft – control panels, joysticks, gimbals and altimeters – but the similarities ended there. Their craft did not rise or fall with aerodynamic forces; there was no ocean of air in which it could swim. The stick in Armstrong's hand was not connected to control surfaces. It did not alter the angle of attack of a hinged flap or a rudder.

When it was moved, the control column didn't pull cables; there was no direct, physical connection between it and the thrusters required to steer through the vacuum of space. Instead the movements of the controller served to throw dozens of switches, which started computer programs running that, in turn, mixed fuels designed to ignite spontaneously and deliver a brief but precisely calibrated force through the nozzles mounted on the outside of the strange vehicle and its spidery legs – thousands of computations happening invisibly in the background, the controls wired in an attempt to match the crew's intent with the vehicle's manoeuvres. The pilot gave the instructions, but the computer worked in the background to do his bidding and hold the entire platform stable.

In Houston the mission-control team was restless – jaws clenched, cigarette smoke curling up into the high ceiling, eyes fixed on the river of data flowing from the lunar module. Armstrong was now jetting along, traversing the lunar terrain below, hunting for a place to land, all the while burning through precious fuel. Nobody had ever seen anyone fly the lunar module in this way in simulation; at least not successfully.

The spacecraft had been designed and built to be as light as possible; anything heavier and even the mighty Saturn V rocket couldn't have launched it to the Moon. That was why it had no seats, tiny windows and thin walls. Engineers had gone further still, shaving the internal frames, beams and trusses, trying to save more weight. All of this enabled them to carry extra fuel, but not much.

With Armstrong now at the controls, thrusters were firing furiously all over the lunar module, keeping it aloft and hovering while pushing it forward, all the while eating into their tiny two-minute fuel reserve.

In the midst of this frenetic finale, CapCom Charlie Duke – the link man between Earth and the lunar module – continued to read information up to the crew. Sitting next to him was the head of the astronaut office, Deke Slayton. With the module now so close to the Moon, Slayton worried that the radio calls themselves might become a distraction and eventually punched Duke in the arm, hissing, 'Shut up and let them land!' Duke nodded and keyed his mic, broadcasting to the rest of the team, 'I think we better be quiet.'

With Armstrong still pushing across the surface, searching for a suitable landing site, *Eagle*'s low fuel-level warning light triggered, showing the crew that they had less than two minutes remaining before they would have to abort.

'Low level,' came the strained call from Bob Carlton, the flight controller in charge of monitoring the fuel state. He clicked the button on a hand-held stopwatch. Carlton, like the rest of the mission-control team, had played through countless simulations in preparation for this moment. But neither he nor anyone else in the room ever expected to be above the Moon with so little fuel remaining. There was nothing that anyone in mission control could now do to influence the immediate success or failure of the mission.

They knew that by this time in any previous simulation Armstrong had already landed. All they could do was wait.

Carlton studied the hand on his stopwatch as it swung round. 'Sixty,' he called, counting down the seconds.

The stopwatch ticked on and the crew continued, with Aldrin calmly calling out altitudes, descent rates and forward velocities. The mission-control team in Houston, who had so effectively managed every second of the descent until this point, had all but melted away. Only the astronauts, peering through their windows and working the controls, were in full possession of the facts on the ground. For the first time in the mission, Armstrong and Aldrin were very nearly alone.

Aldrin continued to call out their altitude and rate of descent.

'Thirty,' called Carlton, who by now didn't believe there was any hope at all that the crew could land successfully.

But in the lunar module Armstrong and Aldrin were mere feet from the surface; they could see the shadow of their vehicle being cast on the landscape below, and the engines kicking clouds of dust around. The swirling particles created the illusion of motion – as though they were hovering in drifting fog – and Armstrong, at the controls, with his senses betraying him, also began to drift. But they were almost there.

And then Bob Carlton, having managed to measure the urgency of his tone until that moment, got ready to yell, 'Fifteen seconds!'

But before he could do so, he heard Aldrin call down, 'Contact light.'

With only eighteen seconds left on the clock, Armstrong and Aldrin shut down their engine and *Apollo 11*'s commander uttered his historic words: 'Houston, Tranquility Base here, the *Eagle* has landed.'

13.
The ballet on the bullet

Michael Collins once described the launch in 1969 of *Apollo*'s mighty Saturn V – the rocket that blasted him and his crew from Cape Canaveral and onwards to the Moon – as being akin to trying to balance a pencil vertically on the tip of your finger. That sense of perpetual instability was present throughout the mission, from the surface of the Earth all the way to the Moon and back again. Tremendous brute force was needed to hurl the astronauts at the Moon – a barely contained explosion with energy enough to propel the crew and their vehicle to speeds of more than 24,000 miles per hour. But for success and survival, all of that had to be married with pinpoint precision and accuracy: a ballet performed on the back of a giant bullet.

There is an art to releasing that kind of destructive force while avoiding being destroyed in the process. The necessary finesse and protection came from feedback loops, which did for the spacecraft what Walter Cannon's concept of homeostasis does for the human body: creating balance in an otherwise unstable system, without the need for constant, conscious control on the part of the human in the loop.

For Project Apollo, it was the Apollo Guidance Computer (AGC) that provided Armstrong and Aldrin with the control that held the vehicle steady and stable in a way that no human pilot alone could, enabling them to focus on a performance that would otherwise have proved impossible. The lunar landing looked superhuman, because it was. Not a thing of fluttering capes and underpants worn over tights, but a feat that was beyond the capability of any human without the augmentation that science and engineering provided. And so they relied almost entirely upon the AGC and its attendant suite of technologies. But the word 'almost' is doing a lot of work here.

The technical system had limits. In the final phase of landing, as the mismatch between digital expectation and reality began to grow, so too did the danger. When you hear the chatter across the mission-control audio loops, and the radio calls between Houston and *Eagle* in those final minutes of descent, you're listening to the human – social – element of the system. And their job was to close the gap between the plan, as laid down in the AGC's algorithms and lines of computer code, and the truth of what was playing out before their eyes.

It was here that the mission was most vulnerable, as it became increasingly dependent on humans to sense and process information and make appropriate judgements and adjustments; vulnerable because all of that came wrapped in the vagaries and uncertainties of human perception, cognition and performance. But at the edge of that chaos lay the human operators' unique advantage over the technical system: that of flexibility and adaptability in real time – their ability to know the difference between the failures that the system could accept and those that needed to be remedied immediately; to improvise responses to scenarios unanticipated by the system's architects. This is how the battle rages on, long after 'the plan' has failed to survive contact with reality: through the people with boots on the ground.

At that point in the mission, with events fracturing away from carefully laid plans, some of the best sources of feedback came from the social parts of the system: from Armstrong and Aldrin peering through their windows at the landing site that the computer wanted to take them to; from the flight controllers making decisions about the severity of the alarms and readings they could see and hear. It is this that I marvel at most of all in the landing of *Apollo 11*: the partnership between the social and technical elements of the system.

How do you best configure a team to take on that role? Schooling people to adapt, to make decisions and stand by them – in high-consequence, single-shot scenarios where there are no second chances and no one else to turn to – takes skill and time.

Many, if not most, of the Apollo flight controllers I've interviewed found themselves in the space programme almost by chance. At that time human space exploration's lore and legend had yet to crescendo; few of them had grown up with dreams of rocket flight. But in the 1960s NASA's new Manned Spacecraft Center in Houston was hiring engineers and scientists hand over fist, in pursuit of John F. Kennedy's ambition to win the race to land on the Moon. If you were a young science or engineering graduate, then NASA was simply where the jobs were.

Unlike the astronauts, the flight controllers weren't so precisely scrutinised before being brought into the space programme. Amid the NASA hiring frenzy, some people simply turned up and found themselves employed on the spot. Others, like guidance officer Stephen Bales, worked their way in through unusual routes – in his case starting out as a space-centre tour guide. That's not to say it was an easy ride. Far from it. Instead, for the flight-control teams, the hard yards of selection, training and testing happened on the job.

The near decade-long build-up to the launch of *Apollo 11*, which saw a flurry of missions – from single-seat Project Mercury flights and longer two-person Project Gemini missions to the first Apollo missions – saw NASA focused on refining its technologies. But at the same time it served as the perfect training ground to develop the unique brand of teamwork they would need to sail across Kennedy's new ocean of space.

The lives of the engineers and scientists at NASA in this time became consumed by Project Apollo, a combination of fierce training simulations run alongside real missions that steadily increased in complexity as the decade progressed. When Alan Shepard became the first American to launch into space in 1961, it was aboard a tiny capsule on a flight that lasted fifteen minutes and twenty-eight seconds, reaching an altitude of just 116 miles above the Earth. By Christmas Day 1968 NASA had hurled three men – Frank Borman,

Bill Anders and Jim Lovell – and their *Apollo 8* capsule one quarter of a million miles into space, and left them enjoying a dinner of thermostabilised turkey, cranberry sauce, stuffing and fruitcake in orbit around the Moon.

The training simulations had a specific purpose. They were unforgiving and exacting; designed, in theory, to be harder than any mission would be in reality, with the goal of trying to push the teams to the limits of their capacity. The simulation supervisors, or SimSups, who ran them were regarded as people with cruel and unusual imaginations. They would play the flight-control teams through outrageous scenarios. Engines would fail, sensor suites and life-support systems would malfunction, conflicting telemetry would flash up on their screens. They would force controllers to make real-time decisions, without access to all the facts, all the while studying their performance under simulated pressure.

It wasn't about testing their ability to follow procedures to the letter. It was about getting them used to incomplete, ambiguous information and faulty data, and seeing if, in the midst of that fog, they were still able to make good decisions. The sims didn't always end well. Even Gene Kranz, while preparing for *Apollo 9*, managed to make mistakes during a training simulation which would have killed a real crew. In that instance, hesitation and a late abort decision on his part smashed their imaginary capsule into the Atlas Mountains in Western Morocco shortly after launch.

The simulations weren't there to make the teams feel good about themselves. They were approached with reverence and trepidation. It was important for the flight-control teams and astronauts to experience failure, to learn from their mistakes and to reinforce the culture of debrief, iteration and learning. It was thanks to an error in a pre-mission simulation, and the learning that followed, that Stephen Bales and his back-room team were equipped to deal with the 1202 and 1201 alarms that flashed up in the final minutes of the *Apollo 11* landing – a prime example of system stabilisation achieved through effective feedback.

Here we see feedback in the social side of this sociotechnical system. Not a computer controlling thrusters, or a biological system rebalancing physiology, but a human team using feedback as a means of updating their understanding and improving their future responses. This is why it is important for all organisations to discuss and deconstruct successes and failures, to greet both with equanimity and to use them as opportunities for learning that contribute to improvement of the system as a whole.

The simulations gave the astronauts and flight-control teams the opportunity to train, learn and bond. Their assignments to early missions enabled them to rehearse their skills of teamwork, leadership and followership during flights where the risk and complexity were real, but lower than they would be for the first landing on the Moon.

As the rockets and capsules got better and more capable, so too did the flight-control team. The engineers built the vehicles and launchers, but it was the flight controllers' diet of steadily increasing exposure to risk and complexity that built their team.

There was no rulebook for what they were doing. They were inventing a go-kart while it raced around the track: developing the people and the technology in tandem. The simulations and the schedule of missions with steadily escalating difficulty helped to expose the flaws in the system and finalise standard operating procedures. But their value to the programme went much further than that.

First, they bound the flight-control teams together, forming and strengthening linkages between the flight controllers. The sims were the ultimate team sport. The team finished each one victorious, or staring at their shoes in the dressing room, ruefully contemplating their defeat. But either way, they did that together, building all-important cohesion in the process.

Second, they helped to filter out those who were less suitable for the demands of the real role. The flight controllers may not have undergone any process that resembled the rigours of astronaut selection before they were hired, but their intense and lengthy mission preparation was every bit as exacting. Along the way some people came to realise that the job wasn't for them; others were gently moved aside when the simulations found them wanting.

Project Apollo was a system set up for anticipation and prevention, the very foundations of High Reliability Organisation theory. But there was the broad understanding that – with this leap into the unknown – they would be forced to operate perilously close to the edge of chaos and that reality could, and likely would, break through their carefully laid defences. At that point, the strategies of anticipation and prevention would be replaced by one of *containment*.

Containing the consequences of failure requires shifting into a different mode. Mission plans and standard operating procedures recede. What becomes paramount instead is the quality of your adaptive responses, and those are, by necessity, the responsibility of the social, rather than the technical, aspects of your systems: the humans in the loop. So the key here is having a team that is *comfortable with risk and ambiguity*, and one that is *practised* in grappling with it. This is where simulation and mission experience honed the skills of the Apollo teams, binding them together while *familiarising them with uncertainty*.

The last step in preparation was to structure the team in the right way, so that it could react in real time.

The flight-control team had all the trappings of a traditional pyramidal team structure. The Mission Operations Control Room was built in tiers, cascading from top to bottom. Gene Kranz, flight director for the *Apollo 11* landing, sat at the centre of the uppermost row, at the top of the ziggurat.

But that wasn't how the team itself was organised, or how the operation worked. The Apollo architecture was vast, complex and fast. It was capable like none other before it in history, but arcane, too. To be across it, to keep up with it, the hierarchical human team needed to open and flatten, creating more points of contact with the technical system, more opportunities to sense, process and effect. And all of that had to happen in parallel.

This flattening alone wasn't enough. Information had to flow.

Even in the presence of Gene Kranz, the battle-hardened ex-marine and arguably NASA's most revered operational leader, the flight controllers had to feel able to speak up, to contribute, to challenge and – where necessary – to oppose directions. The flight directors, in turn, had to be prepared to accept their junior team members' lead.

This had to be about something beyond ordinary command and control. The famous 'Go/No-Go' calls were much more than a ritual. They were an opportunity to speak up, to call a halt, to declare a problem. The poll efficiently made space for that to happen.

But the quality that the *Apollo 11* flight-control team demonstrated more clearly and more powerfully than any other was that of deference to expertise, wherever it lay in the system, and delegation to that authority. By empowering the flight controllers, by giving them ownership of their tasks, they maximised the value that they brought, making the team equal to the moment – a whole far greater than the sum of its parts.

This is how a leader deals with the complexity inherent in modern systems: not by attempting to develop an encyclopaedic understanding of its many sub-systems, but by gathering the best knowledge from the best people, to inform the best decisions and thereby the best actions.

The work of Project Apollo may have taken place five decades ago, but it remains a pioneering and hugely valuable prototype for teamwork in all our modern high-risk, high-reliability, high-performance systems. It shows how the habits and skills required to deal competently with uncertainty and complexity need to be practised and developed over time. Creating a team that is comfortable with distributed leadership, followership, deference to expertise, delegation of authority, and one that feels psychologically safe to contribute and challenge when necessary, is a dynamic process. If you want to draw upon them in a crisis, those attributes have to become habits of normal operation, a feature of everyday work.

There is also something instructive in the story of Project Apollo for our immediate future: as Artificial Intelligence becomes the new general-purpose technology of our time, the question we must ask ourselves is not simply what it can be used for and what we will be capable of once it is integrated into our systems, but what we will do to prepare for the moment when these new, AI-powered systems reach the limits of their capabilities, as they surely will, and the human in the loop is forced to step back in.

According to the ancient Greek myth of Prometheus, technology is a power stolen from the gods on Mount Olympus, one that made us more potent and more capable, allowing us to ascend to ever greater heights. For Prometheus, of course, it came with a punishing curse: that he would be bound to a rock and have his liver eaten from him by an eagle every day for eternity. For us, the curse is that technology will take us to new heights, but sooner or later it will also desert us in the decisive moment, leaving us naked and undefended in the face of new extremes.

These are places where no human alone can prevail, but where teams – configured in the right way – just might.

14.
Graceful failure

On 6 August 2012, I joined a crowd of journalists and space enthusiasts at the Natural History Museum in London, listening to the audio feeds from NASA's Jet Propulsion Laboratory (JPL) as we waited for the *Mars Curiosity* rover to begin its entry and descent into the Martian atmosphere.

The scheme for this landing had been described to me by a friend a couple of years earlier: the spacecraft carrying the rover would hurtle into the atmosphere at 13,000 miles per hour; it would then deploy a giant parachute in the supersonic flow of the Martian atmosphere and finally, as it approached the ground, having not yet bled off enough energy to effect a safe landing, it would be slowed by a rocket platform that would decelerate and then hover 100 feet or so off the surface of Mars while lowering the rover the remaining distance on the end of a cable.

It sounded utterly ludicrous, and the friend who was telling me about it was a space enthusiast rather than a space scientist, so at first I thought he might have got it wrong. But it turned out that was exactly the way the entry, descent and landing phase had been designed. In fact elements of it were even worse: dozens of pyrotechnic charges had to go off at pre-prescribed intervals and at precisely the right time. The rocket platform – which NASA dubbed 'the sky crane' – had to hover, lower the rover and then fly away to avoid crashing into the probe once it was on the ground. And all of that would unfold in a few hundred seconds of drama a couple of hundred million miles from Earth, with no way to influence the outcome remotely once the process had begun; which is why the *Mars Curiosity* engineers had come to call it 'the Seven Minutes of Terror'.

At the heart of this plan was the parachute system. The probe would be designed so that it could be steered in the upper atmosphere at hypersonic speeds; those turns in the upper atmosphere would get the rover above the right spot and, at the same time, would bleed off sufficient energy to get it travelling at a rate that was merely supersonic. But the bigger challenge followed: while it was still scorching the sky, the heaviest, most complicated rover ever built would then deploy the largest supersonic parachute ever seen, at the highest Mach number ever attempted.

This step, untried, untested – indeed, in the confines of Earth's atmosphere, largely untestable – represented a source of single-point failure; something that absolutely had to work. There were other elements of this Entry, Descent and Landing (EDL) phase that were similarly mission-critical, but the parachutes were to be the first true test of the behaviour of this system in the alien atmosphere of Mars. And leadership over this part of the project was handed to Anita Sengupta, a twenty-seven-year-old engineer.

It is difficult to imagine what that level of responsibility must feel like at any time of life, far less in your late twenties. But when I met Anita and asked her about it, she shrugged it off. There is a confidence and an easiness about her that don't in any way smack of superiority – the way you imagine a proper rocket scientist to be. I asked her if she was always the smartest girl in the class at school and she paused.

'I was the quietest girl in the class,' she told me.

If you've ever watched Anita talking about her work in NASA public-relations videos or ever seen her deliver a lecture to a live audience, this statement is hard to credit. She is as good a speaker as I have ever heard. When I push her on that, she tells me that she knew she was scared of public speaking and so she decided she had to do more of it. After she started at NASA's JPL, the centre's speakers bureau came casting around for volunteers to go out and preach about space exploration to the masses. Anita signed up because it scared her, because it was something she might fail at, and because she knew she could only overcome that fear by doing more of it.

This appears to be her guiding philosophy in life. It is OK to be scared of something, but that isn't a reason to avoid it. The fear falls away with experience; most of that fear fades just by trying. Anita tells me that she decided to ride motorbikes and learn to fly planes for precisely the same reason.

That in part explains why she so readily accepted that leadership role at NASA. It wasn't that she didn't have the insight to recognise the magnitude of the responsibility; nor was it simple self-belief. She was confident enough, but any apprehension she might feel would disappear in the endeavour. Anita had learned that this – like so many other things – couldn't be as bad as the idea of it. She had faced this, or something like it, many times in the past and perhaps reasoned that running the parachute team for the multibillion-dollar *Mars Curiosity* rover would be like riding a motorbike.

It's tricky building a parachute that you can never test for real. Trickier still when the function of that parachute is a mission-critical element, on a $2.5 billion space probe, with no room to build in backup systems, should it fail.

For Anita Sengupta, the mathematical modelling wasn't encouraging. The Martian atmosphere is too thin to provide enough resistance for a small parachute to make any difference. But *Curiosity* would be moving too fast to safely deploy larger parachutes. Sengupta's team built parachute after parachute, testing them in the giant wind tunnels at NASA's JPL in Pasadena. Variously they shredded or collapsed, or both. And then one day the realisation dawned that the secret to preventing the destruction of the parachute as it unfurled in the turbulent atmosphere of Mars was to *tolerate failure*.

The result was a parachute that behaves in a genuinely alien fashion. Instead of opening and remaining inflated, it oscillates rapidly between states. The problem for the design team had been how to deal with the turbulence in the supersonic flow. Smaller parachutes didn't reduce the speed of the vehicle sufficiently, but larger canopies – even when properly reinforced – couldn't stay inflated in the supersonic winds.

The solution for Sengupta and her team was to allow the

parachute canopy to be destroyed by the turbulent air, at least temporarily. By letting the canopy collapse and then reinflate, over and over again – opening and closing like a giant jellyfish – it could do its job.

On the morning of touchdown, the giant white jellyfish unfurled in the red skies above Mars in the first minutes of entry, descent and landing, with *Curiosity* still more than six miles above the surface of Mars and travelling at around twice the speed of sound. The probe signalled to the *Mars Odyssey* satellite in orbit around Mars, which in turn relayed the message to Earth across hundreds of millions of miles of space. It took nearly twenty minutes for that signal, travelling at the speed of light, to arrive at the control room in Pasadena. When it did, it told Sengupta what she wanted to hear: her alien parachute, fluttering in the rarefied Martian atmosphere, had worked. Her parachute had been successful precisely because it had incorporated into its design the inevitable and repeated failure of the canopy that they had observed during flight-testing.

As sub-system after sub-system deployed successfully, and the delicious ripples of applause rose from the floor of mission control at JPL, only to be rapidly muted in anticipation of the next hurdle, the audience allowed hope to rise that this impossible vehicle and its absurd cargo might make it all the way to Mars. And then, after seven minutes that crowned years of effort by hundreds of engineers and scientists, the announcement came from the flight controller. 'Touchdown confirmed,' he said, 'we're safe on Mars.'

Nobody in mission control really heard the last part of that utterance. The celebrations in the control room at JPL were fierce enough to be palpable across the ocean, in our room at the Natural History Museum in London. Had *Curiosity* been sentient, I'm sure it would have felt them, too.

When I first met Rob Manning, the chief engineer of the *Mars Curiosity* team, I couldn't help but congratulate him.

'It's so fantastic that everything worked first time!' I exclaimed.

At which point Manning turned to me and said, 'Oh, but it didn't!'

He uttered those words in a somewhat conspiratorial fashion, as though he was about to take me aside and tell me that the rover wasn't actually on Mars; that it was instead roving around on some sound-stage in Hollywood, pretending to be on the Red Planet. Frankly, I might almost have found that easier to believe.

When I asked him what he meant, Manning pointed to the myriad failures in the history of Mars exploration. Since the first probes arrived at Mars in the 1970s, the failure rate had been eye-watering. Shooting stuff at Mars was a risky endeavour. Close to two-thirds of everything that was ever sent there failed to complete its mission, disappearing into space or crashing into the surface of the planet.

'That,' says Manning, 'was the legacy of Faster, Better, Cheaper. We learned the hard way that you couldn't do all three.'

The Jet Propulsion Laboratory famously started life as a kind of exile colony for would-be Caltech rocket scientists whose early experimentation set fire to the campus dormitories. The students were forced off-campus into the San Gabriel Mountains of California, where they continued to experiment, risking life and limb in the pursuit of more advanced rocket engines.

JPL grew quickly and became a sort of monastery for acolytes of the space age. From here the greatest of NASA's robotic missions were dreamed up and made reality. While the human space-exploration teams at Johnson Space Center in Houston were still grappling with the quarter of a million miles that lie between the Earth and the Moon, JPL was firing probes the size of cars hundreds of millions of miles across the solar system. Those ubiquitous images of Mars, Saturn and Jupiter that we take for granted were destinations never seen before the mid-1960s. Our first up-close glimpses of the planets that comprise our solar system were gifted to us by projects hatched on the outskirts of Pasadena.

It is precisely because of this glorious record of achievement that the decade of failure that closed the twentieth century proved so galling for NASA. In 1992, with the United States still reeling from the consequences of the savings-and-loans crisis, federal agencies were being asked to tighten their belts. NASA, by the 1990s, had started to become regarded as rather bloated and inefficient. In 1993 the loss of JPL's *Mars Observer* space probe, just three days before arrival at the Red Planet, with an estimated cost of more than $800 million, seemed to illustrate quite how complacent NASA had become. In response, Dan Goldin, NASA's then newly anointed administrator, ushered in an operating philosophy that he believed would set the agency back on the right tracks and drive it on into the millennium: Faster, Better, Cheaper (FBC).

Robert Manning remembers the early success of that strategy. The *Mars Pathfinder* rover was conceived, built, launched and successfully landed on Mars, for a mere $265 million. In the same year that *Pathfinder* touched down on the surface of the Red Planet, James Cameron's *Titanic* was released, a film that boasted a budget of some $200 million. That NASA had suddenly become capable of putting probes on the surface of another planet, for little more than the cost of a Hollywood blockbuster, became a thing of wild celebration. By 1998 nine out of ten of NASA's new breed of spacecraft had been built and successfully flown.

Commenting on this era, Roger Launius, curator at the Smithsonian's National Air and Space Museum and a former NASA historian, remarks that leadership is as much about timing as anything else. Had Dan Goldin decided to leave NASA in 1998, the world would have regarded him as a genius who had turned around the fortunes of the country's ailing space agency. But the honeymoon didn't last. Faster, Better, Cheaper began to bite.

All told, in the decade that followed the dawn of NASA's FBC initiative, the agency would go on to lose more than one-third of its interplanetary missions. Starting in the late 1990s, as the true cost of FBC started to make itself felt, NASA endured loss after loss. At its nadir, NASA's *Mars Climate Orbiter* – a $200 million project – was lost in the terminal phase of the mission, having steered itself into a collision course with the planet instead of gently entering into a parking orbit. The root cause? One of the instruments responsible for calibrating thrust had been designed and coded in metric, but fed instructions in imperial measurements. Millions of dollars of mission finance and thousands upon thousands of hours of work lost, seemingly because someone, somewhere had used the wrong side of the ruler.

Manning talks about the despair of those times. NASA had become the butt of chat-show-host jokes – a byword for expensive failure. Climbing out of that pit, while keeping his teams of engineers motivated, had been a difficult feat. On the frontlines at JPL, the engineering teams had the sense that projects were being driven too hard and too fast. The apparently enormous cost of space technology derives in large part from the obsessive checking and rechecking of every detail of every component, to avoid precisely the debacle that befell the *Mars Climate Orbiter*. No circuit board costs $1 million. But the armies of engineers who pore over its construction, and over every line of code that it executes, do. FBC delivered products more quickly and more cheaply than ever before, but with less attention to detail and less exhaustive testing regimes.

At first sight, the story of NASA's dalliance with FBC looks like little more than organisational folly, a modern parable telling you what you already knew: that you might want Faster, Better, Cheaper, but ultimately you can only pick two. But Howard McCurdy, professor of public affairs in the department of public administration and policy at the American University in Washington DC, sees it differently.

He thinks that as long as you stick to the rules, you *can* have your cake and eat it. It is perhaps true that Goldin – buoyed by the early success of his FBC mantra – failed to recognise when NASA, striving for still more efficiencies, had gone beyond trimming fat and had strayed into its organisational muscle. But objectively there was much to admire in the strategy. There had been a raft of successes on mission budgets which had been reduced by an order of magnitude. And yes, discrete failure does become more likely, but that in itself is all right, says McCurdy, so long as the overall strategy can tolerate those failures. *Pathfinder* was originally conceived as but one of a fleet of FBC rovers that would pepper the surface of Mars. In that vision, the failure of one or two among dozens would have been neither here nor there. If you can design a strategy that tolerates failure and accepts it as an intrinsic part of the operation, then you can, says McCurdy, achieve a lot more with a lot less.

This is like the difference in survival strategy between mammalian reproduction and viral replication. Mammals have a very finely tuned system for taking the detail of their genetic code, copying it and then handing it on to the next generation. The biological proofreading that that entails – billions of base pairs correctly sequenced and aligned – is simply breathtaking and explains why, over millions of years, mammalian life generates startlingly accurate copies of itself over and over again. Viruses, on the other hand, have a far less resource-intensive system. They bang out quick and dirty copies of themselves, hijacking the machinery of whatever cells they can find to do so. Their strategy values quantity over quality; producing millions of copies in every cell, most of which are so poorly transcribed that they are entirely unviable. And yet there are enough success stories in that haphazard scheme of reproduction to achieve the viruses' mission goal: survival of the species in perpetuity.

But the viral strategy isn't right for all. And McCurdy points out that the FBC approach demands that you accept, and tolerate, regular and recurrent failure. This works well in organisations that operate in fast-moving landscapes where innovation and agility are key. (Witness the co-founder of Facebook, Mark Zuckerberg's one-time mantra of 'Fail Fast, Fail Cheap, Fail Often', which would appear to have served the multibillionaire reasonably well.) But when I ask McCurdy how broadly the Faster, Better, Cheaper strategy can be applied, he readily acknowledges that it has limits. 'You've got to stick to the rules,' he says. 'In systems where the consequences of failure are so grave that they can never be accepted, FBC is not the right strategy.'

Ultimately, NASA called a halt to Faster, Better, Cheaper, with the frontline staff eventually finding the voice to tell the agency's senior managers that they couldn't continue in that vein. There is something to respect in that story of turnaround, too; that an organisation so famous for its monolithic and unswervable character proved responsive to pleas from its operational tier in that way. But by the start of the twenty-first century NASA had learned its lesson.

Robert Manning became overall manager of JPL's Mars programme shortly thereafter. With responsibility for a raft of missions that spanned well into the future, hard decisions had to be made. 'We de-scoped,' says Manning, 'we did fewer things, but we did them better.' They learned from their mistakes and learned to embrace failure for what it was: a chance to discover and improve.

When I last caught up with Manning, seven years after *Curiosity*'s successful landing, he was a little distracted. 'We've just been testing the hypersonic parachutes,' he said, 'and they don't work. In the tests they got shredded to hell!' The parachute failure that he started enthusiastically describing to me, ahead of our meeting, was in a new system that they had designed to help get them onto Mars with bigger payloads. These parachutes would be needed for heavier vehicles, and 'for what comes after that' – by which he meant human missions to Mars. He wasn't in any way downbeat about the canopies that now lay in tatters on a laboratory bench somewhere – far from it. In fact I'd venture to say he was almost excited about it.

'That's not how we view failure here,' he said. 'To us, it's a positive thing – something interesting. A failure at the right time. You want it to happen on Earth while you've got a chance to fix it. Not when you're on your way to Mars.'

His enthusiasm is both boyish and infectious. It's impossible to describe it in any other way. Manning is essentially one of the most senior managers at JPL, but somehow he has managed to hold on to the energy and fascination that first made him seek out a career in rocket science. He's not faking it, either. He really does find intrigue in the failures they experience in testing. To him they are puzzles to be solved; more than that, they are opportunities to learn, to grow, to progress.

None of this is the sort of platitudinal soliloquy that a coach might deliver to the cameras after their team has just taken a terrible drubbing. It's real. Manning embraces failure because within his culture it's a necessary part of how they learn and move forward. Externally, NASA is a place where projects of exploration are designed, executed and delivered. There are armies of people involved, but, says Manning, this is not a machine and those people are anything but faceless. 'When we talk about these machines as resulting from programmes of activity, we don't mean that. They're really built by people – human beings – and humans make mistakes.'

There's an old palindromic adage that management-consultant types like to trot out at team meetings. 'Fail to prepare. Prepare to fail.' For Manning the maxim is even simpler than that: 'Prepare to fail.' This is not a defeatist attitude; rather it is an expression of the process through which engineers iterate their production lines. JPL expects failure, viewing it as a kind of wayfaring point, indicating the route to a successful design.

Today JPL understands that on the way to stunning achievements like *Mars Curiosity*, one has to visit the sort of failures that set dorms on fire or that lose lesser space probes. A culture of benign failure has become part of the DNA of today's projects. But this is about more than the lessons learned. JPL has ceased to be scared of failure in the way that it was. It understands its place in the development of its projects.

At the end of our meeting in California, Manning was still fielding calls about the parachute system, which his team had been trialling in a supersonic wind tunnel. This is where his passion lies – Entry, Descent and Landing. Despite his many lofty managerial appointments, he still describes himself as an 'EDL-er'. The rocket scientists love to tell you that the two hardest feats in all of rocket science are starting and stopping. Stopping is what Manning is all about.

'They still can't get it to work,' he told me with a smile. 'Every time they put it in the tunnel, it falls apart.'

There was no false bravado here, just the fascination of an

engineer for a system designed to operate at the limits of the team's understanding. The failures happen here on Earth; indeed, the teams are encouraged to drive their projects that far, so that the lessons can be learned in wind tunnels and the deserts around Pasadena rather than live on CNN, while staring at the wreckage of a vehicle somewhere on the surface of another planet.

The motto of JPL is 'Dare Ye Mighty Things', and it's an organisation that lives by those words. Anita Sengupta and Robert Manning together have many useful points to teach us: as individuals, as teams and as organisations.

You have to be willing to get past the fear and uncertainty; you have to find the courage to hurl yourself into the void and take on whatever it might throw at you. Anita learned to ride motorbikes and fly planes like that; she came to lead teams at JPL because of it. It's an approach to life that got her a long way – all the way to Mars.

From Robert there is something to learn about failure and what it can teach us. Failure, he says, is an inevitable feature of complex systems and complex endeavours. There is much that you can, and should, do to forestall it and reduce the probability that it happens. But you need to accept that you will fail and, when you do, you need to greet that as an opportunity to learn and to go again, better than before.

While we're talking here about how to fail, and before we leave the rocket scientists and their extraterrestrial rovers behind, I want to share one last lesson that I learned from them.

While researching this chapter I stumbled across a page in the technical specification documents for NASA's *Pathfinder* rovers, one that includes a description of its power system. It tells you that the rover has three rechargeable lithium-thionyl chloride batteries, with capacity enough to run a hairdryer for not much more than ten minutes; or something that would drain the power more gently – such as the systems on a Martian rover – for much longer. There are a lot of other details, mostly of the type printed on the back of almost every electrical device in your home, which (if you're anything like me) you have probably never read. And I almost ignored it, but one section caught my eye, near the bottom of the page:

> **Power Electronics Technical Information**
> Distribution Architecture Single string w/ graceful degradation

'Graceful degradation' seemed like a strangely poetic term to include in the instruction manual for a Mars rover, and I asked Robert Manning about it. He explained that these probes have only a very limited mass budget; that you can't send the thing into space packed with duplicates of everything, just in case something fails. And so the design philosophy accepts that for some components there will be no backup – hence the term 'single string' – but that the system will be engineered such that it can experience multiple discrete failures while continuing with most, if not all, of its function.

I found that a strangely powerful metaphor for the way we should approach our teamwork and our organisations, and perhaps for the way we should approach life ourselves. It's not that these organisations are designed to be error- or failure-free, but rather they are set up in such a way that these errors and failures do not disable them.

PART THREE

15.

System capacity

December 2020: more than 300 days into the Covid-19 pandemic. The hospital had called for help earlier that day. The signal it had sent wasn't the ordinary reporting of long waiting times and people stacked in corridors in the emergency department, or of operating theatres grinding to a halt due to a shortage of beds on the general wards. All of that was standard fare for the National Health Service (NHS) in winter. This was something else entirely.

There was more than a note of desperation in the hospital's plea: the creeping realisation that it was approaching the absolute limit of its capacity; that soon it might all but cease to function. I had been sent with a small team, drawn from hospitals across the region, to see what support we might give.

The surrounding hospitals had formed a tight bond during the pandemic, communicating daily, perpetually reconfiguring their limited resources, trying to absorb the shock and to spread the load between them. They were a fleet of ships at sea in darkness. The call for help was like watching a distress flare go up; in its flickering illumination we could see the silhouette of a sinking vessel.

It was well into the evening when we arrived to find the intensive-care unit (ICU) full and spilling over. The ceiling lights had been dimmed to try and simulate the ordinary rhythms of days and nights, even though all other sense of normality had been shattered. In the quiet darkness of the unit, the glow of monitors at bedsides and the winking lights on the pumps and ventilators were the only movement. There was little outward sign of the approaching chaos, or the imminent terror. But it was there in spades, if you looked for it.

*

Before Covid, this hospital on the outskirts of London had space, equipment and staff to hold just seventeen critically ill patients on ventilators in its ICU. In the past ten months, since the beginning of the pandemic, the team had expanded its physical capacity to nearly twice that: more beds, more ventilators, more kit, but with roughly the same number of specialist staff. It was a painful stretch for the team. But the surge of patients had continued for months and now, with Christmas approaching and a new, more transmissible Covid variant circulating, they could barely keep their heads above water. That evening there were nearly sixty patients across the hospital who were sick enough to need specialist critical care. There was neither space nor staff enough to treat all of them.

Specialist ICU nurses would ordinarily spend their days dedicated to a single ventilated patient. Yet they were now each responsible for up to four patients at a time and constantly worried about what they might be missing. There was little chatter between the staff – there wasn't time for it. Cocooned in their gowns, masks and visors, they were too busy studying the patient monitors. Near-constant alerts filled the air, chorusing gently but insistently, coming from every direction: the sound of a unit in crisis.

The alarms had a different pitch, depending on what emergency they signalled: a racing heart, collapsing blood pressure, a ventilator struggling to push air into stiffening lungs. The nurses acknowledged each one; a tap on a button to mute the audio, giving them brief respite while they adjusted drug doses and tweaked machine settings in an effort to remedy the problem. This was the fine technical skill of the job: constant small – and not-so-small – corrections; trying to step in and restore balance, doing what bodies compromised by Covid no longer could. This was the work of healthcare: a partnership between people, science and technology, one designed to support a patient's failing homeostasis; an attempt to rescue the sensitive and unstable stuff from which we are all made.

'I'm not managing patients here,' Alita, one of the ICU nurses, told me in exasperation as I looked in, 'just alarms!'

They were spread too thinly, across too many patients. They

spent their shifts putting out fires – there was little time for anything else.

ICU teams are well acquainted with death and dying. It is part of the job. They know how to accept it when it becomes an inevitability. They become expert, too, at softening the blow, for the people in their care and for those gathered around them. There is far more at work in ICU than life-support machines. It is the care that is intensive, and not simply the treatment.

But with Covid came something else: death at a rate and at a scale that none of them had ever seen before. Across the course of the pandemic, around one in every three patients in their care had died. And even that figure doesn't paint a full picture. The mortality came in waves, focused in time and space. In the grip of it, the worst-hit hospitals, in units like this, worked through weeks when more than half of all the patients in their care didn't survive.

Intensive care is about the details. About doing the most you can for the sickest patients, one patient at a time. About being able to go home satisfied that you have thrown more than the kitchen sink at it; knowing that nothing more, or better, could have been done. And when death is all that's left, it is about the small comfort that knowledge can sometimes bring to those left struggling in the wreckage. But during Covid – with the diluted staffing, the make-shift bed spaces and the repurposed ventilators – the teams found themselves no longer sure of that, or of themselves.

'At some point it just stops being intensive care,' said Alita.

Sickness rates had been running high among the staff and were still climbing. Covid had taken its toll on them, too. In the run-up to Christmas, more than a few of the nurses – burnt out by months of this grind – had left the NHS. There were now none to spare. And tonight, on this shift, there was no one even to cover their toilet breaks. Unable to leave their patients unmonitored even for a few short minutes, some of their nurses had started wearing adult diapers, while others used the patient commodes.

*

There's a feeling that you get when you stumble across a patient on a hospital ward or out on the road and you realise – even at first glance – they are sick enough that they might die; a fast-rising sense of dread that you have to fight to keep at bay. That was precisely how I felt on seeing that intensive-care unit. I fumbled with my phone, tempted to call in my report immediately, but that would have contained little more detail than the signal flare that the hospital had already put up. I knew I needed to see more.

I joined Subir, an intensive-care doctor, who began a tour of the rest of the hospital. Other medical teams had been referring deteriorating patients to him all day, hoping – in vain – that there might be space for them to be admitted to the ICU. I noticed him wheezing a little as we climbed the stairs. He'd had Covid himself in recent months and hadn't yet fully recovered. 'I was as sick as hell,' he told me.

Hundreds of health and social-care workers had died from Covid since the pandemic began. Compared to the general population, patient-facing NHS staff were four times more likely to be infected with Covid-19, and twice as likely to die. Healthcare workers from minority-ethnic backgrounds were particularly at risk. Vaccines had only recently, and slowly, begun to roll out. Neither Subir nor I had yet received one.

We roamed down the long corridors and looked in on the respiratory unit. There were more than twenty patients there, most of whom would ordinarily have been in intensive care, too, but were now being looked after by specialist ward teams with expertise in advanced respiratory care. The patients here were critically unwell, but still awake and just about holding their own; wearing masks strapped tightly to their faces, with oxygen flowing under high pressure to try and support their breathing and push through the damage caused by the virus.

However bad things had looked on the intensive-care unit, they were far worse here. The respiratory-unit teams had fewer staff – in places, one nurse was stretched between seven or eight patients – looking after people who were often just as sick as those asleep on ventilators up on the ICU. Resident doctors on these wards, early in their careers, had to take on responsibilities that went well beyond their years. Death was all around. For many of their patients the pressurised masks were the limit of what their bodies could tolerate. So much of the staff's time was spent caring for patients who wouldn't survive, making them comfortable when all other therapies had failed.

The pandemic shone so much light on the plight of the intensive-care units. They featured prominently in the daily reporting. It was right that we tracked them so closely: these were the beds in shortest supply and in greatest demand; the resource we thought most likely to be at risk of collapsing first. But there were many places within the walls of the hospital and beyond – in the community, on the road with our paramedics, in our care homes – where conditions were as bad, if not far worse.

We spiralled down the stairwell into the emergency department. The patients in the resuscitation bays were sitting up on their trolleys, glassy-eyed, oxygen hissing, attached to suites of monitoring that threw out steady streams of numbers. There was an orgy of information here: blood pressures, temperatures, heart rates, oxygen saturations, blood results, imaging, ECG telemetry wiggling across the screen, and more besides. But I had learned early in my career that the numbers weren't everything, that stepping back from the bay and watching from the end of the bed often gave you a truer impression. All of that was hard to put into words or capture through data. Sometimes a patient just looked sick. Sometimes you knew where you were heading before the numbers told you.

Three of the five patients in the resus bays were unwell enough to warrant urgent admission to ICU. Nearing the point of exhaustion, they now needed to be carefully anaesthetised and established on ventilators. But how and by whom? And where would they be cared for afterwards? Subir kept a note of them all, adding to his list of demands and unsolvable crises, watching the growing gap between what his patients urgently needed and what the hospital could provide.

I poked my head outside the rear entrance to the emergency department. There was a long line of ambulances, engines running to keep the cabins warm, patients waiting within. Maybe a dozen, maybe more. Subir told me that earlier on in the day somebody had died in that queue in an ambulance, because there had been no space for the hospital to receive them. And it wasn't the first time; the same had happened the evening before.

When you start your training with HEMS, one of the things they teach you is how to respond if you are the first to arrive at the scene of a major incident – a train crash, a terrorist bomb, a motorway pile-up. They give you a strict recipe for reporting in, a checklist of what to say and in what order: a report of exactly where you are, what has happened, whether the scene is safe, how many casualties there are, what resources are on the scene and how many more are required. It exists because otherwise, confronted by the enormity of something like that, it is very likely that you'll push the button on your radio, open your mouth and spout something desperate and unintelligible.

But this *was* a major incident, happening inside the walls of the hospital, everywhere I looked. For a moment I forgot myself and everything I'd been taught. All I wanted to do was climb the stairs to the roof of the hospital, get outside and scream for help, and keep screaming until there was no air left in my lungs. It is the closest I have ever seen any hospital system come to the point of operational collapse.

I paused, took time to breathe and think, picked up my phone and reported in to the network, using something of the rubric that HEMS had taught me, to stop myself from rambling. The surrounding hospitals kicked into gear, magicking up ambulances and transfer crews from nowhere, quickly transferring out a bundle of patients to free up space in the ICU, spreading the burden across the network, creating a tiny sliver of capacity – enough to get them through the night. But by the morning that, too, had been soaked up.

I drove home that night, leaving them behind. I got in and took my clothes off downstairs, putting them in the washing machine. I wasn't entirely convinced it was necessary, but it had become part of the ritual through Covid. I had a strange role, seconded to NHS England as 'National Clinical Adviser in Emergency Preparedness, Resilience and Response for the Covid-19 Incident'. My mornings were spent on calls with the national team, with people calling out case numbers and bed occupancies from across the country, and reports of hospitals under pressure everywhere, like the one I had come from. You could just about stomach it when you read the sterile figures off the data dashboard. It was much harder, later, to marry those numbers to the truth of what was happening on the ground; to see it up close, to feel the fear my colleagues felt in hospitals around the country. There was more to communicate than the statistics ever could.

I cried in the shower that night. I didn't even try to stop myself.

16.
Initial conditions

SARS-CoV-2, the virus that causes Covid-19, crept into our lives insidiously. On the last day of 2019 Chinese state media reported a cluster of pneumonia cases of unknown cause in Wuhan city, Hubei Province, centred around the Huanan seafood market. As a result the World Health Organization (WHO), which had been tracking the outbreak in partnership with Chinese authorities, activated its Incident Management Support Team, gearing up its emergency response.

At this point very little was known about this disease. It had the potential to cause serious illness, but what was its cause? Where had it come from? Could it spread from person to person? Was it already spreading through the population in Wuhan? And, if so, how fast? Was this a familiar threat – a re-emergence of the SARS (Severe Acute Respiratory Syndrome) epidemic of 2003 perhaps – or something entirely new?

By 3 January 2020 there were only forty-four known cases of the disease worldwide, but a quarter of those appeared to be severely unwell. The WHO issued the following advisory: 'There is limited information to determine the overall risk of this reported cluster of pneumonia of unknown aetiology.' The words were carefully chosen. Nobody could be sure what lay ahead. This could still be a statistical blip or an infection that would burn itself out. But there remained the growing possibility that this mysterious outbreak was the beginning of something much worse.

Within a week the cause of the outbreak had been identified as a coronavirus. On 11 January, Chinese state media reported the first death from the virus: a sixty-one-year-old man who had been a regular customer of the Huanan market. By mid-January cases had been identified in Thailand, Japan, South Korea and the United States; at the end of that month the first cases were being reported in Europe. The slow phase of this outbreak was over. With case numbers in East Asia rising, the WHO gave this new disease a name: Covid-19.

Covid-19 was the worst kind of threat: fast-moving, lethal and unknown. The virus was formally complex in the way it behaved: it had no single point of control and was governed by the simple rules laid out in its short genome. It was capable of emergence – new, unexpected behaviours – and over time was able to adapt and overcome many of the measures that we would put in place to slow its progress. Worst of all, it was a threat that would scale in a non-linear fashion – which is to say that it was like a fire that, once started, spread at an ever-accelerating rate. There was no way of outrunning it.

Let's consider that non-linearity: the virus's ability to spread like wildfire. It is only one feature among its many complex attributes, but it is worth understanding, because it helps to explain why we were so quickly overwhelmed, and why our intuitive sense of the scale of this threat led us dangerously astray in some places.

Let's play a quick game. If I start by giving you one penny, and then I double the amount of money you have each second, so that you have two pennies after one second, four pennies after two seconds and so on; how long would it take for you to become a millionaire?

Now one pound is, of course, 100 pennies, so what I'm really asking here: is how long would it take to build a pile of 100 million of them at that doubling rate? I don't want you to pause or think too hard. I want you to shoot from the hip and make your best guess, right now, without using a pen and paper or a calculator, or asking ChatGPT.

OK: time's up. If I start with a penny and double the money you have every second, you would become a millionaire just over 26.5 seconds later. I'm willing to bet you were – like the vast majority of people I have asked – very wide of the mark. Most people give a timespan in hours, days or weeks. A few people guess that it takes sixty seconds. But even guesses like this, which are apparently close, represent a sizeable calculation error: if 26.5 seconds makes you a millionaire, then sixty seconds gives you a quintillion pennies: that's a one followed by eighteen zeros (10,000,000,000,000,000,000), making you a ten-quadrillionaire. This teaches us two things. First, that very few of us have an intuitive sense of quite how fast a non-linear, doubling process like this can grow. And second – as I've just shown – if you're wrong small at the start, then you're wrong big by the end.

During the pandemic it was infections, rather than pennies, that were doubling. In the UK in the spring of 2020 the number of Covid cases was doubling every three days, and possibly faster, creating a flood of hospitalisations, beginning in London and then spreading beyond. The process that had overwhelmed northern Italy had taken root in the UK and was now moving at staggering speed.

Wherever you work, whatever you do, the initial conditions in complex systems are important. That is why much-maligned politicians and senior managers at the blunt end actually have such a crucial and central role. It is their decisions, designs and strategies – made over months and years – that lay the foundation of the response. Their ability to anticipate threats and to build in effective measures of prevention are what set the tone and guarantee the adequacy (or otherwise) of the frontline response. The adaptive capabilities of your frontline teams may be remarkable, but it takes time to train people, to take them from being novices and turn them into teams of proficient experts; time to make sure that they are properly partnered with their technology and that the system has been built around them, so that it becomes a suit of armour rather than an iron maiden. If you haven't done any of that before the onset of a crisis, then you can't expect it to suddenly materialise when the crisis arrives.

Not only that, but small differences in how the system is set up at the start of a crisis, and how the threat is managed, can magnify to become very large differences later. It is why close attention, along with early and definitive action, is so important. And of course to escape a threat that is growing exponentially you have to act fast – long before it becomes obvious to all and sundry that you need to do so. By the time everyone can see it, it is too late.

The state of the NHS at the start of the Covid-19 pandemic in 2019 was unenviable. Since its inception in 1948 the population of the UK had grown, and grown older, in large part precisely because of the success of the National Health Service and of public-health policy in preventing diseases that for most of human history had shortened lives.

But the decade leading up to the pandemic saw the largest-ever sustained fall in NHS spending growth since its foundation. On the eve of the Covid outbreak the NHS had fewer doctors and fewer nurses per head of population than most comparable high-income countries: Germany, the Netherlands, France, Norway and Denmark, for example. We had fewer intensive-care beds, too. On 30 January 2020, the day the WHO declared Covid-19 to be a public-health emergency of international concern, there were, across England, just over 3,600 intensive-care beds, and – as with the beds on general wards – these were already running close to full capacity.

The healthcare workforce meanwhile was facing its own crisis, with more than 100,000 unfilled full-time vacancies and signs of growing stress across the board. None of this was news. Report after report had highlighted this problem and the need for corrective action to address it, but none came.

Seven weeks after the first cases were reported in China, on 21 February 2020 at Codogno Hospital, Lodi, in northern Italy, a thirty-eight-year-old man was hospitalised with Covid-19 – the first Italian patient to be diagnosed. Within ten days hospitals in Lombardy had come under severe pressure.

As we watched these first Covid cases flood Italian hospitals, the NHS began to ready itself for what was to come. Yet the situation was already dire: we had too few doctors, too few nurses, too few beds. Too little of just about everything. Every winter we somehow stretched our limited resources to fill new gaps and barely made it to the spring. We waited for the last straw that would break the camel's back. And then Covid landed, like a pallet of steel girders.

When complex systems fail, it takes a lot to redress the balance. It is why prevention is always better than cure. In the practice of medicine, what you learn through working with people whose physiology has been stretched to its very limit is that there is no single lever that you can pull to restore them. The goal is not to try to cure them in one fell swoop. Critical-care medicine – wherever and however you practise it – is always a partnership between you, the patient and what remains of their underlying physiology.

The art is to try to nudge your patient back into a state where the intrinsic mechanisms that have kept them alive for the whole of their lives can reassert themselves and eventually take over. The goal is not a cure – it is to try and return to that zone of stability created by homeostasis. What you learn is that less is often more; that heroic interventions are often the least effective; that many small moves earlier on are better than some dramatic but futile gesture too close to the finale.

You learn, too, that you can push human physiology pretty hard before it breaks. It is a system built to survive, engineered for resilience through billions of years of evolution. So the skill in this kind of medicine is to recognise when you are within that zone of stability; when biological feedback loops that are more ancient and robust than anything you can muster are once again in control and you can afford to leave well alone. You cannot command your patient's physiology to do anything; you can only facilitate it.

But as we have learned, these systems are fragile at their boundaries. Outside what an engineer would call their 'design limits' – the conditions under which they can reasonably be expected to adapt and self-balance – the system (whether that be your physiology, your organisation or your healthcare service) will collapse. Without remedy, that collapse accelerates rapidly, leaving only the occasional and briefest window before it becomes irretrievable.

At the start of 2020 that is where Covid-19 found healthcare systems across the world: hovering at the edge of their capability, at risk of spilling beyond their zone of stability; realising that over time we had come to rely too heavily upon the remarkable adaptive qualities of the people who worked within them, and wondering what these systems might look like if, indeed, they ever broke.

My colleagues and I in the NHS looked at the mathematical models that described the progress of the Covid-19 outbreak as it swept across East Asia and wondered if it might already be too late. We were out of time, under-prepared and under-resourced. And it crossed my mind that we might be about to see the disintegration of a system in not-so-slow motion.

17.

Day zero

Friday 6 March 2020. Covid was already well on its way, but in the UK we had yet to begin to prepare in earnest. In the NHS our day jobs continued as they always had. I'd been on shift with HEMS: a cold, bright day with scattered cloud and views for miles around. It seems strange now that we should have been in our normal routines even then. Strange, too, that it was so hard to see the future that lay in wait.

We handed over our last patient to the trauma team in the emergency department. We wiped the kit down, gathered our bags and got ready to fly back to the aerodrome at Redhill. The crew slowly made their way to the roof of the hospital, clattering up the steel staircase into the stiff breeze on the helipad. We paused there awhile, looking out across London, taking a moment to soak up the spectacle of the sun dipping on the horizon, bathing the city in its last light. By the time we were airborne, darkness had almost fallen.

I handed over to the team coming in for their night shift and signed off. It took an hour to tidy up the loose ends, finish notes and square away our medical kit. That part of the shift always felt like a too-rapid decompression: from our total immersion in the frenetic events of the day to the mindset of the homeward-bound commuter.

On the motorway driving home an hour later, I turned on the radio to catch up with the news. The first coronavirus death in the UK had now been confirmed; the number of cases had more than doubled in the previous forty-eight hours, from fifty-one to 116. We had been tracking the stories from northern Italy for some weeks, as schools and businesses there had closed and the number of deaths had begun to climb.

In the UK we were still unable to fully accept what was about to happen. This was perhaps just the first stage of our collective grief, manifesting as denial: 'This can't be us, this won't be us.' As a country, we deployed a familiar defence: an overvalued sense of British exceptionalism, that somehow the rest of the world was doing something differently or something wrong, handling the outbreak in a way that we in the UK never would. At the most senior levels of government there appeared to be indecision over when and how to act. And then, as things worsened abroad, we gave up waiting for guidance and began to contact our friends and colleagues in Wuhan and Italy directly, searching in vain for confirmation that we might be dealing with little more than an outbreak of hyperbole.

But by midweek an email was circulating from Professor Maurizio Cecconi, a consultant intensive-care doctor in Milan and, at the time, president-elect of the European Society of Intensive Care Medicine. Here was someone we knew directly and respected, describing the horror of their experience in the first ten days of the pandemic in Italy and the challenges of dealing with the flood of patients that had arrived in their hospitals. One in ten of all patients they admitted with Covid was ending up in intensive care. Given the sheer rate of infection and hospital admission, that was a fearsome percentage. The Italians were imploring us to learn from their experience, to act in order to get ahead of the coming storm. 'We wish to convey a strong message,' Cecconi wrote. 'Get ready!'

Five days later northern Italy went into lockdown and the WHO declared a global pandemic. It is so difficult to convey the scale of the challenge that faced us, or how confronting it was. But in the opening few weeks of the pandemic in Italy, as Covid ripped through the country, in the Lombardy region alone more than 10,000 people died.

On the frontline in the UK there was, at first, an information vacuum that made preparations difficult; there was a buzz in the hospital corridors, but nothing with enough substance to drive our immediate decisions or actions. And yet you could feel it: the distant roar of something awful and unseen.

That week two of our intensive-care consultants built a rudimentary mathematical model of the disease, to try and get a truer sense of where we might be headed. The hospital in London where I work as a senior doctor had yet to see a single case arrive on our intensive-care unit, but the Italians had shaken us out of complacency.

The model was little more than a spreadsheet that dealt with Covid infections as though they would grow like compound interest, day on day. The first results – though only a very coarse approximation – were terrifying, suggesting that our existing intensive-care unit would be overrun within a month.

That same week my mother was admitted to the hospital where I work. She had been diagnosed with bladder cancer only a few weeks earlier, but was now sick after her first doses of chemotherapy. The cancer was advanced; it had spread out of her bladder and into her liver. This was already her second admission in as many weeks. Things were going badly and I began to worry about her battered immune system and the future of her cancer treatment as Covid loomed.

We made some small refinements to our toy mathematical model, making it look less like an accountant's spreadsheet and more like operational research. We recruited some help from a computer scientist at University College London and developed more detailed models and scenarios. The revised figures were no more reassuring: unattenuated Covid-19 would overwhelm our existing ICU capacity in a matter of days.

On Friday 13 March 2020 a small group of senior intensive-care and anaesthetic doctors, about twenty of us in all, gathered in the anaesthetic-department seminar room at University College London Hospital. We challenged and rechallenged the assumptions in the model, but the conclusions were always the same. There was no fine grain to our predictions, no completeness to the information on which it was based, but it was all anyone had, and it told us enough. We had days and not weeks to prepare: we had to start *now*. This was the shape of our decisions, made under conditions of extraordinary uncertainty. This was our decision point. We knew that we had to act and that those actions would be imperfect, but that to do nothing would be to invite catastrophe.

This aspect of the response is sometimes overlooked, because it happens so early in the onset of the crisis. You have to *decide to make decisions*. In the face of uncertainty, that can feel deeply uncomfortable. The information you have may be incomplete, ambiguous or just plain wrong, but you have to decide all the same. And you need to continue and commit to the actions those decisions prescribe until better information arises, or until you encounter failure and are forced to revise. Paralysis is the risk; dynamism is what you need.

We began making preparations deep into the night and across weekends, drawing up plans and delivering them almost as soon as they had been finalised. The hospital would have to pivot hard and transform itself to meet the oncoming wave. There was an air of brutality about all of this. The service would lose much of its nuance in the process, shedding the breadth of its capability, giving itself over instead almost entirely to this single purpose. But there was no alternative.

Our plans were scribbled on whiteboards in seminar rooms. That was where we did our thinking. These were photographed and turned into policies and protocols without much further inspection: there was no time to pore over the detail or turn it all into a neatly formatted document. We would spill out of the intensive-care unit and into a series of ad hoc locations – theatre complexes and general wards. There we would establish makeshift critical-care units: beds in all-too-crowded spaces, ventilators stolen from operating theatres, staff borrowed from other specialties.

We would start by commandeering the operating theatres, which bore at least some resemblance to our formal ICU, and which had teams of anaesthetists already well versed in how to resuscitate and stabilise critically ill patients. We would move on to the recovery suite and then, if the surge was still coming, we would expand upstairs onto wards that were never designed to accommodate patients on ventilators.

This is what the edge of chaos looks like, and is why complex systems have to organise themselves to function at that precipice. The agility that it fosters becomes all-essential here. It is what enables a system – even one as vast and apparently monolithic as the NHS – to transform itself in short order; and it is why, in the face of a fast-moving crisis, central leadership has to give way to the expertise of those closest to the decisions and the consequences of those decisions. We use the term 'human resources' casually. But in a crisis, as we have seen throughout this book, the human teams closest to the threat are your most valuable, agile and adaptable asset.

It was a plan designed to be deployed as a cascade of defences, to be triggered serially as the patient load grew. But while we billed each stage as an expansion of our existing capacity, each new area we were forced to move into would represent a retreat. Every time we spilled over to a new location, staff and equipment would be stretched more thinly. There were no illusions. What we were building was an Alamo of sorts, and no one was sure if – or for how long – it would hold.

Despite the late nights and long weekends in the hospital, I managed to steal away regularly to see Mum up on the wards. She was tucked away in a corner on the eighth floor of the hospital's main tower, and was still well enough that she wondered why she was there and what the fuss was all about. But her kidneys weren't quite right, and if they weren't doing their job, then she wouldn't be able to continue with her chemotherapy. It was sensible to keep her in hospital for now to try and get things corrected quickly, before Covid arrived.

Mum was tiny and chirpy; a Mauritian who had arrived here on a ship more than half a century earlier, and whose success in this country had been down to hard work and her ability to make friends quickly. Having managed Civil Service typing pools for most of her life, she was more than capable of talking the hind legs off any donkey. Whenever I visited she would introduce me to every other patient in the bay, as though I was a guest showing up late to her cocktail party. Later, as I perched on her bed, she would relate the details that she had gleaned of her fellow inmates' life stories.

When I wasn't there, she would potter up and down in the lifts, to shops on the ground floor and back again. After years of not really understanding what I did for a living, Mum was finally getting an up-close and very personal tour of my workplace. The opening days of Covid shackled me to the hospital, but because of that I was able to visit her more regularly, and more often, than might otherwise have been the case.

Over the next week we started to rehearse donning and doffing our Personal Protective Equipment (PPE). On with the duck-bill mask, with its elastic straps biting into the side of your face; on with the clear plastic visor. Then the first pair of sweaty nitrile gloves against your skin, with a gown pulled over the top of all that, and finally a second pair of gloves – taped to your sleeves – so that when you finally tore the gown off, they would come away, too. The ensemble was hot, clumsy and uncomfortable from the moment it went on. But the flimsy layers of paper, plastic, rubber and fabric were our only armour against the virus.

The virus tended to seed first in the upper airways and lungs of infected patients, before spreading to wreak havoc in the rest of the body. The sickest patients would arrive in respiratory failure, with the virus multiplying rapidly in their cells, distorting the architecture and function of their lungs. And when this happened, the intensive-care and anaesthetic teams would don their PPE and step in: to give a struggling patient some rest, to unburden their physiology with machines and drugs and start down the road to life support.

To connect someone directly to a machine upon which their life will depend is no small thing, and is fraught with hazard even at the best of times. But to anaesthetise and intubate these patients – to place a tube in the patient's larynx, so that they could be started on a ventilator – with the virus welling in their lungs was something else entirely.

These patients, already so unwell with coronavirus that they were at risk of dying, would cough out clouds of aerosols loaded with the disease. To do their job and to care for their patient, the anaesthetic team would have to stand directly inside those virus-laden clouds. And when they intubated these patients, they would be staring into the source of that infection, hoping that the mask, the gown, the visor, the double pair of gloves and the sticky tape would be enough to protect them.

These fears were far from irrational. The only comparable event in recent history had been the SARS outbreak in 2003, which had spread quickly in East Asia. During that epidemic a Chinese-American businessman called Johnny Chen – 'patient zero' in the Vietnam outbreak – arrived in the French Hospital in Hanoi in late February and was promptly admitted to intensive care and established on a ventilator. He died two weeks later. But so, too, did the nurse and doctor who had intubated him. More than thirty-eight staff working at the hospital in Hanoi fell ill in the following weeks. Four more went on to die, along with Dr Carlo Urbani, the WHO infectious-disease specialist who had been sent to Vietnam to contain the outbreak.

The SARS epidemic in 2003 was also caused by a coronavirus. It killed many healthcare workers in outbreaks across East Asia and in Toronto, Canada. As the Covid-19 pandemic flared, that was all we knew of the world's last significant coronavirus outbreak.

Getting patients onto ventilators, learning how to manage the risks of working in and around them, took careful choreography. We set up teams to try and anticipate every problem, every source of potentially fatal error – both for the patient and for our teams – and then designed procedures to protect against them. The anaesthetists drew up long checklists, urgently rehearsing and refining them.

This was happening all over the hospital. Upstairs, wards were being cleared, surgery was being stopped, rotas were being redrawn. The government appeared unsure of how best to prepare the NHS for any of this, but at the same time acutely aware of quite how much they were about to ask of its workforce. By rights, there should have been some rallying address: a no-shit call-to-arms. But none came. And while our political leadership continued to deliberate, the frontline teams were already delivering.

The politicians had little of substance to offer in those early days. All of our opportunities to prepare properly had been squandered years before. Pandemic influenza (or a similar respiratory virus) had featured as one of the highest priorities on the national risk register for more than a decade. It was no secret. The twenty-first century had already seen at least four influenza strains and two emergent coronaviruses with pandemic potential. There were countless bodies of research and publications outlining the risks and consequences: too many for anyone to discount. And yet here the frontline staff were, in the moment, making contact with the risk that we – as a nation – had failed to properly insure against.

Short of intensive-care beds and staff, short of ventilators and PPE, absent any useful testing capability that could now be deployed at scale, the government found itself wrongfooted, outflanked and outpaced. There was a yawning gulf between what we needed and what we had, and no better option than to hurl the frontline workforce into that breach, in the hope that they might somehow make up the difference.

The first Covid-19 patient arrived on our ICU on 16 March. By that time my mum had herself been admitted to intensive care, for kidney failure. I remember watching through the glass of a closed double door as a team of my colleagues wheeled onto the unit in full PPE with our first critically ill Covid-19 patient. Behind me, in the side-room, Mum was getting sicker. On the monitors, her numbers were all moving in the wrong direction; her kidneys had all but failed, and she was suddenly weary. No more excursions to the hospital shop, no more chit-chat.

On the screen by Mum's bedside, a junior doctor's note lay open, summarising the grim state of affairs. I glimpsed the last line of the entry, a single phrase and a well-worn euphemism: 'Family discussion required.' And I understood then what I had perhaps known all along: that Mum's journey, across continents, decades and cultures, would end here.

My friend David Brearley – who happened to be the consultant covering the intensive-care unit that day – found me at Mum's bedside. He led me down the corridors towards the Relatives' Room, to start a conversation that I myself had started, so many times, with so many other families. There was such a profound sense of dread as we reached the door to embark on that set-piece. This was the beginning of a ritual that would be followed in short fashion by many others, more ancient. David paused before he turned the handle, looked at me, understood the strangeness of it all and said gently, 'Shall we do this in my office instead?'

A Covid-19 response team from NHS England came down to meet us that night, sharing their information and asking for ours. In a cramped seminar room, our senior anaesthetists and intensivists outlined their concerns, showing them how fast we thought the virus was likely to move, and what that would mean for our hospital and the rest of the country. The NHS England team scribbled notes and furrowed their brows. I held my mobile phone in my hand, glancing at it periodically in case the nurses from the ICU rang.

I was angry by this time, I think, and in no mood to hold my tongue. Whatever the truth, it felt to us that nobody had done their due diligence for Covid. Caught in the glare of its oncoming headlights, we were being led by a government that was not responding quickly enough to make a difference. I found myself stabbing my marker pen into the flipchart on which we had scrawled a graph showing the tidal wave of Covid patients we were expecting. By the end I was almost shouting, trying to get somebody to sit up and take notice.

I crossed the hall to the intensive-care unit. I spent the rest of the night at Mum's bedside. Mum knew that nothing now could make her better, perhaps even more than I did. She was tired. I knew that when she – a true force of nature – decided enough was enough, she wouldn't last long.

We talked quietly about everything that night, in a side-room tucked away from the bustle on the unit and its urgent preparations. The rest of my family had time to arrive. We clustered around the bed, and Dad sobbed like a small child. Eventually everyone else went home, and it was just me and Mum in the side-room. It was close to midnight when her breathing changed. She was comfortable, and I was there with her when she gently slipped away.

The cancer was cruel and fast, multiplying without control. It was too late; there had been nothing we could do to slow its progress. But in the end Mum was cared for in my hospital, by my friends, and I was able to be by her side till the end. There was nothing more, or better, that anyone could have done for us. She deserves a more complete eulogy than this, and a better one than we were able to give a few weeks later after lockdown had begun, during a rushed service in a chapel, with only six of us allowed to attend and the priest telling us to keep our words to no more than two minutes in length. But here it is perhaps enough to say that she was the best mother a boy could ever ask for.

I was seconded to NHS England two days later, as part of the national Covid-19 response team. In the early days of Covid, the Emergency Preparedness, Resilience and Response (EPRR) teams at NHS England were front and centre. They had a range of reflexive responses that they could snap into action almost immediately. These are the teams that you usually get out of the cupboard when disaster strikes, and they were well drilled: terrorist attacks, train crashes and floods had seen to that. But the pandemic was moving fast, at terrifying scale and with a terrible momentum; and EPRR understood that it was more than they alone were equal to.

They gathered a wider team, adding to their ranks, with me caught up in the sweep. I had worked with the Department of Health in the past, in the wake of several major incidents – mostly terrorist attacks, shootings and bombings. I knew something of the challenges presented by sudden surges in demand for critical care and what those scenes really looked like. When we drew up the contract, there was a box for 'Duration of secondment', and my boss looked up at me and scribbled, 'Duration of the Covid-19 Incident'. Even then I thought that meant a role that would last for around six to nine months. I was still there three years later.

Skipton House, the headquarters of NHS England in London, sat in a red-brick office block in Elephant and Castle. By mid-March it had become something of a ghost town, with only essential staff showing up to work regularly. We shared a floor with the newly arrived military, among them a contingent from the army's Royal Logistics Corps. It began to feel quite surreal. Commuting to work through now-deserted streets, and watching the military move into the office, amplified the sense that we had accidentally stumbled onto the set of a post-apocalyptic disaster movie, and that somewhere around the corner – out of shot – reality was running just fine.

And then it was upon us. By 20 March two hospitals in London had declared major incidents, overrun early by the sudden rush of patients with Covid-19. Hospitals across the country, which had prepared in the same way we had, received a torrent of patients. None of us had ever seen anything like it before. A true national emergency.

The supply chains for everything, from ventilators and drugs to gowns and gloves, were stretching and snapping all over the globe. Hospitals were crying out for resupply, but the warehouses were emptying fast. One day, over coffee, we asked one of the Royal Logistics Corps officers from the military if they had a good plan to solve our problems. 'There are no good solutions,' he told us. 'By the time we get involved, all the good solutions have gone. That's why they call us.'

Crises of any scale have the same properties: the opening act is nothing short of chaos, and it takes great skill and leadership to superimpose structure. Covid seemed to warp time: weekdays bled into weekends, weeks ran into one another, hours would sometimes feel like days, and days sometimes flashed by like hours. We came to call it 'Covid Time'; the strange flow that we were all carried along by.

The hospitals themselves were incredible. They deserved their applause every Thursday, and far more besides. I watched them get battered, then regroup, re-form and go again, day after day. But all of that came at a cost. At ground level, the response was a textbook example of how organisations should respond in the face of any crisis. The hospitals committed early and completely to their course of action, pivoting hard to get themselves ready. They prepared against a backdrop of dense uncertainty, knowing that their first solutions would be wrong, but that there would be an opportunity to revise and reiterate along the way. This was what they were trained to do: to make decisions in the impossible moment, to reap the consequences – good or bad – and get ready to go again, and again. Real decisions, real risk, real consequences.

For every decision that we needed to make in those early days, the deadlines for action were very clear: yesterday was already too late; if we were to have any chance of avoiding catastrophe, then right now was all we had left. This is the cadence and character of all major incidents: that sense of moving swiftly in dense fog, with something lethal and unseen dwelling within it, knowing that inaction will only allow it to manifest more fully.

We were under no illusions as to what this might look like. A good friend of mine, an intensive-care consultant in another London hospital, talked about his recurring nightmare across the pandemic, which found him living on a tiny comic-book desert island – a pile of golden sand with a single palm tree – watching a tsunami rolling towards him in the distance, knowing that he couldn't swim away, knowing that building a wall out of the sand would be futile, and watching all the while as the wave continued to roar towards him.

It's hard now to properly capture what we felt in those moments. At times it didn't feel real. For the frontline teams across the country, who were now preparing in earnest, what lay ahead looked insurmountable. What had to be done seemed impossible. They did it anyway.

18.
Estimates

'War' is an overused metaphor in medicine, even more so during the pandemic, and people rightly railed against it. But Covid, particularly in the early days, was more war-like than anything else, in its scale, complexity and uncertainty. And in this the military had plenty to offer. In them lay an understanding of what it took for an organisation to make high-consequence decisions in the absence of all the facts, and of the cadence at which we might have to operate to avoid something still worse.

The military, who arrived on the scene at NHS England around the same time I did, helped me realise that much of what I had learned from past lives – about small teams operating amid dense uncertainty; about psychological safety, leadership, followership, deference to expertise, delegation of authority, failure and iteration – all applied here, albeit on a radically different scale and consequence. My seat at NHS England was the same as the one I'd had when I first climbed aboard the aircraft with HEMS; I was a new crew member, once again scanning the horizon, encouraged to call out the threats as and when I saw them.

I brought a different perspective. I knew enough maths – from my days studying astrophysics – to be able to understand at least some of the disease modelling, but I had also seen enough major incidents up close to appreciate how this might play out at the sharp end. The threats, and their consequences, were far from clear: indefinite shapes, difficult to make out in the distance, some of them closing fast; many of them phantoms. Steering clear of one might put you into the path of another. And yet any one of them, or any combination, might cause the loss of tens of thousands of lives or livelihoods. Collision with some of them would more than likely lead to both.

The work happened largely in silos at first. That is not a criticism; it was the only way. Everyone was in the same boat, setting up their teams, recalibrating their effort, trying to adapt in real time. There were mechanisms for sharing information across boundaries, but the whole thing was a hastily erected Tower of Babel, and we were fractured into many tongues: mathematicians, managers, clinicians, epidemiologists, politicians.

Part of my job was to sit across that, trying to scour the detail and synthesise a picture; seeing if the disparate threats might come together to form a more terrible and unseen whole. There was plenty to call out: too much that set alarm bells ringing, but too little that you could attach numerical probability to. That's not to say that data were scarce. There were dashboards everywhere, with a flow of numbers pouring from them like water from a fire hydrant. But that was paralysing in its own way.

I would sit at my desk, trying to write briefing notes that summarised the oncoming concerns as I saw them, endeavouring to create a signal out of the noise. But it was hard to know how to do that with so very little certainty at hand.

The army was used to managing precisely this problem of having to make assessments – upon which lives could depend – without having the luxury of enough accurate information. They introduced me to the concept of 'strategic estimates'. The strategic estimate answered that most difficult of first questions: 'Where do we start?' It was defined in their doctrine as a structured assessment of the strategic environment – enemy intentions and capabilities; one's own strengths and constraints; allies; geography; economics; technology and time – to inform national decisions in the theatre of war. For the army it was a standardised process, a way of making a formal best guess, to prepare for the possibility of immediate action.

The early, modern origins of the military-strategic estimate come from the eighteenth-century Prussian major-general and military theorist Carl von Clausewitz, who regarded war as a state of irreducible uncertainty. As war became faster and more kinetic, the combat estimate was devised: a tool that enabled troops already in contact with the enemy to make a snap assessment before committing to action.

Estimates of this kind acknowledge the absence of solid information and the evolving nature of a threat. They are forward-looking, assumption-driven and explicitly uncertain. Writing briefing notes with this in mind created a kind of freedom, and the guaranteed imperfection of these notes was what made them useful. It meant they could be written quickly, not as a comprehensive brief or as a solution, but as part of the flow of information that left the leader of the moment best informed. Everything was subject to revision; that was a built-in condition of the estimates, and part of what makes the idea successful – the dexterity and flexibility to be open to change and improvement. Crucially, it was about the pursuit of a goal through rapid cycles of feedback.

This is exactly the model for assessing and treating a critically unwell patient. At the outset we rarely know the source of an injury or the cause of illness; we make our best guess and start our interventions. But we are constantly reassessing, reappraising and revising as we gather new information and the patient responds to treatment. And we always remain live to the possibility that our direction of travel could be wrong. It is why, when out with HEMS at the scene of an accident, or in our hospital teams, we solicit as many diverse opinions as possible. All of us, in our own way, run John Boyd's OODA Loop, preserving our adaptive capacity by Observing, Orientating, Deciding and Acting; running through that in cycles until the problem of the moment is solved.

Constructing the estimate is an essential first step in creating adaptive capacity in the face of any unexpected event; making the best estimate of the problem, with the resources at hand and the time that you have. The process of forming the estimate tells you what you don't know and what you need to know for future iterations, forcing you to identify the many islands of uncertainty.

Your first assessment is always a necessary oversimplification, riddled with assumptions. Overconfidence in it, and fixation upon it, represents a common source of error. The goal of reassessment is to reduce the number of simplifying assumptions and, if necessary, layer on more complexity until you get close enough to what is truly unfolding. And all of that is true whether you're pulling people from wrecked cars on a motorway; are in the jaws of a fast-evolving global pandemic; or are a business finding itself suddenly wrong-footed, at risk and having to set a new direction.

Estimates – no matter how coarse – are useful because they give you a basis for first action. They work only if everyone in the loop understands that the information will change, as may the plan of action. And they are why that positioning of your team or organisation, at the edge of chaos, becomes so important. The faster and more complex a threat is, the greater the necessary frequency of reassessment. And the more likely it is that you will have to pivot and repeatedly reconfigure your response.

Covid was an archetypal complex threat. Finding a way through it was never about coming up with a single solution that would endure. It was about recognising the imperfection of each moment, but perpetually striving for better solutions every single day.

The coronavirus that caused the pandemic became formally chaotic in its behaviours as it continued to spread and, because of that, savagely difficult to predict with any great certainty. To know what our country and our Health Service might have to deal with, we needed estimates of this, too. But good models of how the virus might propagate through the population were fiendishly difficult to produce. They depended upon so many different things that nobody – at the time – knew for sure: the dynamics of the organism, how it transmitted from person to person, how long someone would be infectious for, whether infection would lead to immunity, how complete that immunity might be; the list went on and on. And all of this before you began to consider the dynamics of the population: who and how many people we come into contact with every day, where and under what circumstances; how likely transmission in those environments was; how we might respond to government instructions and restrictions; what we might do without them.

There is a fine skill in knowing how to process conflicting lines of information; in taking account of what you know, what you don't know and everything in between; a skill in attaching guesses to variables and in quantifying that uncertainty. Nevertheless, someone had to try and constrain the possibilities and paint a best-guess picture, given the information to hand, no matter how uncertain. It was a daunting task, but one that teams of mathematicians and epidemiologists, paired with public-health officials, were willing to take on. Not all futures were equally likely. The job of these mathematical modelling teams was to pluck out those that were most probable, while also identifying scenarios that, while less likely, would prove devastating, should they materialise.

The official disease-modelling effort was run by around half a dozen teams of researchers in universities up and down the country, who were purposed specifically for this task. They formed a loose syndicate, brought together under the umbrella of the Scientific Pandemic Infections group on Modelling, better known to all of us now as SPI-M, which existed to provide expert scientific advice in this field to our government. During the pandemic they were an emergency advisory body and, as such, convened in private, to encourage frank, fast and fulsome discussion.

That necessary but closed approach jarred with others in the modelling community. Modellers, whether building remote-control aeroplanes or mathematical simulations of infectious disease, like to show off their creations and what they can do. They like to be able to interrogate one another, to understand the inner workings of the mechanisms they are looking at, so that they can swap ideas and offer constructive criticism. The closed-door approach of the SPI-M group made that difficult for the wider mathematical modelling community.

It felt strange for those of us on the receiving end of the forecasts, too. If you're an anaesthetist, you tend to like to know how things work. That's what the job is all about: being able to look at what is happening to your patient, strip that right back to basic physiology and, through that, find the right way to intervene. And so for us (and for me especially) it felt strange that the mathematical modelling, whose outputs were so central to our expectations of how the pandemic would unfold, seemed to be happening in a black box.

Early in the pandemic I was introduced to a group of researchers in Durham who had been working on building a mathematical model of their own, separately from the SPI-M teams. They were a particle-physics and cosmology group whose work had been interrupted by the pandemic. Epidemiology was far from their native expertise, and I was, at first, sceptical that they would have much to offer. But their team of a dozen PhD students and postdoctoral researchers worked tirelessly.

Particle physicists spend their lives looking at what happens when subatomic objects collide, and then tracing the fates of the fragments that shower forth. They study collisions triggering cascades; cascades triggering avalanches. At a mathematical level, you could see how they might have some insight into how an infection might shower through a population. After all, this too was all about collisions and events.

On a practical level, the Durham team had access to enormously powerful computers, of the type that could run models describing the evolution of the early universe. These were supercomputers that occupied entire rooms, filled with dozens of cabinets the size of Coca-Cola vending machines, each one holding hundreds of processors, generating so much heat that you needed ear-defenders to protect your hearing from the deafening buzz of the cooling fans. And in modelling Covid-19, that monster computing capability would prove useful.

The Durham team was led by the formidable Professor Frank Krauss. Frank was a big-canvas kind of guy, used to thinking about things at scale. A German particle physicist who had contributed to the statistical and computational techniques that helped find the Higgs boson, he was never one to think that any problem might be too big.

Frank approached the Covid pandemic with a combination of art and sheer first-principles brute force. He and his team of researchers developed an Agent Based Model (ABM) that digested the United Kingdom's 2011 census data and proceeded to build a simulation of every individual in England, according to that information. The sort of model that had you marvelling at the attention to detail. He was a particle physicist now trying to build a model of the Covid-19 pandemic in the UK, from the bottom up, particle by particle; hoping to create a simulation that could help us understand how fast and how widely the disease might spread. It was different from the other models. Less efficient, because of its scale and resolution. It would consume huge computing resources, too. But it was Frank's hope that it might yield deeper insights.

The UK census defines populations and their geographical place of residence down to the first four digits of their postcode. The detail is granular: who lives where and with whom; the relationships between them; their age, ethnicity, occupation, employment, job titles, hours worked. Even after it had been processed and anonymised, the data were there in enough detail to allow a high-resolution picture that helped to predict where everyone was and what they were doing, for most hours of any ordinary day.

Broadly, it worked like this: if the census suggested that you were a teacher in your thirties, in a given postcode region, it assumed that you probably worked in one of the handful of schools nearby, then randomly assigned you to one of those schools as your presumed place of work and calculated the distance between the two. That assumption isn't universally valid, of course. Some people commute absurdly long distances to work. But it was good enough for a first approximation.

From that, Frank's squad of data scientists could build estimates of where everyone lived, where they worked, studied or went to school, and use that statistical detail to infer how they might travel from one to the other: plane, train, automobile, and so on. Armed with that framework, the team could construct a kind of self-playing video game. One that would set up the population of England and move millions of simulated individuals through a working week, from one place to another, in one-hour time steps.

I thought, at first, that this model would have far too much detail and diversity in it to work. But it turns out that for most of our lives the vast majority of us are quite vanilla in our habits. Most of the time we're in our own homes. When we're not there, we are generally at school, in higher education or at work. And outside of that, when we're not shopping, we are almost exclusively in a pub, restaurant, cinema, gym or someone else's home. In a first approximation, these destinations capture the whereabouts and activities of most of the population, most of the time. And if you had a good estimate of that, then you could work out where people gathered throughout the day, how they mixed and in what numbers and, importantly, the ages of the people they were mixing with. From there – knowing something about how the virus passed from person to person – you could build a model of how infection spread at a granular level.

This gave us statistical probabilities, not certainties. And it was a model of the disease, not a re-enactment of real life. But it gave me a better appreciation of the challenges and limits of these disease-modelling tools; something that I could factor into my own estimates.

The Durham team would refine code during the day and upload it to the supercomputers overnight. The model took hours to run, and the code often had bugs and glitches and would grind to a halt somewhere along the way. So the students and researchers monitored its progress with extraordinary diligence and dedication, setting alarms to wake themselves up regularly through the night to make sure it hadn't crashed; correcting, resetting and rerunning it, if it had.

Delving into the algebra and the calculus became a kind of cathartic experience for me. Whenever I could, I would spend a couple of hours with them each morning. It was something of a balm to be able to switch my mind away from the horror of what was unfolding on the ground in the hospitals. I would learn about Latin hypercubes, random forests and Bayesian emulators; get my head around the scale of the computer required to run these models; laugh when they told me that the management at Durham University had got upset about the size of the electricity bill required to crank out their answers.

By the end of the summer Frank and the team had a model that could generate half-decent forecasts. They called their model JUNE, named after June Almeida, the Scottish scientist who first discovered the coronavirus – who picked that name because of the crown-like appearance it had under electron microscopy. Like all models, JUNE was far from perfect, but it worked well enough to give me a sense of the broad character of what was coming. The code for JUNE, and details of the model, were published in the Royal Society's *Open Science Journal*, and JUNE's outputs contributed to the estimates that I continued to serve up to the strategic-incident director's team.

When Frank and his group first started their work on JUNE, many in the community told them that it couldn't be done; that it was too computationally expensive, too complex to make useful predictions. But as the pandemic wore on, and as new variants arrived – alongside vaccines, and people who seemed to gain only ephemeral immune protection from infection – that detail became more important. JUNE endured and continued to be useful throughout the pandemic.

Later it would be applied and adopted by several countries and organisations: first by the UN High Commission for Refugees, to model outbreaks in their densely populated refugee camps; later by the New Zealand government as a core pandemic-preparedness tool. Today it forms part of the UK's armamentarium of pandemic-preparedness assets – a lasting testament to the Herculean efforts of a small team of particle physicists, cosmologists, mathematicians and data scientists who gave themselves over completely to the pandemic.

By October 2020 the Durham model was in agreement with the published outputs of the SPI-M group. As Covid began to envelop the whole country, it looked increasingly likely that we would see a peak in hospital admissions that would far outstrip what we'd seen in the spring. The clinical teams needed less nuance and detail than their senior leadership and politicians. What they wanted to know was whether things were going to be bad or worse, so that they could steel themselves and their teams accordingly; so that they could find ways to try and give their teams whatever respite they could ahead of the crescendo.

For the clinicians, the existing estimates – if they could be trusted – told them enough. The first wave brought a surge of patients across the country, larger than we had ever had to deal with before. Covid had already killed more people in the UK than the Blitz in the Second World War. By the end of October almost all the modelling told us that what was coming was going to be substantially worse. By early November the frontline teams already had a sense of the terrible momentum that was building. One morning a text popped up on my phone, from a consultant colleague working in intensive care.

'On a scale of 1 to 10, how f**ked is my Christmas?' he asked.

'Very,' I replied.

19.

Closing the gap

All organisations face the same fundamental problem. How do the people sitting in offices at a strategic level, staring at reports and Excel spreadsheets, know what's actually happening down on the shop floor? And if you're about to descend into crisis, how can you be sure that you're seeing and hearing the right things?

We have come to fetishise data in recent years. We talk of Big Data, and we digest bar charts and graphs. We love a good dashboard – it gives us a sense that we're measuring something meaningful. And lately we've begun to imagine Artificial Intelligence as an engine that will magically turn those raw numbers into money and solutions.

Early in the pandemic, at the headquarters of NHS England, I ran into a clever doctor who had left the NHS many years before and had gone to work for one of the big tech firms. He was wandering around, looking a little dazed, having been called in by the higher-ups to see how digital innovation might contribute to the response. I beckoned him over, asking him how it had gone. Looking weary, he slumped in one of the chairs, head lolling back, eyes to the ceiling. 'If one more politician asks me how AI is going to get us out of this mess, I'm gonna scream!'

We were swimming in graphs and tables of numbers that, between them, summarised what we knew about the state of the hospitals and how well they were coping. There was, at that time, no better lens. But data is not the same as information; and information is not the same as insight.

The data were broadly reassuring: on paper, we appeared to be well within capacity and, for the most part, coping. But that wasn't what the hospitals were telling us. From the office at NHS England, I rang around the hospitals that were getting hit earliest and hardest until one Sunday morning, late in March 2020, while on the phone to one of my friends whose hospital had just declared a major incident, I asked him how they were doing. He sighed deeply and told me that he could try and put it into words, but that it would be better if I just came and saw it for myself.

I drove there the same day. With London truly deserted, it took half the normal time to cover the distance. I pulled up in a nearly empty hospital car park. The intensive-care registrar on duty greeted me at the hospital entrance and led me down a long corridor. As we walked, I noticed panels that whined incessantly, with flashing icons warning that the oxygen supply was nearly exhausted.

Until Covid few of us on the clinical side had ever thought too hard about where the oxygen in our hospitals came from; to us, it was like the water that runs from the tap in your kitchen – you never ask the question until it is suddenly not there. Even under ordinary conditions, large hospitals can use millions of litres of oxygen each day. During Covid, with a deluge of emergency admissions all suffering from severe pneumonia, that requirement increased sharply. It had never occurred to us that a hospital might simply run out of oxygen.

We arrived at the first of the areas they had hastily adapted to create more space for critically ill patients. I donned my PPE and squeezed through their makeshift airlock: sheets of clear plastic, with duct tape and a zip down the middle. Dozens of staff scurried back and forth between beds. It was calm enough, but there was a cacophony nevertheless: ventilators clicking and hissing as they shuttled oxygen back and forth, monitors chirping, alarms sounding, the staff raising their voices to be heard above it all. This was the work of caring for people while at the same time trying to hold a system together. This was the Health Service's *milieu intérieur*, struggling to achieve homeostasis.

They had already reconfigured their operating-theatre recovery areas to hold Covid patients. Here, where they would ordinarily have held people serenely emerging from their anaesthesia after surgery, was a makeshift extra intensive-care unit. There were thirty-six bed spaces, spread over two floors, and all of them were now full, as was their main ICU. I found a nurse squeezing between two beds, packed so close together that neighbouring patients could have held hands.

The narrow channels around the beds were crammed full of the paraphernalia that goes with intensive care: ventilators, dialysis machines and hanging fluids, with arrays of syringe pumps whose lights winked on and off like a forest of Christmas trees. I did my best to introduce myself – my voice muffled through the PPE. The nurse frowned at me, too busy really to stop for long. I asked her how things were, and how she was coping. She spread her hands widely, gesturing at the four patients in her care, all of them unconscious and on ventilators, all of them dying, as far as anyone could tell. 'What do you think?' she said.

'They're setting up a field-hospital facility in Excel London, the exhibition centre in Docklands,' I said, 'to bring all of these patients together. How would you feel about going there, if you were asked?'

There was a flash of fury at the suggestion, her eyes watering as she replied, 'I can hardly do this here, in a place that I know, with people that I know. How do they expect us to go there – to be with strangers and even more patients?'

As the first intensive-care units became overrun in hospitals across the country, we wanted to believe that they were exceptional in some way. Perhaps they had made some fundamental error that led to their unexpected compromise? Perhaps the same would not happen everywhere else. But none of that was true; and, deep down, we knew it. These were people doing the best they could with what they had, facing a scenario in which everything they could think of to do, everything they could muster as a team, still wasn't enough.

Outside a pandemic, there are days when any hospital might experience a sudden and unexpected increase in demand and activity. Those shifts are hard, but the surge eventually abates, over hours or days. Covid was different. The surge came in wave after wave, unremitting and unforgiving. 'It is like a terrorist attack every day,' said the registrar who led me around that first hospital, 'but with Covid you don't know when the attacks are going to stop.'

Large organisations need many tiers of leadership to regulate, coordinate and steer the business. More still to set strategy and make progress. But when trying to gather data to monitor the true state of the operation, those layers act like a fine filter. Much of what is essential gets through, but important detail is lost.

Part of the problem of managing a crisis of any scale is about how you – as an organisation or a team – attend to the detail, in real time, and how you monitor the state of your operation with enough sensitivity to be sure that you are working with the right information. Organisations approaching a state of chaos live and die on the quality of their feedback loops. If you're not sensing the right things, if you're not processing or acting upon the right information or insight, if those feedback loops are compromised, then, as we have seen, you risk catastrophe.

What you sense, how you sense it and how you deliver effect at scale become fundamentally important here. When the rhythm of the operation alters, when the tempo becomes brisk, you need specific strategies and mechanisms to help you do that well, and you need to shift your overall concept of operations to something different.

During Covid the reports that we got directly from the frontline teams were brutal. In the worst-hit hospitals, supplies of everyday essentials ran dry. There was no space to accommodate the waves of critically ill patients arriving, no drugs or equipment with which to treat them and too few staff to cover it all.

Routine work was suspended, staff were recalled and resuscitation trolleys that ordinarily stood sealed at the end of the ward, reserved only for cases of cardiac arrest, had to be broken into and raided for basic items. All the usual trades were here: certainty for time; time for risk; necessary deviations from the norm to avoid something much worse. Only now they were happening at an industrial scale.

On paper, the NHS shouldn't have been able to meet the surge in demand that came with Covid. It was never designed to face down a crisis on the scale of a pandemic and hadn't at any point in its history been properly equipped to do so. Worse still, it looked monolithic in structure: a single organisation of 1.5 million people, not known for its dexterity. And yet in March 2020 it was being forced to pivot hard; a lumbering cruise ship suddenly trying to swing quickly around a marker buoy. For the senior leadership teams there was the broad realisation that their usual strategies at the usual cadence couldn't work. There was a conscious and useful shift away from the inertia of command and control, towards agility and localism.

Authority was delegated; expertise was deferred to, wherever it lay in the system: ICU doctors pored over floor plans, remodelling and expanding their ward spaces; nursing teams restructured their workforces – fielding the pain of stretching them well beyond their usual limits. When supplies of medications ran short, pharmacists found new ways to deliver the same treatments with novel pharmaceutical cocktails. Meanwhile hospital estates teams pulled up floors to rewire and replumb the infrastructure, making sure that we could power and supply the solutions that the clinicians were inventing.

We don't often think about the full spectrum of skills or people it takes to deliver modern healthcare. But during Covid all of us were out of the woodwork, delivering this transformation: physiotherapists, radiographers, occupational therapists, hospital porters – all the way to the people who fed us, mopped up the carnage and reset the wards each day, so that we were ready to go again. We worked harder, we worked longer, we worked smarter. This is what it means to have an organisation innovate with every fibre of its being.

These responses would be recognisable to any student of High Reliability Organisation theory: the appropriate adaptations of a complex, time-pressured system; one with the capacity for catastrophic failure, one now struggling, but continuing to contain the threat day by day and somehow finding resilience. Amid crisis, most of the required adaptation happens at the sharp end in real time. Skilful, confident leadership recognises this necessary pivot and delegation. Within the NHS, senior managers largely got out of the way, shifting from command to facilitation. And through this the frontline teams were able to take their cruise ship apart and transform it into a fleet of racing yachts.

This strategy is essential when dealing with uncertainty of this magnitude: delegation of authority at scale, in a way that empowers the frontline human expertise to absorb the shocks from the unexpected crisis at hand. This is what the final few minutes of *Apollo 11*'s lunar landing illustrated for us so clearly: the delegation of decision-making to the experts, and the trust invested in junior teams and individuals.

In biological systems, when reaction is needed at scale, we find structures that increase the surface area available for contact. Your lungs, for example, move air back and forth, allowing the blood circulating through and around them to exchange carbon dioxide for oxygen. The lungs sit in your chest like an upside-down cone, about one foot tall and around half that width at their midpoint. If they were just a smooth balloon that simply inflated and deflated, the lungs would have an internal surface area of no more than ten to twenty square feet; nowhere near sufficient to absorb enough oxygen, and shed enough carbon dioxide, to keep you alive.

But the airways in your lungs divide like the trunk, branches and twigs of a tree, budding eventually into half a billion microscopic air sacs, called alveoli, around which blood runs in capillaries and into which the air that you breathe flows. You may have a dim recollection of your biology teacher at school telling you that if you unfurled all of those alveoli and laid them out on the floor, you'd have a mat with an area equivalent to half a tennis court: a design that enables the lungs to do something at a scale and rate that they couldn't, if they were a simpler structure.

That's why the approach of delegating authority is so powerful, because it takes your team or organisation and increases the surface area that is available to create effect; multiplying the response, allowing you to keep pace with a threat that would otherwise accelerate away from you. But this has to be accompanied by a shift in emphasis that needs some attention of its own.

Let's briefly revisit *Apollo*'s 'Low Gate', the point in the mission where the uncertainty, pace of change and scale of threat push you off your predetermined path and force you to innovate; one that shifts the balance in the system away from your carefully laid plans and towards something new. For Armstrong and Aldrin, that happened at 500 feet above the surface of the Moon, rendering the data, algorithms and readouts from their guidance computer suddenly less important than what the crew could see of the landscape unfolding immediately before them.

The Low Gate is a useful concept. It describes an imaginary point in space or time, a threshold which, once crossed, marks a change in the trajectory of your team or organisation: a shift away from reliance on distantly designed technical processes and towards the actions and decisions of the people wrestling with reality – those sitting closest to the threat. As a leader, it's important to recognise when you have passed through the Low Gate. Here you are no longer the main character in this drama; it is no longer all about you – if it ever was. You have to let go. And that takes courage. It's why it's important to be practised in that art in your everyday work.

It is why I found my time with the HEMS teams so valuable. They operate constantly within sight of the Low Gate and are so often thrust through it, by everything from hazards in flight and the lurking chaos of the accident scene, to life-threatening injuries and the complexities of their patients' collapsing physiologies. So often they find themselves on the other side of the looking glass, the place where rules have to bend, and sometimes shatter.

As we have learned, when faced with this type of crisis, our apparently superhuman feats are not down to human endeavour alone. They are instead a product of complex sociotechnical systems, the best of which have evolved over time; a product of data, intelligence and experience.

Within these systems, feedback loops provide stability, allowing us to colonise the edge of chaos, and providing the opportunity to engage productively with the unknown. This keeps the system intact, enabling it to continue to be greater than the sum of its parts. But as we have also learned, the more complex the task, and the more uncertain the threat, the earlier those systems are forced to lean on the unique capacities of the humans in the loop of control, the teams they form and the capacity for real-time adaptation that they bring.

Beyond the Low Gate, the partnership between people and technology continues to be important; the technical elements, the automation, the procedures and protocols still form the basis of the platform from which you launch your improvisation. But the balance between the technical and social elements of your system shifts. As we have seen across multiple fields, the capacity to adapt in real time is a product of the people in the system, rather than of their technologies. That social layer exists to deal with scenarios that we couldn't imagine, or failed to prepare for. And during Covid there was a sudden glut of both.

In 2016, four years before the arrival of Covid-19, the UK government had run its own pandemic-preparedness simulation, 'Exercise Cygnus'. It lasted for three days, played through an imagined influenza pandemic and involved nearly a thousand people across government.

Cygnus demonstrated conclusively that the NHS lacked the capacity necessary to deal with a pandemic surge, that our stockpiles were insufficient, that services would quickly reach breaking point and that we would run out of essential equipment and supplies, among them PPE, ventilators and body bags. There was no comprehensive follow-up, and what little there was failed to effectively address the shortcomings unmasked by the exercise. Its predictions, nevertheless, came true.

In the spring of 2020, during the first few weeks of the pandemic, we quickly ran out of properly equipped ICU beds and ventilators.

We closed operating theatres and used the machines there to try to bridge the gap, drawing on the expertise of anaesthetic teams to staff them. But the ventilators that we use during surgery aren't designed to support patients for days at a time; nor were they well suited to support diseased lungs whose gossamer tissues had thickened and consolidated. Their mechanisms would struggle and perpetually alarm. All too frequently their breathing circuits would block, leaving the anaesthetists managing failing physiology with failing equipment.

Short of PPE – of masks that could filter droplets and aerosols laden with virus, of visors and gowns – even as the first patients arrived in our hospitals, teams went to work in swimming goggles and waterproof smocks bought from camping shops, while elsewhere they made do with bin liners and visors fabricated by school workshops. In places the supply of body bags ran out. Nurses described their trauma at having to use nine-foot-long clear plastic sacks, sealed with cable ties, instead.

By October 2020 there had been more than 40,000 deaths from Covid in the UK, accompanied by many tens of thousands of admissions to hospitals across the country. Covid had shoved the NHS through the Low Gate, suddenly and completely. And yet, despite the shortages and the insufficiencies, the staff somehow kept everything running. They made do, perpetually stretching and modifying. We leaned on them hard, and for too long. Adrenaline had kept them going through the first wave, but when Covid returned in the autumn, things were different. By then we had made our modifications, rehearsed our responses; we knew how to stretch our resources. We got better at what we did, found ways to treat this new disease, learned how to save more lives while we held on, and hoped beyond hope that a vaccine might soon materialise. But by mid-autumn a new Covid variant was circulating, one that transmitted more efficiently from person to person. And the frontline teams began to ask themselves new questions. 'How long can we keep going like this? How long can we last?'

That assessment – the question of when the assumed capacity

of the NHS might be breached – was far from straightforward to answer. We had a good handle on the contents of our warehouses, our stock levels, on bed numbers and occupancies. We could plot rates of infection, hospitalisation and death. But we didn't have a true sense of how the staff were in all of this, or how much they had left to give. And so here, firmly on the other side of the Low Gate, the element that we needed to measure the most was something we couldn't count.

20.
Ground truth

Sociologist William Bruce Cameron once wrote on the limits of what can be gleaned from numbers alone. As far back as 1963, at the dawn of the digital technology revolution, he was keen to dampen enthusiasm for the idea that society's most complex problems could be solved simply by pouring data into IBM computers and drawing charts. 'Not everything that can be counted counts,' he wrote, 'and not everything that counts can be counted.'

Beyond the Low Gate the system is held together largely by the rapid adjustment and readjustment carried out by human teams. At this point, now so dependent on people for survival and success, understanding where *their* limits lie becomes centrally important in the strategic leadership of a crisis and the quality of the response.

It was hard for people to imagine the NHS in a state of collapse. Some wanted to believe it could never happen, that those who delivered the care would continue to do what they always did: throw themselves into the growing gap between demand and supply and get the job done. An organisation like the NHS doesn't fail like a nuclear reactor or a rocket ship might. There is no explosive event, no billowing clouds or raining debris. But it can fail nevertheless, quietly and every bit as lethally.

For the NHS during Covid there were many ways of measuring the success, failure and depletion of critically important tech: ventilators, PPE, medication, body bags, beds and more. But there was, I realised, no feedback loop monitoring *the well-being of the staff*, no sensors to track how they were doing, no effector that might restore them to where they needed to be.

My team of resident doctors at NHS England set about trying to address this. At first we pushed out mental-health surveys to staff working on intensive-care units. The questionnaires were brief, designed so that people who were exhausted at the end of a shift might still find the time to fill them in. They included a standardised scoring system that provided a first, coarse measurement of how the teams were doing.

Thousands of staff responded. Among them, around two-thirds met the criteria for probable Post-Traumatic Stress Disorder (PTSD), moderate or severe depression, anxiety or a harmful use of alcohol. The PTSD scores were particularly worrying, comparable in scale to those seen in British military personnel who had been deployed in combat roles during the war in Afghanistan.

We tracked the trends over time. The larger the surge in Covid cases, the worse the staff's mental health. And while none of that should come as a particular surprise, we had until that point lacked the means to describe it or its severity in any detail; as though we had been hurtling down a motorway in a car without a fuel gauge, trying to guess how much petrol might be left in the tank.

It was evidence of how close to the wire the service was running, and how hard we were pushing the teams. And with these high levels of poor mental health came impaired performance in professional tasks. About three-quarters of the people who worked in intensive care reported being unable to perform their daily duties to the best of their ability, because of how they felt. We weren't tapping an infinite reservoir. The stretch came at a terrible cost. Our concerns for the welfare of the frontline teams were born substantially of our sense of duty to them and their protection. But the work came hand in hand with a hard truth: if we didn't care for our carers, they wouldn't be able to care for their patients.

We took these findings and folded them into our reports and estimates, adding them to the threat assessment. But these statistics featured only as scattered lines in briefing documents; we needed more and better information than that to get a complete picture. And that meant – finally – paying better attention to all the things we couldn't count.

*

In the autumn of 2020 I started to take small teams of clinicians into some of the hardest-hit hospitals in the country. For obvious reasons, we had relied heavily and almost exclusively on video conferencing as a means of communication throughout the pandemic. But this came at a price, disconnecting us from the people who were delivering the care.

It took more than a little effort to win the trust of the people we went to see; we could feel the shields go up as we entered the hospitals. We were, in their view, a team put together by NHS England in London; we were distant, people to be suspicious of and possibly to be feared. They had learned through hard experience that visits of this kind, when you were in deep crisis, didn't always go well. And because of that, I was careful about how we ran the programme. If you wanted to circulate among people who were at full stretch, trying to deliver care under extraordinary conditions, then it should feel like neither a royal visit nor the Spanish Inquisition.

Visits that were designed to be casual and informal took careful choreography. Wherever possible, each outbound team was drawn from a hospital of similar size to the one we were visiting. I didn't want this to feel high-handed. We weren't there to judge, to lend superior advice or guidance or to give the false hope of miracle solutions. We were there to share experiences, to reflect and – through that – to support.

The teams comprised a gaggle of clinicians, in jeans and jumpers, arriving without a fixed agenda – deliberately so. We were peers talking to peers. The people I brought with me had to be credible: teams who had faced what our hosts themselves faced, who had felt the fear that they felt and had done what they did; people to whom they might open up. Wherever we went, we made a point of changing into PPE and getting onto the hospital floor to see the set-up ourselves, snatching conversations where and when we could – all in an effort to get the clearest and most accurate impression possible.

On some of our visits we took military medical personnel with us. They had a name for this: they called it 'battlefield circulation' – a way of short-circuiting the flow of information from the frontline to the senior strategic tier. And they had a name, too, for what you saw but couldn't easily put into words. These were the 'atmospherics', the intangibles, the sense you got from being in the room: the eye contact, the hubbub, the feeling of energy or weariness, and a thousand other things besides.

In Iraq during the war of 2003, General Stanley McChrystal, best known for his leadership of the United States' Joint Special Operations Command there, and later commander of the UN's International Security Assistance Force, made 'battlefield circulation' a central part of how he led his troops. To understand better the experience of soldiers on the frontline, he believed that you had to see it for yourself.

For McChrystal, it was about making sure that he knew what was really happening, rather than relying on the reports that flowed up the chain. He wanted troops of any rank to be able to talk to him, honestly and frankly, about what needed to be done, what was missing and what the frontline teams thought he might be getting wrong at a strategic level. They had to do that without fear for their careers or their status. Psychological safety has its place, even in a warzone.

It is hard for a four-star general to visit a forward operating base and feel like 'one of the guys' – probably impossible. But McChrystal would make the effort and spend the time nevertheless. It was important for him that the visits felt more than cursory. 'If you ask the question, you have to stay around long enough to hear the answer,' he once wrote. And I felt much the same.

After a walk-around and a tour of the hospital, we would retire to seminar rooms and be available to talk to anyone who wanted to speak to us over coffee and tea and tins of biscuits. We carved out the best part of a whole day for each visit, something that often puzzled our hosts, who always wondered how we would possibly fill the time. But from the start we had learned that once you sat down together with people who had seen the same awful things on opposite sides of the country, once people started talking, comparing and sharing experiences, it didn't stop. There was always more to say than could be said, more to learn than we had time for.

It's hard even now to write about what we were told in those meetings. Retelling it, thinking about it, is a little like feeding pruned branches into a wood-chipper: you worry that if you push too hard it might also drag you in, chop you up and spit you out.

We visited more than fifty hospitals and units in total; spent hundreds of hours talking to hospital staff of all kinds. There is too much to tell here; too many haunting atmospherics. It takes great effort to capture experience properly, to process it, to report it accurately and in a way that does justice to the people who shared with you in good faith; but you have to try.

This, in part, is why it took so long for us to evaluate the human-experience part of the pandemic response, even though it was all essential to meeting the surge. It wasn't blind oversight. Initially we counted what we could count most easily: stuff rather than staff. And early in the pandemic, as a first estimate of the adequacy of our response, that was perhaps just about good enough. But in late autumn 2020 – with pressure still building – we had reached a point of transition where stuff wasn't the most important thing to pay attention to any more.

In high-performance systems we inspect and check our critical equipment daily. On the HEMS teams, the pilots crawl over their aircraft with torches peering under engine cowlings, while we methodically examine the contents of our medical bags, check batteries, make sure everything is where it should be and is functioning.

We do that right down to the least significant bit of kit. Even our handheld medical suction unit – a little portable vacuum that we use to hoover up secretions and blood – gets carefully checked. We make sure it can generate sufficient power and has enough battery left, so that when we reach for it in a tight moment, we know it will be there and it will work. But these are equipment checks: the technical side of the system. And if the key to dealing with complex crises is webs of people and things, then the question we must ask is: who, precisely, is running those checks on the humans in the loop?

Covid was hard – the hardest thing I've ever done. It was hard every day, for more than two years. Don't ever let anyone tell you otherwise. It's difficult to convey the full horror of what the clinical teams went through. We toured the country in empty trains, wearing FFP3 masks, going wherever we were invited. Our hosts and visiting teams shared their experiences: what they had learned, what they had gained, what had hurt them. They compared and swapped notes on what worked and what didn't. They always seemed relieved to know that someone, somewhere else, was going through the same experiences they were.

There is so much that sticks out from the accounts we heard: the theatre staff who talked about watching the bodies roll out on trolleys at night, one after another, like rail carriages; the consultant working in a hospital without enough onsite accommodation, who took to sleeping in the boot of his Ford Galaxy; the nurse who talked about the terror that came with the start of each shift, and who found herself vomiting on the way into work, out of fear for what the day might bring; the ICU matron who told us about the day that ten of their patients died, among them two members of her own hospital staff.

For ICU teams, death and dying has always been part of the job. But during Covid it came in waves, and at a scale none of them had ever seen before. 'I just got tired of putting people in body bags,' one of the junior nurses told me. Care at the end of a patient's life is something that people who work in ICUs pride themselves on; what they do doesn't stop just because there is no rescue to be had. Being able to help those gathered around the bed, knowing when to be there for them and when the time has come to excuse yourself and give them some privacy, is an important last act of care and service.

But every unit we visited talked of how difficult that became during the pandemic. With no visitors allowed, nurses found themselves using mobile phones and tablets to talk with their patients' loved ones; breaking the news that this was now the end, turning their cameras so that families and friends could say their last goodbyes. It was important, and the best they could do. But it left them a constant witness to a family's grief, having to listen to the tears and the anguish, unable to escape it.

And it wasn't just the clinical staff. The operational managers took a beating, too. As the surge in Covid reached its peak in the winter, one hospital ran so short of nurses and healthcare assistants on the wards that it had to redeploy its corporate staff – finance managers, HR teams, information officers – to help feed and wash patients. I sat in an office with a chief operating officer in tears. 'It hurts them, to do the things we ask them to do,' he said, 'it hurts to have to ask them to do it.'

It was the smaller hospitals that were hardest hit; these tended to be located in more deprived neighbourhoods, serving populations who were more vulnerable to Covid and its complications. In 1971, in a paper for *The Lancet*, Welsh GP Julian Tudor Hart introduced the concept of the 'Inverse Care Law'. 'The availability of good medical care tends to vary inversely with the need for it in the population served,' he wrote. Which is to say that healthcare systems too often set themselves up so that wherever the care is most needed is where the resources are least likely to be. Covid, and the way it found the vulnerabilities in our healthcare system, proved Tudor Hart all too correct, and at a devastating scale.

To relieve pressure on the smaller units, surrounding hospitals would send critical-care retrieval teams to collect some of their intensive-care patients and transfer them to their less-pressured wards, helping them free up space. We called this 'decompression'. It was just about all we could do to support hospitals that were in trouble. But it had its own unintended consequences. The portable battery-powered equipment that we use in the back of ambulances isn't as capable as the larger power-hungry kit that plugs into the wall on the wards. This meant that only the most stable intensive-care patients could tolerate the journey and be safely transferred. And so, after a decompression, the unit would be left with only their sickest and most unstable patients: those least likely to survive.

Staff at a small district general hospital that we visited told us that, in the weeks after a rash of transfers to keep their heads above water, almost every single patient left in their care went on to die. 'You would see three, maybe four patients die each day. Three was normal,' their nurses told us. 'You would hand over and go home, come back the next morning and the person you had been looking after would be gone.'

I had underestimated how isolated staff at some of these hospitals felt, how disconnected from the rest of the vast NHS system they felt. Operating as they had been at that time – in an information vacuum – they couldn't be sure of what was happening to them, or why. And worse still, with so many deaths, they couldn't help but wonder if perhaps some of it might be their fault.

On a visit to one of these hospitals we spent so long talking that we nearly missed our train home. Everyone had wanted to say their piece, and we had wanted to hear them. We said our farewells and hurriedly made for the door. As I was gathering my notes and papers, I wondered what to say to the ICU matron who had led them through those terrible weeks. It felt like there should be more than a simple 'goodbye'. There was no easy fix for what they had already faced, or what still lay ahead. I had so little to bring by way of support, beyond the information we had shared, and I began to wonder if we had done them any good at all by being there.

But while I was fumbling for something other than a platitude, the ICU matron turned to us and said, with an audible sigh of relief, 'Thank you for coming. We thought we were alone. We thought we were doing it wrong.'

21.

Resilience

In the wake of the terrorist attack on the Ariana Grande concert at Manchester Arena in 2017, a post-incident debrief was held, for all the agencies directly involved in the response. Dozens of people sat in rows, in front of a lectern and projector screen in a darkened seminar room, listening to the different perspectives of their colleagues recounting how events had unfolded. I had been invited to attend as an outside observer, to try to build on what we knew from other major incidents and look for the common threads.

Major incidents are by definition difficult for all, but the attack on this event, attended by families and young children, had been unusually so. There had been hundreds of casualties. Twenty people died at the scene, ten of whom were teenagers; three more in hospital; twenty-two adults and six children were admitted to intensive care.

These debriefs happen after every major incident; a scaled-up version of the 'Death and Disability' meetings that we run with our HEMS teams to review our most difficult cases. They have the same purpose: to give the teams a chance to make sense of what happened to them and the people in their care; and to help them – and their organisations – learn so that they may better armour themselves against disasters in the future.

Most of it was technical in character, a presentation of facts and figures, times and actions, injuries and hospital admissions; an unpacking of the incident with the acknowledged benefit of hindsight, in search of lessons to be identified and learned. But part of it, too, was about the people in the room who had been present at the scene; an acknowledgement that this attack was unlike anything they had ever encountered before.

Late in the morning a pair of psychiatrists specialising in PTSD took to the stand. This session focused on the needs of the first responders – a chance for the teams to reflect on their own experience and how they might have been affected, and a signposting of the symptoms to watch out for, as well the services that were available for them to access, should it be necessary.

There was reassurance that, while they should expect events like these to be deeply affecting, the vast majority of them would recover without any further action being required. And that their day-to-day coping strategies – of confiding in colleagues, friends and family – were very often more than good enough to see them through. But there was a reminder, too, that experience varies from person to person and that you don't have to manage it alone. The psychiatrists' work with military veterans from the wars in Afghanistan and Iraq had shown the value of supporting the mental health of the frontline teams, both during and after traumatic incidents.

The British military had taken the psychological well-being of their personnel seriously. As a result, the median time for service personnel presenting with PTSD, after leaving military service, had fallen dramatically, from nearly fourteen years to just over two; a reflection of the investment that the service had made in monitoring their workforce more closely and raising awareness. They were now seeing people earlier, with a better chance of preventing many of the consequences of problems that had gone undiagnosed and untreated for too long.

At the end of the presentation there was a call for any questions. The room went quiet and the teams shuffled a little uncomfortably in their seats. If you spend your life caring for others, it is a peculiar thing to pause and consider what your experience might be doing to you. After a long pause a single hand went up. 'If some people take fourteen years to present with PTSD,' the paramedic asked, 'how can any of us sitting here be sure that we're actually OK?'

I have heard a version of that same question asked by practitioners in every part of medicine that I've worked in. 'Are we just storing it all up?' 'Are we really OK?' 'If I'm still here after all this time, carrying on regardless, what does it say about me?' We wonder if everything we do and everything we see wears us down over time, makes us somehow harder and shallower.

Until recently there was a vogue in the NHS for sending people on resilience training courses, as though the answer to all your worries was to go to the pharmacy, get a prescription of concrete dust, take two spoonfuls before bed and hope you harden up by the morning. This, of course, is not the answer. It mischaracterises resilience and puts the focus on the individual and their personal fortitude, rather than understanding it as a property of the system as a whole. When it comes to the human teams, it is important to understand precisely what resilience is and what we can do to bolster it; important because the limits of capacity of our high-performance sociotechnical organisations are so dependent upon it. And after spending some time researching the concept of resilience, I came to understand it as something very different from what I – and, I think, most of us – had assumed.

All systems have finite capacity. It seems odd to have to say that, but well-configured organisations and teams can render the illusion of near-infinite adaptability. For good systems, which ordinarily exhibit high levels of reliability and performance, the idea that 'they'll cope somehow, because they always do' is all too familiar. For a system like the NHS that marches through successive winters, tackling the crises that each one brings, and that shrugs off everything from cyber-attacks to terrorist bombings, apparently without collapsing, it is tempting to believe its reserve might be limitless.

But at a strategic level, it's important to know – in some detail – what the limits of that finite capacity are. As we've shown, these systems are remarkably capable and robust up until a point, but fragile thereafter. Failure occurs gradually, and then all of a sudden. Knowing where the limits of the system lie helps us better understand how to extend that capacity and how to protect it when failure looms.

From studying other major incidents, we had learned that accommodating even small surges of critically ill patients within the NHS was a challenge. To cope with – and provide the best care possible to – as many patients as possible, hospitals trigger major-incident action plans: recalling staff, extending shifts, stopping routine work to free up additional capacity, and so on. After a major-incident surge involving dozens of critically ill patients it takes days, and sometimes weeks, for hospitals to recover and return the service to normal. This takes a toll on everyone involved.

In the first eighteen months of the Covid-19 pandemic intensive-care units across the country admitted more than 37,000 critically ill patients, alongside many tens of thousands of seriously ill patients being treated in respiratory units and on the general wards. The mathematics of these surges, and our capacity to absorb them, followed the pattern of other more conventional major incidents. But previous major incidents tended to be isolated events – traumatic and destabilising, yes, but with a time limit. In every crisis there would be a point at which practice could return to normal. Until Covid we hadn't ever probed the limits of that capacity. And what the mathematical models told us was this: the system would flex and adapt and find ways to cope, until it didn't.

We know now that high-performance systems are a complex blend of people and technology. The technical element – the buildings and vehicles you operate from, the stock in your warehouse, the SOPs and guidelines you have crafted – tend to be where senior leadership focuses its attention. But in the face of uncertainty, the social dimension – the people delivering the work and the care – become the system's principal asset in reshaping and adapting a response that is no longer fit for purpose. And so looking after the people in your system is about something more than compassionate leadership. It becomes an operational imperative: your best chance of preserving and developing your adaptive capacity.

During the early days of the Covid response I had looked up Professor Neil Greenberg, who worked as a psychiatrist at King's College Hospital and who had spent his life studying how to look after teams in the midst of traumatic events.

I'd known Neil for many years. Bespectacled, jocular and calm, he was the textbook image of a professor of psychiatry. But beyond that first meeting, Neil confounded all other expectations. Enlisting in the Royal Navy while at medical school, he had later qualified and served as a submariner, completed the Royal Marine Commando course and earned their coveted green beret. I'd always imagined military psychiatrists sitting in comfy chairs in softly lit offices, not crammed into bunks aboard hunter-killer subs or crawling around in the mud, but that was how Neil had spent much of his military career.

He had deployed to Iraq in 2009 to assess and study troops fighting on the frontline. The focus of his work wasn't solely about protecting mental health. For Neil, it was also about how to optimise team performance while the troops were deployed. 'You want service personnel to be psychologically fit when they're at war,' he said. 'You want them to do their job well, which means they need to be psychologically healthy.'

Neil realised that he had to collect data in the field in order to study the soldiers properly, so he took his team of researchers into Forward Operating Bases (FOBs) and Patrol Bases in Iraq. He asked troops who were in the midst of combat deployments to complete mental-health surveys, screening them for signs of common mental-health disorders. Participation was voluntary, but it helped that Neil had made the effort to be where they were: at war.

The FOBs were semi-permanent military bases, acting as logistic and command hubs, supporting several hundred troops close to the fighting frontline. Patrol Bases, by contrast, were small, exposed frontline positions held by smaller numbers of troops, used to maintain presence, dominate the ground, launch foot-patrols and provide rest, resupply and planning space between operations. It was important to Neil to capture the information while the teams were in the midst of their operational tasks; he reasoned that if he wanted to find measures to protect their mental health, then he had to be there with them. 'We went everywhere the troops went,' he told me.

*

The idea of resilience training for individuals isn't entirely without merit. Resilience is a trait that varies between individuals and is something that can be fortified, to a degree. Furthermore, there's at least some evidence that repeated exposure to stress, so long as it's not too frequent or too severe, can be inoculating.

In a study of breast-cancer survivors, researchers found that those who had experienced adversity earlier in their lives – events such as bereavement, divorce, injury or serious illness – tended to have better mental-health outcomes after treatment than those who hadn't. There was a similar finding among military veterans when researchers looked at their risk of developing mental-health problems after deployment.

Intermittent stress, in your personal or professional life, in the right dose, with the opportunity to recover, appears to promote a degree of mental resilience – or 'steeling' as the researchers call it. In turn, this might protect you from mental-health problems, including PTSD. Indeed, it might open the door to something else: the possibility of post-traumatic growth, helping people to thrive under pressure and gain strength through adversity. And so, in theory at least, the ambulance crews and other first responders, sitting in that seminar room at the Manchester Arena bombing debrief, might well have been more able to cope than any ordinary member of the public watching from afar, because of the sum of their previous experiences.

But resilience is also a dynamic variable. It changes from moment to moment and from context to context. And it is in fact the shape of your life *outside* work that best predicts how you deal with additional stressors *at* work. The issues that catch you out unexpectedly often arise from an entanglement between the two.

Of all the cases I've ever had to deal with over the years, one that particularly sticks in my mind was that of a seriously ill nine-week-old who came into our emergency department with severe sepsis, at the time when my eldest son was exactly the same age. The little boy was rushed into our resuscitation bays by the ambulance crew. It was hard work, but after a flurry of activity he was soon out of danger and went on to recover completely.

That experience shouldn't have been remarkable for me; I've seen many things far worse, with worse outcomes. But the context of being in that resuscitation bay, trying to hold and care for a child who looked so much like my own – who felt and smelled the way he did, who wore the same nappies and wriggled in the same manner he did – caught me off-guard, to the point where, for a little while during our resuscitation, I found it difficult to do my job. A prime example of resilience coming and going with whatever the day serves up and wherever you are in your life.

This is the key question: in the face of potentially overwhelming challenge – the type of challenge that Covid-19 presented – what can be done to protect teams and individuals so that they can continue to do their job effectively, as their own resilience swings between highs and lows?

'Resilience,' said Neil Greenberg, 'is something that lies *between* people more than it lies within any individual.' What is true of the technical side of systems is also true of the social aspect. If the bonds and connections between people are properly formed – like those that we create through the rituals, briefings and coffee-room conversations in our HEMS teams – then the whole counts for more than the sum of its parts. Professor Greenberg's studies of the military in Afghanistan showed that the quality of relationships between members of any fighting unit, and the quality of their leadership, helped protect them from the consequences of the traumatic experiences they faced on the battlefield.

Neil explained to me that there were four leadership factors that made a critical difference to a team's resilience: first, if people felt that their leader genuinely cared for their welfare; second, if that leader treated each member of the unit equitably; third, if they didn't berate any individual in front of their peers; and the fourth element was perhaps the most important: a supportive leader was seen as someone able to have meaningful conversations about traumatic experiences and personal difficulties – someone in whom people could confide honestly and frankly.

This last point isn't simply about being an empathic and emotionally intelligent leader. Those qualities might help, but Neil believes that it is a skill that can be taught and learned; that people can learn to approach, in a sensitive but structured way, a colleague who may have experienced something troubling or traumatic. It is about beginning a conversation and, where necessary, having the confidence, skill and training to take it beyond the point where it would usually end.

'You ask someone how they're doing and they tell you they're "fine",' Neil said to me, 'and the conversation usually stops there, doesn't it? But they don't actually always mean that they are OK. Sometimes what they're trying to tell you is that they're F.I.N.E. – Fucked Up, Insecure, Neurotic and Emotionally unstable.'

One of the qualities of leadership that appears to help build resilience in a team is the ability to know the difference between 'fine' and 'F.I.N.E.' and to be able to get beyond that word when you're having conversations with your team about their well-being. Neil told me that some of their study data showed that troops who perceived themselves to be well led, with supportive senior officers, had rates of PTSD around ten times lower than those who felt unsupported. In these high-risk situations, a good leader can be transformative: not just in the moment, but for the life that the team leads long after they have left the service.

Deploying this insight in medical settings with teams of practitioners has been challenging in the past. Medical teams have historically been reluctant to reach out for help. They work within closed units and tightly knit teams, and while that sense of belonging is itself protective to a degree, it also tends to make it harder for them to solicit help from outside their ranks.

Neil Greenberg's early work looked at leaders and the quality of their leadership in a military context – structures with more clearly defined vertical hierarchies. But we have seen that in complex systems, leadership is a distributed property, and that during any task leadership is like a ball that passes from person to person according to their expertise and the demands of the moment. This opens up the possibility that you might empower and equip many members within a team to have better-quality conversations about mental health and to lead discussions and reinforce the resilience of the unit as whole. Here well-being becomes about something more than the relationship between a single identifiable leader and their subordinates, and instead becomes about *the quality of relationships between peers in a team*.

When transferring what he had learned from his time in the military to the civilian sphere, Neil and his colleagues developed structured programmes to help people have better conversations about well-being in the wake of traumatic events – training leaders and peers how to ask the right questions at the right time. Those conversations, between peers, were sometimes enough. But the training also taught teams to recognise the difference between 'fine' and 'F.I.N.E.' and how to direct their colleagues to get help, should they need it, lowering the traditional barriers to entry for psychological and psychiatric services.

This is not about offering counselling or clinical therapy; that is the domain of healthcare professionals. It is about empowering peers within a team to have better-quality conversations, in the wake of what might have been a troubling incident; about creating the conditions that destigmatise conversations about mental health, encouraging people to talk openly and being able to signpost the way to formal help, where needed.

It's important to say that this is not a panacea for PTSD or the protection of the mental health of operational teams. But for services like the military, police, fire service, doctors, nurses and indeed our own HEMS teams, who have traditionally eschewed this type of help and have in the past found it hard to engage with psychological services and therapies, it is a good first step; the beginning of a process.

Importantly, in Neil's approach, emotional resilience is a function of the connectivity between individuals in a team. It's why the events that happen outside the office – away-days, social events after work, Christmas parties, and the like – are so important to the fabric of an organisation; this is the glue that binds; this is how you foster the sense of belonging that protects; this is how a team develops the cohesion that helps them absorb the shocks and keep going.

So far we've departed from the idea of resilience as the fixed property of any individual, casting it instead as something that can be modified by experiences (past and present), the team that surrounds you and the quality of your connection with that team. But we can go further still and look at resilience as a property of the system as a whole. The design of the system, it turns out, can contribute to the resilience *of our human teams*.

When I first stumbled upon the theory of Resilience Engineering I felt as if the work spoke to my experience at the sharp end of medical practice in a way that few other organisational theories did; in part because of the breadth of experience among its key protagonists. It is a theory that extends the concept of resilience beyond individuals and the teams they work within, and considers it as a defining property of complex systems.

Erik Hollnagel, David Woods and Nancy Leveson published the first treatise on the subject in 2006. Hollnagel and Woods are psychologists by training, with a long history of studying and advising high-risk, high-performance industries: nuclear, aerospace and healthcare among them. David Woods served as an adviser to NASA's *Columbia* Accident Investigation, in the wake of the loss of the space shuttle during re-entry in 2003. Nancy Leveson was cut from a different cloth, with a background in mathematics, computer science and systems engineering. The trio were joined by Richard Cook, a former software engineer who went on to train as a doctor and specialise as an anaesthesiologist, and whose seminal work 'How Complex Systems Fail' laid much of the bedrock for the field.

Resilience Engineering built on existing concepts, notably High Reliability Organisation and Normal Accident theories. I think of them as close cousins, even though from time to time they are cast as sibling rivals.

But Resilience Engineering somehow managed to more accurately and completely describe the impossible moments that we, as operators and practitioners, faced every day. It recognised the greyness of the real world, and the realities of sharp-end practice. This theory inverts the usual approach to learning in safety-critical systems, which tends to focus only on what goes wrong: the calamities and catastrophes. It highlights that these events, though important, are generally rare. And while they should rightly be reviewed and investigated, there is at least as much value – if not more – in considering and learning from what goes right, all day, every day.

It puts a different lens, too, on the humans in the loop of control, pointing out that we tend to regard them as a weak link: a point of vulnerability, the reason why things sometimes go wrong; when in fact – for the overwhelming majority of the time – they are the principal reason that things go right. The NHS should have ground to a halt early in the pandemic, collapsing under the sheer volume of patients who suddenly arrived. That it didn't was a function of the inventiveness of the workforce and their ability to improvise.

In the Resilience Engineering framework, variability in performance isn't necessarily something that needs to be ironed out. Indeed, when working in real-time, complex, uncertain environments, variability in human performance is regarded as something of an asset precisely because it is what provides the platform for innovation, creativity and improvisation.

Resilience Engineering refers to this concept as the gap between Work as Done (WAD) versus Work as Imagined (WAI). As we have seen throughout this book, sooner or later that gap will become apparent. This is not because our managers and executives are terrible at what they do, but because it is impossible to imagine the infinite possibilities that exist in the real world and the ways in which they are able to confound even the best-laid plans. Good systems, and good leaders, focus on trying to narrow the gap between WAI and WAD. They do this by paying close attention to the work as it is actually practised and the people who deliver it, and constantly revising their policies, guidelines and expectations accordingly.

The field of Resilience Engineering asks us to regard plans as a *resource* rather than a script, and suggests that we should *expect* to part company with them. In short – when operating in the context of complexity and uncertainty – we should not be surprised by surprise.

Accordingly, the actions that a team takes after the onset of a surprise event are not some imperfect version of normal work or some scramble to regain composure. Those actions *are* the work: the work of continuous adjustment and perpetual adaptation to close the gap between our plans and reality. And in this context, humans in all their variability and inconsistency, their adaptability and nimbleness are the essential advantage. What makes a system able to deal with surprise – what makes it capable of absorbing the shocks – is that adaptive function.

It is why I love teams and the idea of teamwork, why I have such deep respect for the people who took a national healthcare system (one never designed or prepared to cope with the demands of a global pandemic) and between them transformed it into something fit for purpose. Given the state of the NHS in 2019, this should have been impossible.

Resilience Engineering is a branch of organisational theory that dedicates much of its spotlight to what happens after the first five minutes – after the plan has failed to survive. When I was wrestling with how to think about what happened to us in the UK during Covid, I turned to Professor David Woods to try and explore it from his perspective.

For David, the way healthcare systems were forced to respond to the unexpected challenges that every day of the pandemic brought is emblematic of the themes encapsulated in the theory of Resilience Engineering. In his casting, the resilience of a system is not a static property of that system. It is not merely the adequacy of the stores in our warehouses, or the supply of consumables. It is a measure of the system's ability to reshape itself, and the degree to which it can continue to do so in the face of a growing and ever-changing threat.

David and his team have come to define 'resilience' in systems teams as 'adaptive capacity'. In the wake of Covid it is, for me, a definition that rings clear and true. In our complex sociotechnical systems, technology provides a platform from which we can operate. But the humans provide the continuous adjustment, correction and iteration that enable us to make progress; it is from them that the adaptive capacity stems.

It is why our assessments of the capacity of a system like the NHS, in the face of surging pressure, need to take closer account of the system's principal asset: its staff. And why the resilience of the system is so closely married to the resilience of those human teams. My friend was right: in the darkest days of Covid we should have been counting something more than beds. It was never furniture that we were running out of; it was adaptive capacity.

Epilogue: Anatomy of hope

In early April 2020, from my office at NHS England, I rang a respected virologist, asking for her best guess on how soon a Covid vaccine might be ready. 'Yeah, we were talking about that around the lab this morning,' she told me, 'we think maybe a couple of years . . . maybe as many as four.' I recoiled in my seat at the news; whatever effort we, in the NHS, had left in us, it wasn't years.

But at the end of December that same year, less than nine months after that conversation, I sat in a hospital cubicle with my sleeve rolled up, ready to receive my first dose of the Pfizer mRNA-based vaccine. It was like watching the cavalry arrive. The development and deployment of effective Covid vaccines within months of the virus's first discovery will one day shine out in history as a scientific and technological marvel to rival *Apollo 11*'s first landing on the Moon. It was an innovation that rescued us all.

Over the past century, science, technology and engineering have, together, helped create outrageous expectations of life and survival. I have shown how our Helicopter Emergency Medical Service is one extreme example of that blend. But we have pushed at the boundaries of possibility everywhere in the field of medicine. So much that was routinely fatal when I qualified as a doctor nearly thirty years ago has become the stuff of routine survival today.

HIV, for example, which I once believed we would never find an effective treatment for, is now manageable, with near-normal life expectancy. Ten-year survival rates for people diagnosed with breast cancer have risen to nearly 80 per cent. More recently we have seen gene-editing offer the first hope to people with disabling and lethal inherited conditions.

When I started writing this book, I began with the opinion that there were no more heroes to be found; that the spectacular rescues we celebrated were almost entirely a product of technology woven into systems. We are so fortunate to live in a time when our vehicles are so stable and reliable, our medical devices are so capable and our drugs are so potent and forgiving. And so in my mind I had relegated the role of humans; they appeared to feature so infrequently, as little more than cameos in a wider scene.

This was important, I thought. It was good that we should stop believing in the fantasy of comic-book superheroes and their fictional omnipotence and hyper-competence, because to do so was to force ourselves to believe in the opposite: the supervillain and their single-handed ability to wreak havoc. If we could reject the heroic narrative altogether, and see the remarkable things that we are capable of today as products of complex systems, then perhaps we could make better progress.

But while all of that is true, I realise now that my framing was not quite right. We are in many ways the product of our technology and the opportunities it brings. But we operate enmeshed with that technology, and the relationships between people and the devices they deploy are as important as the capability of the underlying technology itself. The wonderful things we do are best seen through the lens of complex sociotechnical endeavour: the hybridisation of science, technology, engineering and human controllers. And through this perspective there is a more important role for the humans in the loop of control – one that in a crisis becomes central and fundamentally important. The technology holds our hand, walks us up to the edge of chaos and the interface with reality, helps us hold station there. But after that it is people who engage productively with the volatility, uncertainty, complexity and ambiguity that follow. What happens after the plan fails to survive the first five minutes of contact with reality is *us*.

I began writing this book long before Covid, when I first set out flying with my air-ambulance crews. Sometimes we succeeded, sometimes we failed. The experience was often bruising. On occasions the accident scenes were so violent, so fast, so chaotic that it didn't always feel as if my interventions had made a difference. And

I wondered if others could perhaps teach me how to cope better with that.

I have spent my career touring other organisations, looking for lessons that we in medicine might learn, searching for ways that we might improve. But the pandemic, and the actions of our NHS teams in the face of it, has become a masterclass of its own and one that I now try to teach to others. I used to think that we lived in a post-heroic age. But Covid taught me a different lesson about the place of humans in the face of something awful and unstoppable. All of us are heroes, though none of us alone; we are at our best when we belong to something, connected within a whole that is greater than the sum of its parts.

For me, the most remarkable photo in all of spaceflight history is not Armstrong's picture of Aldrin standing on the Moon in the summer of 1969, but the black-and-white photograph of the *Apollo 13* crew in 1970, out of their capsule, bobbing in life-rafts on the Pacific Ocean, having been successfully rescued from the jaws of certain death.

The command module *Odyssey*'s door hangs open; Jack Swigert is in the foreground, getting ready to be winched aboard the helicopter; Fred Haise is lost in a blur to the left as the rescue craft rolls on the ocean swell; but in the background Commander Jim Lovell is clearly visible, still wearing his spacesuit, with a life-vest now around his neck, hatched from the ailing capsule on which his life has depended until now, drawing in the first lungfuls of fresh air since blasting off six days earlier.

Space aficionados often say that in the history of American human space exploration, NASA have had four fatal accidents: *Apollo 1*, in which three astronauts perished in a fire during ground-testing; *Challenger*, which claimed the lives of seven crew members seventy-three seconds after launch; *Columbia*, in which another seven astronauts died after the failure of its thermal-protection system during re-entry; and lastly *Apollo 13*, which many regard as a fatal accident in which, somehow, nobody died.

Many weeks before the launch of *Apollo 13* a spherical oxygen tank, about the diameter of a bicycle wheel, had been fumbled and dropped in the production facility, long before being installed in *Apollo 13*'s service module. It fell only a couple of inches, but the damage was enough to set in train a cascade of events that left the spacecraft catastrophically flawed.

On the third day after its launch *Apollo 13* suffered an explosion in that oxygen tank, 200,000 miles from Earth and heading towards the Moon. The cataclysm took out their power, life-support, guidance system and means of propulsion, leaving their command module dead in the ocean of space. While there is a lot of bravado regarding their refusal to accept failure, the truth was very different. Many among the team in mission control briefly entertained the possibility that they might be about to lose a crew in space; so too did members of the *Apollo 13* crew.

How do you survive something like that: a physical system so intrinsically flawed, and a failure so total, as to be apparently unrecoverable at source? I spent a lot of time reading and thinking about this. I chased down the flight directors and flight controllers, the astronauts and the engineers, to understand it better. I spent nearly three days interviewing Jim Lovell in a library somewhere near Chicago, trying to unpick the details of his story.

We love the idea of the 'failure is not an option' mindset that has come to embody the can-do attitude of the astronauts and their flight-control team. But those words are plucked from the script of the 1995 Hollywood retelling of the mission. Gene Kranz, *Apollo 13*'s famed lead flight director, later borrowed them for the title of his autobiography, solidifying the mythology.

Failure patently *was* an option. I asked Jim Lovell directly if, given the severity of the situation they were in, he thought there was a chance that he and his crew might perish. He half chuckled. 'Oh, I had a very good idea that we might not survive,' he said. Many among the mission-control team felt the same way. And so it wasn't that they refused to believe that failure was an option; rather that the crew and the flight-control team chose to devote little or no time to its contemplation.

I have heard similar stories from other survivors of near-fatal accidents, Chesley Sullenberger – captain of the ill-fated Flight 1549, which so famously ditched on the Hudson River – among them. I don't think this is a fundamental expression of fortitude. Rather, I think it's a matter of bandwidth: you have a limited ration of attention and cognitive capacity, and so in a fast-moving crisis it is best to focus it on the immediacy of the threat in front of you. Amid a rapidly evolving life-and-death scenario, time spent contemplating the horror of mortality is only going to make that spectre more likely to materialise.

The *Apollo 13* crew and flight-control team did precisely that: they prioritised, solving the problems most likely to kill the crew today, deferring death until tomorrow, and then repeating that process over and over again for four days, until they got themselves all the way to splashdown in the warm waters of the Pacific Ocean.

They are not the only team to have faced odds so steeply stacked against them, but they are among the rare few who have prevailed nevertheless. There is of course some considerable luck at work in this type of accident, but that alone is not enough to guarantee survival. To get yourself all the way out of the black sky above and to splashdown below, you have to be able to capitalise upon every resource available to you, and then sweep all of that together to create the tiniest kernel of hope.

There are common organising principles for all teams facing these impossible, fast-moving threats. First, you have to be able to make decisions in the face of frank uncertainty. This isn't easy or comfortable – facing decisions with profound consequences, your instinct is to temporise and ask for more information. But time, in crises of this type, is rarely on your side, and so decisions have to be made in the moment. That is what the formation of estimates is all about, coupled with the courage to then hurl yourself into the waiting uncertainty.

Next you have to commit to those decisions fully (imperfect though they are), because to do anything else – to doubt the action, to delay unnecessarily – is to risk stalling and grinding to a halt. And loss of momentum for an organisation in this perilous state is lethal. After that, you need to delegate authority and defer to expertise wherever it lies in the system. This is how you start to match the pace of the accelerating threat that faces you, by multiplying the scale of your response across as many people as you possibly can. This means giving people responsibility, and by that I mean being prepared to give true mission-critical responsibility to some of the most junior people in your organisation.

If any part of you believes in your hiring processes – and if you believe in your people and what they can do – then there is more potential in your workforce than you usually ever get to deploy. You need to be able to delegate and defer in that way, regardless of your own proficiencies. Because while it is possible (though unlikely) that you might be the best person to execute the entire catalogue of tasks that are now required, there simply aren't enough of you to do so.

The next task is to use those decisions, and the amplification of effort achieved through delegation, to innovate and transform the team's immediate response. Make no mistake: transformation in the face of existential crisis is required, because your organisation is at that point, by definition, not fit for current purpose. (If it were, then you wouldn't be in crisis.)

The next imperative is to experience failure. Failure in the moment, under these circumstances, is inevitable because of the pressure of time and uncertainty baked into the decision-making. You will fail, and you will do so at scale, but you must do so gracefully.

And if all of that sounds like a manifesto for organisational guesswork, then perhaps that is what it is. But what makes this plan powerful is the final element: the ability to go again, having learned from the last iteration, and to guess again, with new information, new decisions and new uncertainties.

I still cry sometimes when I talk about Covid. I'm not sure how anyone who was there during the worst of it manages not to. But I think that's all right. One of the things I learned in the wake of the major incidents was that it was OK not to be OK. I count myself lucky here to have had teams around me who had my back in every moment of the job and every moment afterwards. Here, too, we are a system. This is where resilience lies.

I still wonder how we came through it, how we didn't just give up and go home. But surviving something like that is about all those elements: uncertainty, commitment, deference, delegation, innovation, transformation, failure and iteration. Those last two are essential. You *must* learn the art of graceful failure, and be prepared to go again, knowing that you will fail again. None of that is easy. None of that is without cost. But that is what the teams did: every day they were wrong in a million different ways, but they went again; and every day they were a little less wrong, until one day they were almost right, which in the face of catastrophe was good enough – indeed, more than good enough. That is how we survived. That is the anatomy of hope.

This book starts with a description of teams and teamwork. The HEMS crews I fly with are among the best and closest units I have ever had the pleasure of working with. I still get nervous, sometimes, when we lift; a little fearful of the unknown. I still wonder if I'll be up to whatever the scene will throw at me. But the confidence comes from knowing that you are part of something bigger, which makes you something more. Good teams learn to partner with their technology, knowing its limits, how it might help and where and when it might hurt them.

There is no technology that explains how we were able to keep going through Covid. There is only the baying chaos that lay on the other side of the Low Gate, and the remarkable performance of the people who rose to face it. We are too often keen to paint the human as a point of vulnerability, as the reason that things go wrong, when exactly the opposite is true. Overwhelmingly your human resource is precisely that: a resource, a source of strength, agility, adaptability; the reason that the mission is able to continue at all. The successful organisations of this era will be those who understand that best; those who co-create technologies with the humans in the loop of control, designing them in partnership with those people, rather than instead or in spite of them.

Early in January 2021 I was back at my hospital, with my anaesthetic team, finishing an overnight shift supporting our colleagues in intensive care. The hospital was overflowing. More patients were on their way. We had yet to reach the peak of that wave.

In the small hours of the morning the crash-pagers were ringing again, the sixth cardiac arrest of the night. The sixth death. I was tired of wearing gowns and gloves, tired of the mask that bit into my face and of the visor that somehow always fogged. Tired of how it all felt. The clinical teams had been at this for more than 300 days.

However, the vaccination programme was under way – we were already nearly a month into the campaign. Vaccines delivered in record time, against the odds, against expectation. Science is a wonderful thing. There was, for the first time, a glimmer of hope.

I came away from the makeshift ICU on the sixth floor, where patients and ventilators were crowded into every corner. I rode the lift down to the main unit below, which had long since been overwhelmed. I pushed through the doors, plastered with signs warning you that this was a Covid-19 area, that we were at risk here and should don PPE. But inside there was something unusual happening: people were – for a moment – away from their stations, crowding the windows, camera phones in hand.

It had been a cold night, and snow cloud lay like a solitary blanket low above the city, as far as the eye could see. Out to the east, underneath it all, the sun was coming up, setting it on fire, a spectacular blaze of colour washing across the whole sky and now bathing the unit in its warm glow. And this was the last, but most important, lesson the pandemic had to teach us: that no matter how dark the night is, the sun always comes back.

Further reading

Those of you who are students and scholars of organisational science, complexity theory and safety science will recognise fragments of those scattered throughout the book. It is not intended as a comprehensive lay summary of those fields. Rather, as a recipient and occasional student of those teachings myself, I wanted to try and describe what the sum of those theories feels like when put to the test in practice. The non-initiate should regard this volume merely as a portal to a vast and exotic universe of new ideas: one which encompasses systems, systems thinking, risk, complexity and uncertainty. What follows is a bibliography and some further reading for those who would like to extend their exploration a little further.

Athanasiou T, Krasopoulos G, Nambiar P, Coats T, Petrou M, Magee P, Uppal R. Emergency thoracotomy in the pre-hospital setting: A procedure requiring clarification. Eur J Cardiothorac Surg. 2004;26(2):377-386. doi:10.1016/j.ejcts.2004.03.016.

Aylett-Bullock J, Cuesta-Lazaro C, Quera-Bofarull A, Icaza-Lizaola M, Sedgewick A, Truong H, et al. June: Open-source individual-based epidemiology simulation. R Soc Open Sci. 2021;8(7):210506. doi:10.1098/rsos.210506.

Beck CS. Wounds of the heart: The technic of suture. Arch Surg. 1926;13(2):205-227. doi:10.1001/archsurg.1926.01130080054002.

Boyd JR. A discourse on winning and losing. Hammond GT, editor and compiler. Maxwell Air Force Base (AL): Air University Press; 2018.

Cannon WB. The way of an investigator: A scientist's experiences in medical research. New York (NY): W.W. Norton & Company; 1945.

Cannon WB. The wisdom of the body. Rev. and enl. ed. New York (NY): W.W. Norton & Company; 1939.

Carayon P, Schoofs Hundt A, Karsh BT, Gurses AP, Alvarado CJ, Smith M, Brennan PF. Work system design for patient safety: the SEIPS model. Qual Saf Health Care. 2006;15(Suppl 1):i50-i58. doi:10.1136/qshc.2005.015842.

Carayon P, Wooldridge A, Hoonakker P, Schoofs Hundt A, Kelly MM. SEIPS 3.0: Human-centered design of the patient journey for patient safety. Appl Ergon. 2020;84:103033. doi:10.1016/j.apergo.2019.103033.

Catchpole K, Russ S. The problem with checklists. BMJ Qual Saf. 2015;24(9):545-549. doi:10.1136/bmjqs-2015-004431.

Chartered Institute of Ergonomics and Human Factors. Human factors in health and social care. London: Chartered Institute of Ergonomics and Human Factors; 2018. Available from: ergonomics.org.uk/resource/human-factors-in-health-and-social-care.html

Christianson MK, Sutcliffe KM, Miller MA, Iwashyna TJ. Becoming a high reliability organization. Crit Care. 2011;15(6):314. doi:10.1186/cc10360.

Clark TR. The 4 stages of psychological safety: Defining the path to inclusion and innovation. Oakland (CA): Berrett-Koehler Publishers; 2020.

Cook RI. How complex systems fail: Being a short treatise on the nature of failure; how failure is evaluated; how failure is attributed to proximate cause; and the resulting new understanding of patient safety. Chicago (IL): Cognitive Technologies Laboratory, University of Chicago; 1998. Available from: how.complexsystems.fail/

Cooper GE, White MD, Lauber JK, editors. Resource management on the flightdeck: Proceedings of a NASA/Industry Workshop, San Francisco, California, June 26-28, 1979. Moffett Field (CA): NASA Ames Research Center; 1980. NASA Conference Publication 2120.

Coram R. Boyd: The fighter pilot who changed the art of war. Boston (MA): Little, Brown and Company; 2002.

Coulter JW. Impact of the war on South Sea islands. Geogr Rev. 1946;36(3):409-419.

Cox SJ. H-025-2: the USS Enterprise (CVAN-65) conflagration, 14 January 1969. Washington (DC): Naval History and Heritage Command; 2019 May 3. Available from: history.navy.mil/about-us/leadership/director/directors-corner/h-grams/h-gram-025/h-025-2.html

Dall'Ora C, Saville C, Rubbo B, Turner L, Jones J, Griffiths P. Nurse staffing levels and patient outcomes: A systematic review of longitudinal studies. Int J Nurs Stud. 2022;134:104311. doi:10.1016/j.ijnurstu.2022.104311.

Davies GE, Lockey DJ. Thirteen survivors of prehospital thoracotomy for penetrating trauma: A prehospital physician-performed resuscitation procedure that can yield good results. J Trauma. 2011;70(5):E75-E78. doi:10.1097/TA.0b013e3181f6f72f.

Dooley LN, Slavich GM, Moreno PI, Bower JE. Strength through adversity: Moderate lifetime stress exposure is associated with psychological resilience in breast cancer survivors. Stress Health. 2017;33(5):549-557. doi:10.1002/smi.2739.

Edmondson AC. The fearless organization: Creating psychological safety in the workplace for learning, innovation, and growth. Hoboken (NJ): John Wiley & Sons; 2018.

Eisen LA, Savel RH. What went right: Lessons for the intensivist from the crew of US Airways Flight 1549. Chest. 2009;136(3):910-917. doi:10.1378/chest.09-0377.

Flin R, O'Connor P, Crichton M. Safety at the sharp end: A guide to non-technical skills. Aldershot (UK): Ashgate Publishing; 2008.

Fong K. Moon landing: Space medicine and the legacy of Project Apollo. Lancet. 2019;394(10194):205-207. doi:10.1016/S0140-6736(19)31568-5.

Fong KJ, Summers C, Cook TM. NHS hospital capacity during Covid-19: Overstretched staff, space, systems, and stuff. BMJ. 2024;385:e075613. doi:10.1136/bmj-2023-075613.

Fong KJ. Risk management, NASA, and the National Health Service: Lessons we should learn. Br J Anaesth. 2010;105(1):6-8. doi:10.1093/bja/aeq139.

Foster RS Jr. Luther Leonidas Hill Jr. In: Encyclopedia of Alabama. Auburn (AL): Encyclopedia of Alabama; 2010 Oct 13. Available from: encyclopediaofalabama.org/article/luther-leonidas-hill-jr/

Freedman L. Strategy: A history. New York (NY): Oxford University Press; 2013.

Gawande A. The checklist manifesto: How to get things right. 1st ed. New York (NY): Metropolitan Books; 2010.

Greenberg N, Langston V, Jones N. Trauma risk management (TRiM) in the UK Armed Forces. J R Army Med Corps. 2008;154(2):124-127. doi:10.1136/jramc-154-02-11.

Greenberg N, Wessely S. Mental health interventions for people involved in disasters: What not to do. World Psychiatry. 2017;16(3):249-250. doi:10.1002/wps.20469.

Greenberg N, Weston D, Hall C, Caulfield T, Williamson V, Fong K. Mental health of staff working in intensive care during COVID-19. Occup Med (Lond). 2021;71(2):62-67. doi:10.1093/occmed/kqaa220.

Griffiths P, Ball J, Drennan J, Dall'Ora C, Jones J, Maruotti A, Pope C, Recio Saucedo A, Simon M. Nurse staffing and patient outcomes: Strengths and limitations of the evidence to inform policy and practice. Int J Nurs Stud. 2016;63:213-225. doi:10.1016/j.ijnurstu.2016.03.012.

Hall CE, Milward J, Spoiala C, Bhogal JK, Weston D, Potts HWW, et al. The mental health of staff working on intensive care units over the COVID-19 winter surge of 2020 in England: A cross-sectional survey. Br J Anaesth. 2022;128(6):971-979. doi:10.1016/j.bja.2022.03.016.

Haynes AB, Weiser TG, Berry WR, Lipsitz SR, Breizat AH, Dellinger EP, et al. A surgical safety checklist to reduce morbidity and mortality in a global population. N Engl J Med. 2009;360(5):491-499. doi:10.1056/NEJMsa0810119.

Helmreich RL, Merritt AC, Wilhelm JA. The evolution of Crew Resource Management training in commercial aviation. Int J Aviat Psychol. 1999;9(1):19-32. doi:10.1207/S15327108IJAP0901_2.

Hogan H, Healey F, Neale G, Thomson R, Vincent C, Black N. Preventable deaths due to problems in care in English acute hospitals: A retrospective case record review study. BMJ Qual Saf. 2012;21(9):737-745. doi:10.1136/bmjqs-2011-001159.

Holden RJ, Carayon P, Gurses AP, et al. SEIPS 101 and seven simple SEIPS tools. BMJ Qual Saf. 2021;30(11):901-910. doi:10.1136/bmjqs-2020-012538.

Holden RJ, Carayon P, Gurses AP, Hoonakker P, Hundt AS, Ozok AA, Rivera-Rodriguez AJ. SEIPS 2.0: A human factors framework for studying and improving the work of healthcare professionals and patients. Ergonomics. 2013;56(11):1669-1686. doi:10.1080/00140139.2013.838643.

Hollnagel E, Woods DD, Leveson N, editors. Resilience engineering: Concepts and precepts. Aldershot (UK): Ashgate Publishing; 2006.

Hollnagel E. Safety-I and Safety-II: The past and future of safety management. Boca Raton (FL): CRC Press; 2018.

Hollnagel E. Safety-II in practice: Developing the resilience potentials. Abingdon (UK): Routledge; 2018. doi:10.4324/9781315201023.

Jones N, Seddon R, Fear NT, McAllister P, Wessely S, Greenberg N. Leadership, cohesion, morale, and the mental health of UK Armed Forces in Afghanistan. Psychiatry. 2012;75(1):49-59. doi:10.1521/psyc.2012.75.1.49.

Kanki BG, Helmreich RL, Anca J, editors. Crew resource management. 2nd ed. Burlington (MA): Academic Press; 2010. doi:10.1016/C2009-0-02518-5.

Kelly FE, Frerk C, Bailey CR, Cook TM, Ferguson K, Flin R, et al. Human factors in anaesthesia: A narrative review. Anaesthesia. 2023;78(4):479-490. doi:10.1111/anae.15920.

Kohn LT, Corrigan JM, Donaldson MS, editors. To err is human: Building a safer health system. Washington (DC): National Academies Press; 2000. doi:10.17226/9728.

Langton CG. Computation at the edge of chaos: Phase transitions and emergent computation. Physica D. 1990;42(1-3):12-37. doi:10.1016/0167-2789(90)90064-V.

Leary A, Walshe K. Rookie factor: Why healthcare workforce policy needs to embrace experience. BMJ. 2024;387:q2836. doi:10.1136/bmj.q2836.

Liberati EG, Peerally MF, Dixon-Woods M. Learning from high risk industries may not be straightforward: A qualitative study of the hierarchy of risk controls approach in healthcare. Int J Qual Health Care. 2018;30(1):39-43. doi:10.1093/intqhc/mzx163.

Lockey DJ, Brohi K. Pre-hospital thoracotomy and the evolution of pre-hospital critical care for victims of trauma. Injury. 2017;48(9):1863-1864. doi:10.1016/j.injury.2017.03.034.

Lockey DJ. Research questions in pre-hospital trauma care. PLoS Med. 2017;14(7):e1002345. doi:10.1371/journal.pmed.1002345.

Mazzocchi F. Complexity in biology: Exceeding the limits of reductionism and determinism using complexity theory. EMBO Rep. 2008;9(1):10-14. doi:10.1038/sj.embor.7401147.

McChrystal S, Collins T, Silverman D, Fussell C. Team of teams: New rules of engagement for a complex world. New York (NY): Portfolio/Penguin; 2015.

Meadows DH. Thinking in systems: A primer. Wright D, editor. White River Junction (VT): Chelsea Green Publishing; 2008.

Mindell DA. Digital Apollo: Human and machine in spaceflight. Cambridge (MA): MIT Press; 2008.

National Transportation Safety Board. Loss of thrust in both engines after encountering a flock of birds and subsequent ditching on the Hudson River: US Airways Flight 1549, Airbus Industrie A320-214, N106US, Weehawken, New Jersey, January 15, 2009. Washington (DC): National Transportation Safety Board; 2010. Report No.: NTSB/AAR-10/03.

Noble D. Claude Bernard, the first systems biologist, and the future of physiology. Exp Physiol. 2008;93(1):16-26. doi:10.1113/expphysiol.2007.038695.

Noble D. Systems: What's in a name? Physiology (Bethesda). 2011;26(3):126-128. doi:10.1152/physiol.00014.2011.

Packard NH. Adaptation toward the edge of chaos. In: Kelso JAS, Mandell AJ, Shlesinger MF, editors. Dynamic patterns in complex systems. Singapore: World Scientific; 1988. p. 293-301.

Peerally MF, Carr S, Waring J, Dixon-Woods M. The problem with root cause analysis. BMJ Qual Saf. 2017;26(5):417-422. doi:10.1136/bmjqs-2016-005511.

Pereira J, Eusebio C, Sherlaw-Johnson C, Black S, Punshon G, Hardy S, Leary A. Understanding the relationship between care hours per patient day and summary hospital-level mortality indicator in English hospitals: A time series approach. J Patient Saf Risk Manag. 2025. doi:10.1177/25160435251410480.

Perkins ZB, Greenhalgh R, ter Avest E, Aziz S, Whitehouse T, Read S, et al. Prehospital resuscitative thoracotomy for traumatic cardiac arrest. JAMA Surg. 2025;160(4):432-440. doi:10.1001/jamasurg.2024.7245.

Perrow C. Normal accidents: Living with high-risk technologies. Updated ed. Princeton (NJ): Princeton University Press; 1999.

Reason J. Human error. Cambridge: Cambridge University Press; 1990.

Reason J. Managing the risks of organizational accidents. Aldershot (UK): Ashgate Publishing; 1997.

Roberts KH. Some characteristics of one type of high reliability organization. Organ Sci. 1990;1(2):160-176. doi:10.1287/orsc.1.2.160.

Rochlin GI, La Porte TR, Roberts KH. The self-designing high-reliability organization: Aircraft carrier flight operations at sea. Nav War Coll Rev. 1987;40(4):76-92.

Rona RJ, Burdett H, Bull S, Jones M, Jones N, Greenberg N, Wessely S, Fear NT. Prevalence of PTSD and other mental disorders in UK service personnel by time since end of deployment: A meta-analysis. BMC Psychiatry. 2016;16:333. doi:10.1186/s12888-016-1038-8.

Ryan KL. Walter B. Cannon's World War I experience: Treatment of traumatic shock then and now. Adv Physiol Educ. 2018;42(2):267-276. doi:10.1152/advan.00187.2017.

Sapkota N, Karwowski W, Davahli MR, Al-Juaid A, Taiar R, Murata A, et al. The chaotic behavior of the spread of infection during the COVID-19 pandemic in the United States and globally. IEEE Access. 2021;9:80692-80702. doi:10.1109/ACCESS.2021.3085240.

Seery MD, Holman EA, Silver RC. Whatever does not kill us: Cumulative lifetime adversity, vulnerability, and resilience. J Pers Soc Psychol. 2010;99(6):1025-1041. doi:10.1037/a0021344.

Shojania KG, Dixon-Woods M. Estimating deaths due to medical error: The ongoing controversy and why it matters. BMJ Qual Saf. 2017;26(5):423-428. doi:10.1136/bmjqs-2016-006144.

Shorrock S, Williams C, editors. Human factors and ergonomics in practice: Improving system performance and human well-being in the real world. Boca Raton (FL): CRC Press; 2017.

Sujan M, Pickup L, Vosper H, et al. Making human factors and ergonomics work in health and social care: Chapter 1 - Introduction. London: Chartered Institute of Ergonomics and Human Factors; 2022. Available from: ergonomics.org.uk/resource/hf-in-health-and-social-care-ebook-chapter-1.html

Sullenberger CB 3rd, Zaslow J. Highest duty: My search for what really matters. New York (NY): William Morrow; 2009.

Summers C, Cook TM, Fong KJ. Covid Inquiry module 3 reveals critical gaps in UK health system resilience. BMJ. 2026;393:s846. doi:10.1136/bmj.s846.

Sutcliffe KM, Paine L, Pronovost PJ. Re-examining high reliability: Actively organising for safety. BMJ Qual Saf. 2017;26(3):248-251. doi:10.1136/bmjqs-2015-004698.

Sutcliffe KM. High reliability organizations (HROs). Best Pract Res Clin Anaesthesiol. 2011;25(2):133-144. doi:10.1016/j.bpa.2011.03.001.

Tamuz M, Harrison MI. Improving patient safety in hospitals: Contributions of high-reliability theory and normal accident theory. Health Serv Res. 2006;41(4 Pt 2):1654-1676. doi:10.1111/j.1475-6773.2006.00570.x.

Trewavas A. A brief history of systems biology: 'Every object that biology studies is a system of systems.' Plant Cell. 2006;18(10):2420-2430. doi:10.1105/tpc.106.042267.

Tversky A, Kahneman D. Judgment under uncertainty: Heuristics and biases. Science. 1974;185(4157):1124-1131. doi:10.1126/science.185.4157.1124.

UK Covid-19 Inquiry. Module 2, 2A, 2B, 2C report: Core decision-making and political governance. London: UK Covid-19 Inquiry; 2025. Available from: covid19.public-inquiry.uk/documents/module-2-full-report/

UK Covid-19 Inquiry. Module 3 report: The impact of the Covid-19 pandemic on the healthcare systems of the United Kingdom. London: UK Covid-19 Inquiry; 2026. Available from: covid19.public-inquiry.uk/documents/module-3-full-report/

Van der Kloot W. William Maddock Bayliss's therapy for wound shock. Notes Rec R Soc. 2010;64(3):271-286. doi:10.1098/rsnr.2009.0068.

Vaughan D. The Challenger launch decision: Risky technology, culture, and deviance at NASA. Chicago (IL): University of Chicago Press; 1996.

Vernon PE, editor. Creativity: Selected readings. Harmondsworth (UK): Penguin Books; 1970. (Penguin Education; Penguin Modern Psychology Readings).

Vincent C, Amalberti R. Safer healthcare: Strategies for the real world. Cham (CH): Springer International Publishing; 2016. doi:10.1007/978-3-319-25559-0.

von Bertalanffy L. General system theory: Foundations, development, applications. New York (NY): George Braziller; 1968.

Wall RJ. Successful roadside resuscitative thoracotomy: Case report and literature review. J Trauma. 1994;36(1):131-134.

Walshe K, Smith J, Lamont T, Leary A. Workforce research priorities for resilience to future health shocks-and the workforce crisis. BMJ. 2024;387:e078997. doi:10.1136/bmj-2023-078997.

Wears RL, Sutcliffe KM. Still not safe: Patient safety and the middle-managing of American medicine. New York (NY): Oxford University Press; 2019.

Weick KE, Sutcliffe KM. Managing the unexpected: Sustained performance in a complex world. 3rd ed. San Francisco (CA): Jossey-Bass; 2015.

Weick KE. Sensemaking in organizations. Thousand Oaks (CA): Sage Publications; 1995.

Weick KE. The collapse of sensemaking in organizations: The Mann Gulch disaster. Adm Sci Q. 1993;38(4):628-652.

Weisse AB. Cardiac surgery: A century of progress. Tex Heart Inst J. 2011;38(5):486-490.

Wise D, Davies G, Coats T, Lockey DJ, Hyde J, Good A. Emergency thoracotomy: How to do it. Emerg Med J. 2005;22(1):22-24. doi:10.1136/emj.2003.012963.

Wolfram S. A new kind of science. Champaign (IL): Wolfram Media; 2002.

Woods DD, Branlat M. Basic patterns in how adaptive systems fail. In: Hollnagel E, Pariès J, Woods DD, Wreathall J, editors. Resilience engineering in practice: A guidebook. Farnham (UK): Ashgate Publishing; 2011. p. 127-143.

Woods DD, Dekker S, Cook R, Johannesen L, Sarter N. Behind human error. 2nd ed. Boca Raton (FL): CRC Press; 2010.

Woods DD. Four concepts for resilience and the implications for the future of resilience engineering. Reliab Eng Syst Saf. 2015;141:5-9. doi:10.1016/j.ress.2015.03.018.

Woods DD. Outmaneuvering complexity: Creating safety by engineering resilience. Farnham (UK): Ashgate Publishing; 2015.

World Health Organization. WHO surgical safety checklist. 1st ed. Geneva: World Health Organization; 2008. Available from: who.int/docs/default-source/patient-safety/9789241598590-eng-checklist.pdf

Acknowledgements

This was not an easy book to write, for lots of reasons. I realise now that I had to go through some stuff and get out the other side before I could put it to bed. And though it often felt like torture it was in the end its own kind of therapy. Which is to say that it took altogether too long to finish, and so my first thank yous go to my eternally patient editor Will Hammond, at Bodley Head, and my equally patient literary agent Will Francis and his crew at Janklow & Nesbitt; in particular Corissa Hollenbeck and Michael Steger. Thank you for waiting for this and for keeping the faith even though mine occasionally faltered.

Thanks also to the wider team at Penguin Random House, to Ana Fletcher for her early and essential resuscitation efforts, to Matt Broughton for our fabulous (and fabulously orange) jacket design, to Mandy Greenfield for tracking the text so carefully and spotting my many crimes against grammar and punctuation, to Rhiannon Roy for following in her wake getting us to the finish line (and for telling me the funniest story I have ever heard about nightmare copy-edits), to Florence Ward for nudging us across the line, and to marketeers Mia Quibbell-Smith and Sam Rees-Williams for a campaign Helmuth von Moltke the Elder would have been proud of.

There should by rights be a whole chapter on how grateful I am to Juliet Brooke, who I cannot thank enough and will likely never stop thanking. Having wrestled with so many versions of this not infrequently chaotic text, I of all people should have guessed that it was rapid cycles of the right kind of feedback that I needed. Juliet delivered that in spades. She was at times quite the surgeon (there are whole chapters that lie discarded on the operating room floor). But there was reassurance too, in the dark teatime of the soul that accompanied the first draft, that the vital organs were salvageable if I would only persevere. I will genuinely miss our one-man, one-woman, one-book, book club.

Minute Six opens with tales from my time flying with teams at Air Ambulance Kent Surrey Sussex (AAKSS), for whom I have nothing but admiration. Not just for the paramedics and the pilots but the remarkable team at the charity and its visionary leaders, who labour to keep all of us flying and the mission moving forward. AAKSS is what any organisation should aspire to be: formidable and unflappable in the decisive moment, deeply impressive down to the last individual, but even better together than they are alone. Most importantly they are family when family is what you need. I count myself lucky to still be amongst them after all this time.

My heartfelt and undying thanks to the mighty anaesthetic department at University College London Hospital who have looked after me since the earliest days of my clinical career and generously supported my many weird and wonderful excursions. I've been able to follow this unique trajectory only because of their generosity.

And in a similar vein, thank you to my academic colleagues in the Department of Science, Technology, Engineering and Public Policy at University College London, and particularly to Nigel Titchener-Hooker and Joanna Chataway who together found themselves able to see past the strangeness of my curriculum vitae, hire me, and then let me out on a long, slack bungee to go in search of lessons that might make all our systems better.

The real heavy lifting in the field of organisational theory, safety science, human factors and ergonomics and complexity theory is done by the academic community. I have learned so much from conversations with the likes of David Woods, Kathleen Sutcliffe, Steven Shorrock, Ken Catchpole, Alison Leary, Martin Bromiley, Mary Dixon-Woods, Aidan Fowler and many more besides over the years, all of whom have shaped my own thinking and helped me make sense of the literature.

The spine of this book – and I guess my career – is built around the first lessons I learned, about teams working up close to science, technology and risk to human life, sitting in Building 272 at NASA's Johnson Space Center, in rooms air conditioned to such a chill that I had to layer up just to go to work. In common with the constellation of people and organisations that have supported me, the NASA life and medical sciences team have continued to be as patient and generous to me, as they were to the kid who rolled up at their front gate in Houston, nearly 30 years ago, wide-eyed and not knowing where the journey might lead him. Thank you as always Steve, Judy, Bill and Mike.

The last act of this book opens a narrow window on the National Health Service during Covid, on my colleagues in acute hospitals up and down the country and – in particular – our anaesthetic and intensive care teams. They deserve far more than simple acknowledgement. In all my travels, in everything I have seen teams do, of all the stories I have heard, I have never come across anything that holds a candle to what the NHS did in facing down the threat of the Covid-19 pandemic.

The NHS is its people. They are that most wonderful of all things, the hope when all other hope has faded; there for us 24/7, wherever we are, whoever we are. The pandemic showed us how remarkable they truly are, but taught us too that their capacity is not limitless. We would do well to care for them so that they might continue to care for us. This book is dedicated to the people who help to deliver that care everywhere in the NHS, every day. Things are hard right now, but the sun always comes back.

Thanks to my readers, Mike Herd, Dan Snow and Neil Nixon who saw and commented on the draft at various stages. And extra special thanks to Dill Paul who helped shape the final cover layout, read the book closely enough that he almost deserves credit as a copy-editor and who has been a reliable source of wisdom across the years.

Throughout all of this it has been family and friends who have kept me going. Thanks to all those who assemble faithfully each year to celebrate Kevstock, most of all Anthony and Louise Cullen, who have been such constant stars; to the crew of the Command Module with whom I have sailed many new oceans. And of course deepest thanks to my sons Noah and Jack and my wife Dee, who have suffered the interminable days of me doing battle with the manuscript. It is within and between you all that my resilience lies.

Finally for my parents who journeyed across continents and oceans, starting with next to nothing but who were somehow able to give me everything. All of this I owe to you.

Index

Kevin Fong (OBE) is a medical doctor specialising in anaesthesia and intensive-care medicine and is the lead for major-incident planning at UCL Hospitals. He also flies as a doctor with a Helicopter Emergency Medical Service, has worked with NASA's human spaceflight programme and was the writer and presenter of the number-one hit podcast *13 Minutes to the Moon*. In 2020 he was seconded as National Clinical Adviser to the NHS England Covid-19 Emergency Preparedness, Resilience and Response Team. He holds degrees in astrophysics, medicine and engineering.

To support the life-saving work of Air Ambulance Charity Kent Surrey Sussex or simply to learn more about the work we do, scan this QR code:

or follow this link:
aakss.org.uk/minutesix